Republicans
and Reconstruction
in Virginia, 1856–70

Republicans
and Reconstruction
in Virginia, 1856–70,

Richard G. Lowe, 1942 –
///

University Press of Virginia

Charlottesville and London

The University Press of Virginia
Copyright © 1991 by the Rector and Visitors
of the University of Virginia

First published 1991

Library of Congress Cataloging-in-Publication Data
Lowe, Richard G., 1942–
    Republicans and reconstruction in Virginia, 1856–70 / Richard
Lowe.
        p.   cm.
    Includes bibliographical references and index.
    ISBN 0-8139-1306-3
    1. Reconstruction—Virginia.   2. Republican Party (Va.)—
History—19th century.   3. Virginia—Politics and
government—1865–1950.   I. Title.
F231.L68   1991
324.2755'04—dc20   90-44920
                                                                    CIP

Printed in the United States of America

For Cheron

Contents

Maps

Acknowledgments

As usual with such research projects, many individuals contributed to my understanding of the subject. Special thanks go to the late Edward Younger of the University of Virginia. He suggested the topic and contributed penetrating criticism from the first day of research. Professors F. N. Boney of the University of Georgia and Andrew Buni of Boston College read an early version of the manuscript and saved me the embarrassment of several errors. My colleagues at the University of North Texas, especially Randolph Campbell, Donald Chipman, Robert La Forte, and the members of NT-LASH, read and criticized a later revision of the study. The Faculty Research Office of the University of North Texas provided released time from teaching to prepare the manuscript for publication. James T. Moore of Virginia Commonwealth University and the two referees for the University Press of Virginia raised important questions and measurably improved the book.

The staffs of the University of Virginia Library, the Virginia State Library and Archives, the Virginia Historical Society, the Library of Congress, the West Virginia University Library, and the Duke University Library were invariably cooperative and often went beyond the usual bounds of their duties to assist me along my way.

I am greatly indebted to my late wife, Cheron F. Lowe, who held down a job during the day and typed deep into the night to help me complete an earlier version of this study. Without her aid in those golden days and warm nights in Charlottesville, this whole project could never have been undertaken.

Introduction

READERS interested in the history of the Old Dominion and its place in the larger story of the nation have been well served by historians. Scholars have traced the life of the state from its beginnings at Jamestown in 1607, through the glory years of the Revolution and early republican period, on through the tragedy of civil war, and down to the late twentieth century. One particular chapter in this long history—Reconstruction, especially the Republican side of the story—is the focus of this book.

The first histories of Reconstruction in Virginia appeared early in the twentieth century with the publication of Hamilton James Eckenrode's *The Political History of Virginia during the Reconstruction* (1904) and John P. McConnell's *Negroes and Their Treatment in Virginia from 1865 to 1867* (1910). Eckenrode's and McConnell's Reconstruction studies were two of many produced by young southern scholars in the early 1900s. Indeed, a whole school of Reconstruction history was built around these books and articles, many of which originated in William A. Dunning's seminars at Columbia University. The Dunning school interpreted Reconstruction as a miserable period of radical Republican misrule in the South, marked by corruption, the domination of educated whites by ignorant and illiterate blacks, and the emergence to power of vindictive carpetbaggers and grasping, unprincipled scalawags. According to this view, long-suffering Virginia white conservatives endured insult and injustice from the radicals until 1869, when they finally merged with the more moderate wing of the state's Republican party to overthrow the radicals. By 1873 the rising conservative tide was able to sweep away even the moderate Republicans and restore home rule to the Old Dominion. [1]

While this traditional interpretation of Reconstruction dominated historical writing in the first half of the twentieth century, it did not go unchallenged, especially by black scholars. Perhaps the best-known such work by a black author was W. E. B. Du Bois's *Black Reconstruction in America, 1860–1880* (1935). But even earlier, another black historian, Alrutheus Ambush Taylor, rewrote the story of Virginia's blacks during Reconstruction. In *The Negro in the Reconstruction of Virginia* (1926), Taylor stressed the social and economic aspects of black life after the Civil War and concluded that blacks were not the shiftless, degraded, and ignorant radicals that the Dunning school had described.

Taylor's work was followed by that of an all-black unit of the Virginia Writers' Project, organized originally under the Federal Writers' Project of the Works Progress Administration. *The Negro in Virginia* (1940), a survey of black Virginians from Jamestown to the New Deal, included four chapters on Reconstruction and seconded Taylor's view that black leaders of the Reconstruction period had represented their constituents "sincerely and intelligently."[2] Five years later another black writer, Luther P. Jackson, published *Negro Office-Holders in Virginia, 1865–1895* (1945), providing biographical sketches of over one hundred state-level black officeholders during and after Reconstruction. These sketches disputed the traditional view of Virginia's black Republicans by demonstrating that many of them were educated (some even before the Civil War) and responsible property owners.

Following the lead of these black scholars and a few white writers of the 1920s, 1930s, and 1940s, the historical profession as a whole, responding to the Second Reconstruction of the 1950s and 1960s, adopted a revisionist view of the first Reconstruction. The revisionists completely overturned the traditional school of thought. They regarded Reconstruction as an honest and sincere attempt by black and white Republicans to convince the American people to live up to the ideals of the American republic. The revisionists placed southern blacks closer to center stage in the story of Reconstruction, denied the existence of black rule in the southern states, outlined the important reforms accomplished by southern and national Republicans, and described Reconstruction as tragic only because it was not more successful.[3]

The flood of revisionist writings since the 1960s has included numerous works that either concentrate or touch on Virginia's Reconstruction. Several have investigated Reconstruction in the Old Dominion's cities. Michael B. Chesson's history of postwar Richmond, William D. Henderson's study of Reconstruction in Petersburg, Peter J. Rachleff's work on black labor in the state capital, and John T. O'Brien's article on post-Appomattox Richmond all portray politically sensitive and intelligent freedmen working to bring about needed reform in Virginia's urban areas. Revisionists have not limited their investigations to city scenes alone, however. An examination of black life at Hampton in the late nineteenth century provides a revealing look at Reconstruction in rural and small-town Virginia. Biographical treatments of important Reconstruction figures include studies of General John M. Schofield, black radical Willis Hodges, and Reconstruction governors Francis H. Pierpont, Gilbert C. Walker, and Henry H. Wells.[4]

Most of the works falling in the revisionist school of Virginia's Reconstruction historiography examine particular localities or individuals. But Jack P. Maddex's history of the Virginia Conservatives is a masterful study of the party that would eventually adopt the Democratic label. In addition, Richard L. Hume's article on the membership of the 1868 constitutional convention provides a systematic and reasonable breakdown of the participants in the Underwood convention. A recent and convenient overview of political Reconstruction in Virginia can also be found in my 1986 article in *Civil War History*. Several unpublished theses and dissertations also examine broad themes of Virginia's Reconstruction, especially those by William T. Alderson and James Douglas Smith.

While the revisionist school of thought seemed to carry all before it for almost twenty years, not every historian of the period was completely convinced that Reconstruction was a truly sincere and radical attempt to reform the South and the nation. In the 1970s and 1980s a third interpretation of the postwar years began to take shape in the writings of several, mostly younger, scholars. These postrevisionists agreed with the revisionists that significant and wide-ranging reforms had been needed to make Reconstruction successful, but they denied that the Republicans of the 1860s and 1870s had attempted (or were even capable of) such changes. Instead, the postrevisionists regarded the Republican party and the North as essentially conservative, caught up in old ideas about laissez-faire economics and the limited power of the Federal government. They saw the Civil War and Reconstruction as mere bumps in the path of history, not a great watershed when the nation attempted to cut loose from its past. The postrevisionists, in an admirable attempt to reexamine

Reconstruction from the black point of view, ironically placed black Southerners once again outside the mainstream of Reconstruction as they stressed racist manipulations by white conservatives. While some studies of Virginia's Reconstruction have implications that shade into postrevisionism, this most recent trend has not dominated accounts of the postwar years in the Old Dominion.[5]

One facet of Reconstruction in Virginia that has not been treated in a full-scale history is the story of the state's Republican party. This has been unfortunate, for the Virginia Republican party led an exciting and, at times, important existence during the 1860s. Its history included courage and cowardice, victory and defeat, joy and sorrow. At times it changed the course of Virginia history. Republicans dominated the loyalist state government formed during the Civil War and were crucial to the success of the West Virginia statehood drive. They devised an antislavery constitution in 1864 that began the work of Reconstruction a year before Appomattox, pressured Congress in 1865 and 1866 to reject President Andrew Johnson's conservative Reconstruction program and adopt a new one, and drew up another constitution in 1867–68 that served as Virginia's basic law until 1902.

Along the way, these Republicans produced some long-needed and significant reforms in postwar Virginia and displayed a maddening tendency to endanger those reforms by dividing into factions that slid and shifted to and fro with political developments in Washington and Richmond. Leading the various factions were such interesting men as John C. Underwood, a New Yorker who had moved to Virginia in the 1840s to reform the state from within; Francis H. Pierpont, a western Virginia Unionist who had refused to accept his state's secession; James W. Hunnicutt, the fiery South Carolina white preacher who became a leader of the Old Dominion's radical blacks; Franklin Stearns, the wealthy New England native who had lived and prospered in Richmond since the 1830s; John Minor Botts, the antebellum Whig politician who had sat out the war at his Virginia home; and two carpetbaggers, Henry H. Wells and Gilbert C. Walker, who occupied the Governor's Mansion in the late 1860s. How these and other Republicans accomplished as much as they did and why they failed to do more—these are the subjects of this study.

The reader of this history of the Virginia Republican party will soon detect a revisionist flavor in its interpretations. In these pages the Old Dominion's Republicans are generally portrayed as sincere and farsighted reformers who understood that sweeping change was necessary to take Virginia out of its slaveholding antebellum past into the new age of the late nineteenth century. These Republicans demanded more reform than they were able finally to achieve, but their eyes were on the advanced notion of civil and political equality for all Virginians. And some of them, especially black Republicans, peered into the future hoping to see social and economic equality as well.

Postrevisionist writers have added valuable new insights to our understanding of Reconstruction. Their emphasis on the northern Republican party's unwillingness to make a long-term commitment to reform in the southern states is especially revealing. More campaign funds channeled to southern Republican parties, additional incentives to southern mountain whites alienated from established political structures to come into the Republican camp, a willingness to continue martial law until white conservative abuse and intimidation of freedmen and white Unionists were eradicated—northern Republicans by and large refused to consider such measures very seriously. If they had, the story of Reconstruction might have been different. In making this point, postrevisionist historians have enriched our appreciation of the story of Reconstruction.

On the other hand, by dwelling on the failures and shortcomings of Republican leadership, postrevisionists sometimes seem to give short shrift to the real advances made by Republicans in the southern states. Virginia Republicans managed to place over 120,000 black men, most of them slaves until very recently, on the voting rolls. They faced social ostracism and physical and mental abuse yet still produced a reform constitution that brought new classes of Virginians into the commonwealth's political life, democratized state and local government, put state finances on a firmer foundation, and erected the Old Dominion's first free public education system. They stumbled here and there, but they accomplished much against great odds, and their story deserves an empathetic ear.

CHAPTER I

Virginia Republicans and the Civil War

I T IS MORE than a little ironic that Virginia—scene of English North America's first experiment with slavery, the state where Gabriel Prosser's and Nat Turner's slave rebellions were crushed, nursery of some of the most renowned of all Confederate generals, and home of the capital of the Confederate States of America—that Virginia would also be the southern birthplace of Abraham Lincoln's Republican party. And yet the Old Dominion was the only Confederate state with a Republican party when the southern states seceded from the Union in 1860 and 1861.

Born in the turbulent politics of the 1850s, this initially tiny party formed the hardest core of unconditional Unionism in the state during the secession crisis. When, despite their efforts, Virginia's withdrawal from the Union was assured, the state's Republicans led the campaign to form a loyalist state government in the hills of western Virginia, a government that purported to represent the entire state. Having created this "Restored" government, western Republicans and Unionists then succeeded in their efforts to have their Unionist regime recognized by President Lincoln and Congress as the only true government of the Old Dominion. With the blessing and cooperation of the Federal government, western Unionists raised Virginia regiments for the United States Army, sent Virginia senators and representatives to the Capitol in Washington, and paid their Federal taxes.

Not content to remain part of a state dominated by slaveholders and stained by secession, Virginia's western Unionist-Republicans also provided strong leadership in the movement to separate the northwestern third of the Old Dominion from its ancient ties and to form a new state west of the Shenandoah Valley. When the statehood campaign was successfully concluded in 1863, the Virginia Republican party found that the bulk of its membership and leadership were now citizens of another state—West Virginia. Severely reduced now in numbers and credibility, a nucleus of Republicans nevertheless carried the Unionist Restored government to the soil of old Virginia.

With their state capital now located in Union-occupied Alexandria across the Potomac River from Washington, Virginia Republicans tried, with mixed success, to operate the Restored regime as a legitimate state government for the remainder of the war. Despite interference from Federal military authorities and only minimal cooperation from Washington, the Restored government claimed legal authority over the handful of Union-occupied counties of northern and eastern Virginia from 1863 to 1865 and managed at least to keep its legal existence intact.

More important, perhaps, the Republicans of the Restored state government in Alexandria wrote a new antislavery constitution for the Old Dominion that brought about many of the reforms associated with postwar Reconstruction in other Confederate states. When the Confederacy finally collapsed in 1865, the Republican Restored government moved to Richmond and became for the first time what it had always claimed to be—the government of all of Virginia. As such, the state's outnumbered and widely despised Republicans would lead the Old Dominion through the turmoil of President Andrew Johnson's postwar Reconstruction.

Thus, despite its embarrassingly small numbers, Virginia's Republican party had an amazingly powerful impact on the history of Virginia during the Civil War. Republicans comprised the core of unconditional Unionism during the secession crisis, led the movement to create a Unionist Restored state government in 1861, provided the cutting edge for the dismemberment of the old state in 1863, wrote a loyalist and antislavery constitution in 1864, and dominated the state government recognized by President Johnson to lead the Old Dominion through Reconstruction. Seldom in American political history has such a small party shaped the destiny of a state so dramatically.

The Birth of the Virginia Republican Party

When outraged northerners in Wisconsin and Michigan reacted to Senator Stephen A. Douglas's Kansas-Nebraska bill in 1854 by forming anti-Douglas and anti-Nebraska organizations, few could have foreseen that within six years the party created by this upswell of northern protest would sweep an obscure Illinois lawyer into the White House. Fewer still could have predicted that this new Republican party, born in the North and based on widespread free-soil sentiment, would take root on unfriendly southern ground.

In the Old Dominion hostility to slaveholders, not sympathy for the bondsmen or concern about the status of western territories, was the primary force pushing white men into the Republican party. Most Virginia Republicans cared little whether blacks lived in bondage, and many were openly contemptuous of the black race. They seldom complained about the black man's plight but invariably protested their own.[1] Their Republicanism sprang from the cleavage between northwestern Virginia and the rest of the state.

The forty counties of farthest northwest Virginia, separated from the east by the Appalachian Mountains, had been quarreling with the eastern two-thirds of the state since the American Revolution. Most westerners, like most settlers of the Midwestern states, owned small family farms, and very few of them owned slaves. But the state government was dominated by slaveholding easterners who made sure their own economic and political interests were protected, at the expense of the west if necessary. Westerners were underrepresented in the state's General Assembly and congressional delegation because slave property, located mainly in the tidewater and piedmont, was counted for purposes of representation. Westerners carried a disproportionate share of the tax burden because their property was taxed according to market value while easterners' slaves were not taxed at all until the age of twelve, and then their value was set at the low rate of only three hundred dollars.[2]

Unfair taxation, discriminatory representation, laws designed to benefit slaveholders, a long history of sectional hostility, and the conflicting economic and political interests of east and west—all these angered and frustrated the northwest. Most westerners in the 1850s attempted to right things by working through the established political parties. A smaller number, despairing of any help from the old organizations and seeing a new party arise out of the old Northwest Territory, joined the Republicans because they were most outspoken against slaveholders and slavery, the primary causes of western subordination to the east.

Originally, their ranks were painfully thin. After several local organizational meetings in the politically charged summer of 1856, a few hundred northwesterners formed a state Republican party in September in a convention at Wheeling, a bustling manufacturing center in the panhandle pinched between Ohio and Pennsylvania. Farmers, merchants, and professional men—most of them former Whigs—made up the bulk of the assembly. Despite their high spirits, the Republicans made only a weak showing in the presidential election. Their last-minute appearance in the campaign, the state's viva voce method of voting (which discouraged all but the stouthearted from voting for the "black Republican" Frémont), social pressure, threatened and actual violence against Republicans, and their small numbers resulted in a mere 291 Frémont votes, mainly in the panhandle.[3]

Undaunted, the little band of Republicans continued to organize and gain strength during the late 1850s. Their ranks were increased by the immigration of several hundred northern families into northern and western Virginia between 1857 and 1860. Moreover, three newspapers—the powerful *Wheeling Daily Intelligencer* and the smaller *Wellsburg Herald* and *Ceredo Crescent*—joined the party and served as its political organs. The ambitious Virginians even managed to attract the 1860 Republican national convention to Wheeling until grim-eyed John Brown staged his famous raid in 1859; then the site was shifted to Chicago to avoid southern hostility.[4]

Disappointed that they had lost the national convention, Virginia Republicans nevertheless plunged into the 1860 presidential campaign, sending a large delegation to the party's Wigwam Convention, organizing bands of "Wide Awakes" (Republican marching clubs), and raising numerous liberty poles throughout the northwest. But the same old problems plagued them in 1860: social ostracism, physical violence, the viva voce system, and the majority opinion that Republicans were a sectional, abolitionist party. As a result, Abraham Lincoln, the victorious Republican candidate, received only 1,929 votes in Virginia, mainly in the northwestern panhandle.[5]

Thus, the state Republican party that existed when Lincoln was elected in 1860 was primarily a middle-class white man's organization devoted to the interests of the northwest. Northern influence was especially prominent within the Virginia party: several of its most important leaders and spokesmen were either born or educated in the North, many of the votes Abraham Lincoln received in 1860 were cast by northern immigrants, and northern capital had helped to establish its few newspapers.[6] Most of its members cared little about the plight of the slave and firmly believed in white racial superiority, but all were bitter enemies of eastern slaveholders. Although they counted only a few thousand members in 1860, they would provide a rock-solid nucleus of unconditional Unionism when the Old Dominion began to flirt with secession during the winter of 1860–61.

Republicans and Secession

Lincoln's victory in the 1860 election frightened and outraged the cotton states of the lower South. It appeared to them that the hated "black Republicans" would soon undermine all the South's defenses for slavery, that the ascendant North would pen slavery within its present borders and then attack it even there, destroying the South's wealth and social system. To avoid this dreaded probability, the lower southern states began seceding from the Union in December 1860, with South Carolina leading the way.

Compared to South Carolina, Virginia was quite calm about the Republican threat. Most Virginians were content to remain in the Union on the condition that the North refrain from abusing or coercing the seceding cotton states. A smaller number, especially in the northwest corner of the state, were unconditional Unionists and would have nothing whatever to do with secession. The westerners owned few slaves and had no grievances with the North. Why should they fight other people's battles, especially when those other people happened to be their old antagonists from eastern Virginia? Besides, if the Old Dominion was to secede, northwestern Virginia would be pinched between southern armies in the tidewater and the northern masses of Ohio and Pennsylvania. Few residents of trans-Allegheny Virginia wished to see their homes and farms turned into battlefields.

This coalition of conditional and unconditional Unionists held Virginia in the Union throughout the critical winter months of 1860–61. Indeed, as late as April 4 the special state convention that had been called to consider the national crisis voted down a secession proposal. But the

Union coalition disintegrated two weeks later. Confederate batteries in Charleston, South Carolina, opened fire on Fort Sumter on April 12, the Federal commander surrendered on April 13, President Lincoln called for 75,000 troops on April 15, and the Virginia convention voted to secede on April 17.[7]

Unconditional Unionists of the northwest, especially Republicans, denounced the April 17 ordinance and immediately began organizing resistance to secession, scheduled for a May 23 popular referendum. Dozens of local Union meetings and scores of editorials urged westerners to resist, to crush secession in the approaching canvass. Northwestern Democrats and former Whigs who had been aiming venomous attacks at Virginia Republicans only a few months earlier now joined with those very same Republicans to oppose secession. Antebellum party lines were cracking and crumbling. A new party, a Unionist party, was emerging from the decay, and it would control the political life of the northwest for the next ten years.[8]

A strong undercurrent running through many of the Union rallies was the renewed western desire for separate statehood. Westerners had talked about this for decades, but with the threat of secession looming, the talk increased in frequency and volume. By April observers as far away as New York were mentioning the trans-Allegheny sentiment for a division of the state.[9]

Meanwhile, the Richmond secession convention was taking Virginia out of the Union step by step, even before the secession ordinance was submitted to the voters on May 23. Between April 17 and May 1 the convention canceled the congressional elections scheduled for late May, entered into an offensive and defensive alliance with the Confederacy, ratified the Confederate constitution, elected members to the Confederate Congress, absolved all Virginians from their allegiance to the United States, and seized the Federal arsenal at Harpers Ferry along with the navy yards at Norfolk and the customs houses in Richmond and Norfolk. The May 23 referendum, then, would be meaningless.[10]

By this time virtually all western Unionists realized that local protest meetings, however outspoken, would not be enough to prevent Virginia from joining the Confederacy. Accordingly, about 450 western Republicans, Whigs, and Democrats gathered in a Wheeling mass meeting on May 13 to settle on some common reaction to the crisis. What they would do was not clear, even to themselves. No single solution to their problem had jelled by mid-May. All opposed secession and most were willing to take up arms against southern invaders, but there unity ended. There was obvious sentiment for the formation of a new state out of the northwestern counties, but few clear ideas about how to erect one. Some spoke of forming a provisional state government; others, of annexing the northwest to Pennsylvania or Ohio. Many confused a provisional government with a new state. Because of this uncertainty, the First Wheeling Convention simply condemned secession and called for a second meeting in Wheeling if the secession ordinance should be adopted.[11]

Ten days later, to the surprise of no one, the voters of Virginia approved the secession ordinance by an overwhelming margin (roughly four to one) and cut the final thin thread between Richmond and Washington. Nearly all the votes against secession came from the northwest, where the ordinance was defeated almost two to one. Western Unionists could delay no longer. They were forced now to acquiesce in secession or to take some action against it.[12]

Acquiescence was out of the question, so the Second Wheeling Convention, representing thirty-five northern and western counties, assembled on June 11. The convention members, some elected as delegates by their neighbors and others attending on their own, were still confused and uncertain about what should be done. Some wanted to form a new state immediately. Others looked forward to separate statehood but saw too many constitutional obstacles to an immediate move. Another possibility, one that had been steadily gaining favor during the spring, was to form not a new state but a new Unionist government for the old state, a "Restored government of Virginia." This course would enable Virginia Unionists to maintain official ties with the North. At the same time it would pave the way for the future formation of a new state since a prerequisite for West Virginia statehood would be consent by the Virginia legislature.

The man who transformed this general idea into a specific proposal for the convention was Francis H. Pierpont, a lifelong Whig from Fairmont near the Pennsylvania border. Born near Morgantown in 1814, he was a graduate of Allegheny College in Pennsylvania, a prominent lawyer for the Baltimore and Ohio Railroad, and a prosperous small manufacturer. His massive head, framed by a mop of curly dark hair and a full beard, gave him an aura of strength and stability. His legal and business success and his calm demeanor inspired confidence. Diligent and conscientious, he felt compelled by his strong Whig Unionism and his educational and business ties with the North to speak out against secession. In June 1861, at forty-seven years of age, he was just beginning a political career that would catapult him to the governorship and a leading position within the Virginia Republican party. [13]

Although Pierpont did not invent the idea of the Restored government, he did give it some legal underpinning and transform it into a specific program of action. His plan was based on the Lockean right of revolution and the Supreme Court's 1848 decision in *Luther* v. *Borden* (7 Howard 1). Since state officials supposedly had led Virginia out of the Union, Pierpont reasoned, the Wheeling convention, as a representative of the people, should declare that seceding state officers had abused their powers and that the loyal people were exercising their right to reconstitute the state government. Then the convention should turn out all disloyal public officials, appoint new ones, invite the Union army in to preserve order and secure the northwest, and ask for recognition of the Restored state government by Congress.

This recognition doubtless would be forthcoming because by the decision in *Luther* v. *Borden*, Congress, in its capacity to guarantee a republican form of government to every state, could decide which government in a state was the legal one. And Congress surely would not recognize the Richmond government. Once the state government was reorganized on a Union basis and recognized in Washington, it could consider a division to form a new state. [14]

Whether the Lockean right of revolution extended to states as part of a federal system Pierpont did not tarry to consider. Nor did he worry that only about one-fifth of the state was represented in the Wheeling convention or that some of the convention members were self-appointed. These were critical times, and theoretical niceties were subordinated to immediate practical needs. [15]

The June convention, with little opposition, adopted the Restored government formula. Acting for the loyal citizens of Virginia, it declared vacant all state offices occupied by rebels and appointed Pierpont governor of the state. To assist him, the convention also named a lieutenant governor and a five-man governor's council, all former Whigs except for one Republican. Their pride in this accomplishment was not at all diminished by the outraged reaction of the *Richmond Enquirer*, which called them "miserable tools and pimps" of the despot Lincoln. [16]

The Lockean portion of the Restored plan had been completed, and recognition by Washington would conclude the process. Although he apparently took no active part in the formation of the Unionist state government, President Lincoln delighted the Virginians on June 25 when his secretary of war, Simon Cameron, assured "Governor" Pierpont in a letter that the Federal government would soon send aid to western Virginia and that meanwhile the governor could commission officers and enlist troops for the Union army. The next day Secretary of the Interior Caleb B. Smith informed "Governor" Pierpont of the new apportionment of Congress based on the 1860 census. The most dramatic executive recognition came in Lincoln's July 4 message to Congress when he mentioned the Restored government and declared that "those loyal citizens, this government is bound to recognize, and protect, as being Virginia."[17]

Lincoln refused to speculate on the constitutional questions raised by the Virginia experiment, but he did return to the subject in December 1862 when he was considering a bill to create the new state of West Virginia. Some members of his cabinet questioned the legality of the bill because they doubted that the tiny Restored government, which had given Virginia's consent to the formation of the new state, was the legitimate government for the Old Dominion. Lincoln, however, once again declared that the Restored government, even though small, was the only legal authority in Virginia. The only real constitutional question, he said, was whether the Restored legislature was legal. He believed it was because all Virginians had been invited to participate in the Restored government and vote on the West Virginia statehood issue. If many had ignored the call, it was their own fault. Indeed, he continued, "it is not the qualified voters, but the qualified voters, who choose to vote, that constitute the political power of the state."[18] Thus, if Confederate sympathizers refused to recognize the Pierpont government, they were merely removing themselves from the political process, not destroying the state government.

The recognition process continued into the second week of July. The Restored legislature—those members of the Richmond General Assembly who refused to recognize secession—met in Wheeling on July 1. Consisting of only eleven senators and forty-nine delegates, representing 48 of Virginia's 150 counties, the legislature elected two United States senators to replace James M. Mason and Robert M. T. Hunter, who had vacated their seats to join the Confederacy. The new Restored senators—John S. Carlile, a Unionist Democrat from the northwestern town of Clarksburg, and Waitman T. Willey, a Morgantown Whig and friend of Governor Pierpont—were sponsored by their fellow southern Unionist Andrew Johnson of Tennessee and seated in the Senate on July 13 after some ineffectual opposition by border-state senators. Restored Virginia's representatives had been seated in the House on July 4. Thus, recognized by President Lincoln, the Senate, and the House, the upstart Restored government became the de jure authority for all of Virginia. [19]

Early in the war, before most people realized how long and costly the conflict would be and when "reconstruction" meant simply the return of the southern states to their allegiance to the Union, the Virginia Restored government represented an important accomplishment. [20] It was the first Confederate state to be reconstructed (in the initial sense of the word), and it was widely regarded as a useful precedent that would be followed in other rebellious states. Lincoln's attorney general Edward Bates supported the Pierpont government partly because it would further the Federal government's efforts to restore the Union. The administration's plan, he wrote, was this:

> When a state, by its perverted functionaries, has declared itself out of the Union, we avail ourselves of all the sound and loyal elements of the State—all who owe allegiance to, and claim protection of the Constitution, to form a State Government, as nearly as may be, upon the former model, and claiming to be the very State which has been, in part, overthrown by the successful rebellion. In this way we establish a constitutional nucleus around which all the scattered elements of the Commonwealth may meet and combine and thus restore the old State in its original integrity. [21]

It was generally understood throughout the North that the Virginia Restored government was a model for the restoration of other rebel states. The *New York Times* rejoiced in the creation of the new government, for it was "the beginning of a system which will sooner or later be inaugurated in all the seceded States." Congressman Martin F. Conway of Kansas also mentioned this as an administration plan, and even private citizens fully expected to see similar governments established in the other Confederate states. In Virginia, Governor Pierpont, Archibald Campbell (the energetic Republican editor of the *Wheeling Intelligencer*), and members of the June Wheeling convention predicted that the example of the northwest would be followed in other states to the south.[22] In the minds of President Lincoln, his cabinet, some congressmen, and many northerners, the Virginia experience was a rehearsal for Reconstruction.[23]

The widespread assumption that the Union war machine would quickly gobble up other Confederate states and apply the Virginia formula all over the South proved unfounded. As the cost of the war mounted in blood and money, the North determined to change the South, to reconstruct not only the Union but also the laws and institutions of the southern states. When that determination was made, Congress dropped the Virginia formula; it was too lenient, inadequate to ensure significant reform. But the Restored government retains significance as a concrete example of exactly what the nation meant by "reconstruction" in the early months of the war.

Of further importance, the Wheeling experiment probably contributed to President Lincoln's own thinking about Reconstruction. According to his attorney general, Lincoln in 1861 expected to apply the Virginia formula in other rebellious states. Moreover, his famous "Ten Percent Plan" of December 1863 bore obvious similarities to the Virginia precedent. Both depended on a local core of Unionists who would take the initiative to form a minority loyalist government—a constitutional nucleus, in Attorney General Bates's words—that would serve as the de jure government of the state during the war. In both cases it was assumed that as the Confederacy crumbled, the restored, or Unionist, state governments would gradually absorb those ex-Confederates willing to swear allegiance to the Union. Eventually, the restored governments would represent the entire state population.

Finally, the Pierpont regime was significant as an instrument of reform. Despite opposition from Confederates on one side and some radical northerners on the other, the Restored administration would continue to govern Union-occupied areas of Virginia for the remainder of the war. And surrounded by enemies on all sides, Virginia Unionist-Republicans would draw up a new state constitution that would incorporate many of the basic reforms usually associated with postwar Reconstruction.

The Alexandria Government

Once the Restored government was recognized by the president and Congress as the de jure authority in Virginia, the way was open for advocates of separate statehood to form a new state out of western Virginia. The Restored government provided loyal civil authority for westerners, but it also gave them a state government that would readily consent to the creation of a new state, for the leaders and supporters of the Pierpont administration were also the leaders and supporters of separate statehood for the northwest.

Wasting no time, westerners called a special convention that drew up a constitution for the new state in November 1861. Although Confederates and conservative Unionists refused to participate in the state-making process, statehood advocates ratified the document in April 1862, the western-dominated Restored legislature gave its consent in May, and in December Congress passed a statehood bill providing for gradual emancipation. Despite serious doubts about the constitutionality of the West Virginia bill, President Lincoln signed it on December 31. After West Virginia added the required gradual-emancipation clause to its constitution, it entered the Union as a separate state on June 20, 1863.[24]

The new state's creation left the Wheeling Restored government in an embarrassing position. It was the legal government of old Virginia but found itself sitting in the far corner of West Virginia. Even more discouraging, the creation of West Virginia lopped off most of the popular support of the Pierpont regime. The 20,000 or so politically active Unionists of the former northwest, including most members of the Restored government, were now citizens of another state. This left only the few counties near Washington, the two Eastern Shore counties of Accomack and Northampton across Chesapeake Bay, and the extreme southeast tip of Virginia around Norfolk and Hampton—all areas occupied by Federal military forces—under the Restored government's authority. The remainder of Virginia was controlled by the Confederates. Nevertheless, the Pierpont regime was the recognized government for all of Virginia, and the governor and his assistants packed their belongings and records and reestablished their offices in Alexandria, across the Potomac River from Washington, in August 1863.

The problems facing this tiny migrant government would have staggered even the most vigorous and powerful administration. Pierpont's most pressing task was to strengthen Unionist law and order in the Restored counties of war-torn eastern Virginia. The governor hardly knew where to begin. Confederate sympathizers in Accomack County elected their friends to office in the Restored government; Federal and state tax officials were several months and thousands of dollars behind in their collections due to unsettled conditions and harassing raids by Confederate cavalry; Portsmouth city policemen resigned en masse because the city had not collected enough revenue to pay them; the state circuit court in Alexandria had not met for two years; Alexandria, crowded with soldiers, runaway slaves, and other refugees, was threatened by deadly epidemics; Norfolk's trade all but vanished, its schools and newspapers shut their doors, and its municipal government limped along with less than 20 percent of its usual income.[25]

Governor Pierpont and the legislature attacked these problems one at a time. New state judges and tax collectors moved into the Restored counties to preserve order and gather revenue. Pierpont cooperated with military and local officials in programs to provide social services and sanitation. Nevertheless, Restored Virginia remained politically and economically unstable until the end of the war.[26]

Restoring order in the midst of wartime confusion would have been a large enough problem for any energetic administration. Unfortunately for the Restored government, however, that was only the beginning of its troubles, for Union general Benjamin F. Butler soon arrived in Virginia to complicate life further. Butler, a portly "political general" from Massachusetts, was given command of the Department of Virginia and North Carolina in November 1863 after a stormy and controversial administration as occupying commander of Louisiana. His activities in Virginia soon sent a stream of protests from Unionists in Norfolk and Portsmouth to Governor Pierpont. The general's provost marshals were making arrests in purely civil cases, the provost courts were deciding cases that had nothing to do with the military, Butler himself was ordering Norfolk and Portsmouth city officials and banks to turn over their records to him for his inspection and criticism, and new military taxes were being placed on civilian activities.[27]

Butler, suspicious of southern Unionism, including the Restored government, soon suspended civil government in Norfolk and arrested a Restored state judge who tried to hold court there. He removed various Unionist public officials in the Norfolk area and replaced them with his New England associates. The general also confiscated one newspaper's presses and took soldiers from the field to run his own paper, the *Norfolk New Regime*, later suppressed by Federal authority. To compound these problems for Pierpont, there was ample and solid evidence that General

Butler and his Massachusetts friends were making handsome profits smuggling cotton out of the Confederacy.[28]

Governor Pierpont's loud and frequent complaints to Butler and President Lincoln brought only private denunciations of the general's actions by cabinet members.[29] Lincoln, hard-pressed to win reelection in 1864, could hardly afford to alienate General Butler's radical and abolitionist admirers. The president did draft a letter to Butler in early August, admonishing him for handling affairs that did not concern the military and advising him to keep a full account of the public's money. But Lincoln prudently filed it away for later use. After his reelection in November, however, the president took the advice of General Ulysses S. Grant (who was frustrated by Butler's constant military blundering and embarrassed by his tendency toward scandal) and removed the rotund general from his command. It was a victory for the Restored government, but belated and hardly decisive.[30]

Buffeted on one side by Virginia Confederates and on the other by the shady General Butler, the reeling Restored government was hardly prepared for still another blow, this one delivered by a supposed friend, the Congress of the United States. Congress's attitude toward the Restored regime had shifted gradually since the exciting summer days of 1861. In the early months of the war, Congress saw the Restored government as a powerful ally, an embarrassment to Richmond rebels, and a model for Reconstruction in other Confederate states. By 1863, however, conditions had changed. The Pierpont administration no longer represented many thousands of Virginia Unionists; West Virginia had taken most of them with it, leaving the Restored government the master of only a few counties in eastern Virginia. Rather than a strong ally for the North and an embarrassment to the South, the Alexandria government was now more of an embarrassment to the Union because of its Lilliputian size.

In addition, the expectation that the Restored government would be a precedent for rapid Reconstruction all over the South had proved unfounded. The war did not end quickly, and Congress had determined to require more of the southern states than a simple willingness to return to their former allegiances. Indeed, the Restored regime's value as a model had begun to dwindle as early as the first battle of Manassas in July 1861.[31]

Virginia Unionists learned of their reduced status during the winter and spring of 1864 when three newly elected congressmen from Restored counties presented their credentials to the House of Representatives. To the Virginians' chagrin, the Committee on Elections recommended that they be denied House seats because their districts were incapable of conducting full and free elections due to the turmoil of war. With the help of some border-state congressmen, the would-be representatives defended their claims in several learned and witty speeches. Moved by the eloquent defenses of the Virginians, Henry L. Dawes, chairman of the committee, assured them that if feelings alone could decide the case, they would be seated immediately. The question, however, was one of majorities and minorities among Virginians, and he urged the House to reject their claims. This the representatives did by a vote of 94 to 23, with most of the no votes coming from the border states. Thus, except for senators Lemuel J. Bowden (who had replaced Waitman T. Willey) and John Carlile, the Restored government was unrepresented in the Thirty-eighth Congress.[32]

The long string of humiliations continued during the political campaigns of 1864. In May, Virginia Unionist-Republicans appointed a five-man delegation to the Republican national convention scheduled to meet in Baltimore on June 7. Upon arriving, however, the Virginians were denied voting privileges even though other Confederate states (Louisiana, Arkansas, and Tennessee) were given full and equal status. Louisiana and Arkansas, undergoing Reconstruction according to President Lincoln's Ten Percent Plan, could hardly be snubbed by a convention overwhelmingly devoted to Lincoln himself. Tennessee, home state of Andrew Johnson who would be nominated for the vice-presidency by this same convention, was necessarily given full representation. But Virginia, despite its recognition by the president and Congress, was shunted aside along with maverick groups claiming to represent Florida and South Carolina. And even though Virginia Republicans campaigned for Lincoln and Johnson in the North as well as in the Restored counties in 1864, they had been shut out of their party's councils. Once again, the Restored regime's small size had proved a crippling handicap.[33]

Beset on all sides by enemies as well as supposed friends, Virginia Republicans nevertheless persevered in their determination to maintain their Restored government. Their only major accomplishment during the Alexandria years—other than legal survival—was the construction and adoption of a new state constitution. The moving force behind this project was Governor Pierpont himself. During the summer of 1863 he conferred several times with Secretary of the Treasury Salmon P. Chase and President

Lincoln about straightening out Virginia's slave laws. Lincoln's Emancipation Proclamation had freed all slaves in Virginia except those in the Union-controlled districts of northwestern Virginia (now West Virginia) and the areas around Alexandria, the Eastern Shore, and Norfolk. Yet Virginia's 1851 constitution recognized the peculiar institution, and its statutes regulated it. What would happen when the rebellious parts of the Commonwealth were reclaimed for the Union? National policy forbade slavery in those areas, but state law protected it. There would be innumerable court cases, suits, and controversies arising from this conflict in the lawbooks.

To avoid such confusion, Pierpont discussed with Chase and Lincoln the possibility of calling a constitutional convention to adopt a charter more in conformity with national standards—in short, an antislavery constitution, something the governor had wanted for a long time. The three men worked out a plan, and by autumn 1863 Pierpont was ready for the Restored legislature to call the convention.[34]

The Restored General Assembly, consisting of only six senators and eleven delegates representing nine counties and the city of Norfolk, met in the Alexandria city council chamber on December 7. Most of the legislators were farmers, but a few lawyers, merchants, and artisans represented the cities of Alexandria and Norfolk. Most were property owners, and all were educated to some degree. A large proportion, perhaps one-third, were natives of northern states who had settled in Virginia before or during the war. Former Whigs predominated in the rather conservative Unionist-Republican Assembly, but at least one radical Republican, New York–born John Hawxhurst of Fairfax County, was present to urge fundamental reform.[35]

Two weeks after convening, the General Assembly followed Pierpont's lead and called for a constitutional convention to meet in Alexandria on February 13. Delegates were to be elected on January 21. Any Virginian who had not adhered to the rebellion since September 1, 1861, could serve as a delegate, and anyone who had remained loyal to the Union since January 1, 1863, could vote in the election. Although the requirements for voting and officeholding appeared quite liberal, the *New York Times* castigated the Restored government for excluding ex-Confederates who had taken President Lincoln's amnesty oath of December 1863.[36]

The convention met on February 13 in the United States District Court room in Alexandria. Again the minuscule dimensions of the Restored government were reflected in the small number of delegates present. Seventeen members representing thirteen counties and the cities of Norfolk, Portsmouth, and Williamsburg were all the Virginia Unionists could muster for this important convention. The delegates included several members of the General Assembly and were generally drawn from the same background—middle class, educated, former Whig, and politically moderate.[37]

In two months the convention legally destroyed much of what was old Virginia and laid the constitutional groundwork for a new society. The new constitution abolished slavery in all counties of the state; gave Governor Pierpont the power to appoint state judges, thereby assuring a Unionist and antislavery judiciary; extended the franchise by reducing residency requirements for voting and officeholding, thus enabling recently arrived northerners and returning Unionist refugees to participate in state government; disfranchised nearly all Confederate soldiers and civilians, leaving the state in the hands of Unionists and recent northern immigrants;[38] established Virginia's first system of free public education;[39] changed from the voice vote to the ballot, thereby increasing the political independence of Republicans and the poorer classes; substituted annual for biennial sessions of the legislature; made all property taxable according to assessed value, thus erasing the long-standing discrimination in favor of planters; and repudiated the Confederate national and state debts. These and several lesser reforms legally overturned the old order and substituted a more democratic political system.[40]

This radical departure from the past, however, was destined to have only small influence on the wartime history of Virginia. Most Virginians were Confederate soldiers or supporters and refused to recognize the new Restored constitution. Indeed, Governor Pierpont and most convention delegates feared that even in the Restored counties Confederate sympathizers would vote the charter down if it was submitted for ratification. To avoid that embarrassment the governor and convention simply declared the 1864 constitution to be Virginia's new fundamental law. While the new charter governed only those counties and cities within Federal military lines during the remainder of the war, still it was significant. This was the constitution under which Virginians would live after the war, at least until the 1870 adoption of the radical constitution of 1868, and the 1864 charter anticipated many of the changes that were later associated with radical Reconstruction throughout the southern states.[41]

While the governor and other Unionists could look back on the constitutional convention with some measure of pride, they still faced one last embarrassment before the war dragged to a halt. By the spring of 1865 virtually everyone knew the southern cause was hopeless. General Grant's powerful war machine was pounding away at the ragtag remnants of Robert E. Lee's Army of Northern Virginia in the trenches around Petersburg, and General William T. Sherman's western army was burning its way through the Carolinas. On April 2 the Confederates evacuated their capital and trudged toward Lynchburg in southern Virginia. The next morning Union forces marched through the burning city of Richmond and prepared for a visit by President Lincoln.[42]

What happened in the next few days is not clear, but it doubtless threw a scare into the Restored government. On April 5 President Lincoln arrived in the fallen Confederate capital and toured several parts of the city. While in Richmond he suggested to John A. Campbell, a former justice of the United States Supreme Court and assistant secretary of war in the Confederacy, that the rebel legislature of Virginia be called into session. According to Campbell, the General Assembly was to withdraw the state's troops from Lee's army, still fending off Grant southwest of Richmond, and thus force a quick surrender. But the Assembly also was to remain in session and handle the numerous problems attending the return of Virginia to its normal status within the Union. In such a case, the Restored government in Alexandria would be repudiated, at least by implication. Lincoln, on the other hand, later denied that he had meant to abandon Pierpont's regime. According to the president, the rebel General Assembly was to withdraw the state's soldiers and then adjourn. In his eyes, the Richmond legislators were simply war chieftains who had the de facto power to withdraw troops from the field and thus bring a speedy end to the war. The Pierpont government would then oversee the readmission process. The evidence is so conflicting and Lincoln's statements are so ambiguous that a certain judgment of the president's intentions is impossible. In any case, Governor Pierpont had little occasion to rejoice.[43]

The question of how to withdraw Virginia troops from the Confederate army became academic on April 9 when General Lee met General Grant at Appomattox Court House. When the news of Lee's surrender reached Alexandria early on the morning of April 10, excited Unionists, like those across the river in Washington, draped flags from their windows, rang bells, and fired salutes to the Federal triumph. That night two large public meetings rejoiced and heard speeches by Governor Pierpont and other prominent Unionists. The suffering had finally ended, and the Union had emerged victorious.[44]

What had Virginia Republicans contributed to the Union cause during the preceding four years? They had spoken loudly and bravely for the Union when such words were hateful to most Virginians. They had formed a loyalist state government within a few weeks after Fort Sumter and had received the blessings of the president and Congress. Governor Pierpont had raised regiments for the Federal armies among northwestern Unionists, and his Restored government had consented to the formation of the new state of West Virginia. Fending off Confederate raiders and arrogant Union generals, the Restored regime in Alexandria had managed to write a new constitution that brought Virginia out of the antebellum era and into modern America. Perhaps most important, Pierpont and his Unionist allies had managed to keep their government alive throughout the war and thus enable it to lead the Old Dominion through postwar Reconstruction.

CHAPTER 2

A Year of Disappointments

THE REMAINING months of the year of victory, 1865, seemingly were filled with bright prospects for Governor Pierpont and his Republican allies. The hated Confederacy finally had been reduced to defeat, the White House and Congress were controlled by Republicans who would guide the nation through Reconstruction, and the Restored government could now move its offices to their rightful place in the old capital of Richmond. Picking up the pieces of the Old Dominion and fashioning a new Virginia would require hard work, perhaps, but the suddenly potent Republicans in Alexandria were anxious to begin the task.

The tough little band of Unionists who had survived all manner of insults and dangers for four years would suffer more of the same in 1865, unfortunately for them.[1] While the Restored government ultimately did move to Richmond and begin the state's reconstruction, a number of unforeseen problems materialized in the summer and fall that would shatter the wartime unity of the Unionists and leave them once again a minority in their own state government. Former Confederates proved to be more aggressive than Governor Pierpont expected, wartime Republican allies vigorously opposed his policies, and the fall elections produced a state legislature bent on dismantling many of the reforms accomplished by the Alexandria government. By the end of the year, Virginia's Republicans were appealing to the Republican Congress in Washington for protection and aid, just as they had during the secession crisis in 1861. Reconstruction, like the war, would not be accomplished as quickly and easily as some Republicans had hoped.

Pierpont's Reconstruction

Four days after the noisy victory celebrations in the streets of Alexandria, President Lincoln's cabinet held its first postwar meeting across the Potomac River in Washington. Lincoln expressed his fear that chaos and anarchy might grip the southern states unless civil governments were established quickly. Secretary of War Edwin Stanton proposed that Federal troops be used to establish loyal governments in the former Confederate states. Secretary of the Navy Gideon Welles, wary of centralized power, quickly objected that Virginia already had such a government and would require no military action. "The President," Welles wrote in his diary, "said the point was well taken. Governor Denison [Postmaster General William Denison of Ohio] said he thought we should experience little difficulty from Pierpont. Stanton said none whatever." Thus, the Restored government, battered and humiliated so often for the past two years, regained some of its dignity. It would guide Virginia through the postwar years.[2]

Several hours later, however, President Lincoln accompanied his wife to Ford's Theater a few blocks from the White House. When John Wilkes Booth shot the president that night, the Restored government's status became uncertain once more. How would the new president regard the tiny Alexandria establishment? President Andrew Johnson, former war governor of Tennessee, dispelled all doubts on May 9 when he issued an executive order recognizing the Pierpont regime as the legal state government of Virginia.[3] After all, it was Johnson who in 1861 had presented to the Senate the credentials of the Restored government's first senators-elect. And the Unionist state government established in Tennessee in 1862, with Johnson as governor, was based partly on the precedent set by the Pierpont administration in Virginia. President Johnson's acceptance of the Restored government was one of the few victories Virginia Republicans would enjoy in the first year after Appomattox.

Two weeks after President Johnson's recognition, Governor Pierpont was ready to make the move to Richmond. As he sailed down the Potomac River toward the state capital on May 24, the governor doubtless pondered the many problems plaguing the Old Dominion.[4] How would President Johnson deal with the defeated Confederate states? Pierpont had some idea of the president's policy, for he had visited the White House a few days earlier to discuss national readjustment. There Johnson had read part of his forthcoming proclamation on Reconstruction and asked the governor's opinion. Pierpont had approved in general, but the objections he made revealed him to be more lenient than the president in one respect. Governor Pierpont argued that the confiscation of rebel estates, a possibility in the tentative presidential plan, would only engender bitterness and opposition toward the Federal government in the South. It would be better to leave the property to its owners. Pierpont, unlike the president, believed that wealthy southerners had been the last to rebel, not the first; they feared war would wreck them economically. To exclude from amnesty all southerners worth more than $20,000, therefore, was wrong and probably would create more problems than it would solve.[5]

After leaving the Potomac and proceeding down Chesapeake Bay, the governor's steamer turned westward and chugged past the entrance to one of Virginia's most important ports, Norfolk, situated near the mouth of the James River. Whitelaw Reid, the noted northern journalist, had passed this same way only a few weeks before the governor and described the aftereffects of war on Norfolk. Reid saw a city almost devoid of activity. "There is scarcely any business," he wrote in his travel account. "No trade comes or can come from the interior. The people have no produce to spare, and no money with which to buy." About one month after Pierpont's passage through the area, another touring northern journalist, John Richard Dennett, described Norfolk as a rough city indeed. In the first few months after the war, law and order seemed to have disappeared. Fistfights, cheered on by rowdy street crowds, erupted in the city's main thoroughfares, and there were no police to intervene.

Conditions in the rural areas along the banks of the James River were little if any better. Hundreds of miles of fencing had gone up in the smoke of army campfires; innumerable homes and barns had collapsed in flames; railroads and canals had been destroyed by the competing armies; Confederate money was now worthless; farm implements, wagons, and draft animals had been stolen, destroyed, or worn out. Even in areas of the state not visited by wartime destruction, the conflict had left its mark. The observant journalist Dennett traveled on to Lynchburg in south-central Virginia in July and reported that "trade is dead, the people have no money, nor is there a prospect of their soon getting any. . . . The shelves of the shops are scantily supplied with poor goods."[6]

If the governor had traveled to Richmond overland rather than by the water route, he would have observed similar scenes of desolation. Northern traveler J. T. Trowbridge wrote that between Alexandria and Manassas in northern Virginia "the country for the most part consisted of fenceless fields abandoned to weeds, stump-lots, and undergrowth." Advancing to Fredericksburg in the central part of the state, Trowbridge found that city little recovered from the terrible battles in 1862 and 1863. "Scarcely a house in the burnt portions had been rebuilt. Many houses were entirely destroyed, and only the solitary chimney-stacks remained. Of others, you saw no vestige but broken brick walls, and foundations overgrown with Jamestown-weeds, sumachs, and thistles."[7]

Farther west, conditions were just as depressing. Charles Douglas Gray, an unconditional Unionist farmer of Augusta County who had stayed home during the war, described the pitiful state of the lower Shenandoah Valley:

> From Harper's Ferry to New Market, which is about eighty miles, from one mountain to the other, the country was almost a desert. There were no fences. Speaking of the condition of the valley after General Sheridan retired, I described wheat-fields growing without any enclosure; some one asked me whether the stock would not destroy the wheat. I said, "Certainly, if General Sheridan had not taken the precaution of removing all the stock." We could cultivate grain without fences, as we had no cattle, hogs, sheep or horses, or anything else. . . . Large armies, whether friendly or hostile, are devouring animals.[8]

To the south of the governor's river route to Richmond lay Petersburg, scene of General Grant's ten-month siege of 1864–65. "Its business was shattered," Trowbridge wrote. "All the lower part of the town showed the ruinous effects of the shelling it had received. . . . In the ends of some buildings I counted more than twenty shot-holes." The prospects for farmers in the countryside seemed almost hopeless: "Their fences destroyed, buildings burned, farming implements worn out, horses, mules, and other stock consumed by both armies, investments in Confederate bonds worthless, bank-stock gone, without money, or anything to exchange for money, they had often only their bare lands on which to commence life anew; and could not therefore give much encouragement to the freedman, whatever may have been their disposition toward him."[9]

The governor's destination, the capital of Richmond far up the James River, had suffered terribly during the war, especially upon the evacuation of the Confederate army in early April. More than twenty square blocks of the business district, particularly the area between Thomas Jefferson's state Capitol and the river, had been burned and looted on the night of April 2. Ninety percent of the commercial part of the city was destroyed; 228 businesses were in ashes; estimates of the financial loss ranged in the tens of millions of dollars. "For a quarter of a mile one passes nothing but toppling walls, forlorn-looking chimneys, heaps of bricks, with here and there a ruined safe lying in the midst, warped and red from the effects of intense heat," Dennett wrote back to his northern readers. Even the Governor's Mansion, next to the Capitol, had caught fire briefly during the Confederate withdrawal. In the confusion of the fire and the evacuation of Confederate columns, persons unknown had looted the mansion of silverware and linens. [10]

In the midst of Virginia's physical ruin and economic dislocation were more than 500,000 freedmen, no longer slaves but not yet completely free, no longer property but not yet equal citizens. Nearly three-fourths of the state's former slaves were homeless in the first few weeks after Appomattox. And if they expected little in the way of relief from their former masters, they were disturbed that many of their liberators, the northern soldiers of the Union army, seemed insensitive to their plight and hostile to their race. Clearly, the Federal government, the only agency capable of providing relief, would have to make some arrangements for these propertyless and homeless people. [11]

Fortunately for Governor Pierpont and the freedmen, Virginia blacks were not left to shift for themselves completely. On March 3, 1865, Congress had created the Bureau of Refugees, Freedmen, and Abandoned Lands and had made it responsible for the well-being of four million southern blacks. During the Reconstruction years this agency issued millions of rations to destitute blacks and whites, oversaw the rudimentary education of tens of thousands of freedmen of all ages, arranged labor contracts for black laborers and white employers, settled disputes between freedmen and whites in bureau courts, and generally made the transition from slave to citizen easier and less bewildering. [12]

In Virginia the bureau would be established on May 31, 1865, under the direction of Assistant Commissioner Orlando Brown, a Connecticut native and Union army officer who had served as superintendent of Negro affairs in the Federal-held portions of Virginia during the war. A northern missionary who had witnessed Brown's work among the freedmen described him as "over six feet; large, and handsome, not elegant in manner. . . . Very warmhearted and affectionate, [Brown] . . . shows great capacity for organization." While Assistant Commissioner Brown and many of his subordinates were certainly sympathetic to the plight of the freedmen and did all in their power to help, still the Freedmen's Bureau could not protect every black from every injustice. Racism among some bureau personnel, inadequate resources and staff, and the overwhelming proportions of the task sometimes resulted in insensitive treatment and little protection. Nevertheless, the bureau often did protect and advise the freedmen, encouraging them to become independent and to take advantage of their new rights. Virginia blacks, like those in other parts of the Confederacy, were better off with the bureau than they would have been without it. [13]

The attitudes toward the Freedmen's Bureau displayed by conservative whites and by Republicans in Virginia are revealing. While many white Virginians saw the bureau as an acceptable alternative to the confusion and near anarchy of the first weeks after Appomattox, their position hardened once they realized that local and state governments elected under the Johnson plan could replace the bureau. They regarded the bureau as a "fomenter of mischief," a source of black impudence, and a symbol of the hated Yankee. Black Virginians and some white Republicans, on the other hand, depended on the bureau for protection, legal advice, and aid to the destitute. They almost always praised the bureau for its services and worked to keep it in the Old Dominion. Their support was not unquestioning and childlike; they protested loudly when they believed the bureau or its agents had wronged them. But in general, the freedmen were strong believers in this first Federal social program. [14]

Those who lived through the Reconstruction period knew that the bureau was a significant departure from past practices. The northern journalist Dennett wrote that the bureau had "familiarized the minds of the Negroes and their former masters with the fact, not learned at once, that the slaves had been really emancipated." The very fact that white conservatives hated the bureau was a sure sign that it was benefiting black Virginians. One of the state's most radical black leaders, Thomas Bayne of Norfolk, understood this perfectly. In the 1867–68 constitutional convention Bayne informed Conservatives that Republicans would support the bureau "because the opposite party, or those who are opposed to reconstruction do not like it. That is reason enough for me; just so long as the enemies to this Government hate any particular thing, that is the thing I want." [15]

Only five days before the Freedmen's Bureau opened its offices in Virginia on May 31, Governor Pierpont stepped off his steamer onto the Richmond docks. A reception party of prominent Richmond citizens—including Franklin Stearns, reputedly the wealthiest man in Virginia and a Unionist-Republican—conducted Pierpont in a slow rain through the burned district up to Capitol Square, the pleasant park surrounding the state Capitol and the Governor's Mansion.[16] A few remarks by Pierpont to a small crowd gathered in the square, followed by a fifteen-gun salute by Union soldiers and a reception in the Governor's Mansion, introduced the governor to the city of Richmond, cockpit of Virginia politics.[17]

Pierpont's course in the next few weeks, much to Richmond's joy, was exceptionally liberal and conciliatory toward the ex-Confederates. He believed that they had learned their lesson at Appomattox, that they would heed the counsels of the North, repudiate their old leaders, and deal fairly with the freedmen, and that they would do all these things of their own free will. The governor, traditional in his racial views, expected the freedmen to resume their livelihoods as agricultural laborers with little or no friction. Like many other white Unionists in the first few weeks after the war, he foresaw no black code, no elections to high office of prominent Confederates, no conflict between Congress and president or between North and South. To the governor, the war had accomplished the nation's objectives: it had destroyed a wasteful labor system and shattered the destructive doctrine of state sovereignty.[18] All that remained for men of goodwill was to join with the wartime Unionists, establish the Restored government in Richmond, and begin the work of rebuilding the state's economy. The governor envisioned a white Unionist party, now enlarged by prewar Whigs and the conditional Unionists of 1861, leading the Old Dominion into a new era of peace and prosperity.[19]

The governor had begun this work even before he left Alexandria for Richmond. On the second Monday after General Lee's surrender at Appomattox, Pierpont had helped to found the First National Bank of Richmond. Most of the seventeen directors of the bank were Virginia Republicans or northerners, and they eventually established their offices in the Richmond building that had housed the Confederate Treasury Department. Not surprisingly, given the founders, the bank became an official United States depository. With Pierpont's cooperation and help, Union army engineers began the laborious task of removing wartime obstructions in the James River, opening the channel from Norfolk to the capital. The governor consulted with New Jersey businessmen in June in an effort to rebuild the burned district in Richmond using northern capital. Of course, Pierpont also received numerous complaints and requests for aid from citizens trying to recover from the ravages of the recent conflict. The court of Henrico County asked for the governor's protection from "armed bands of marauders" who were terrorizing the citizens of the countryside on Richmond's outskirts.[20]

In an effort to restore civil authority throughout the state, Pierpont received deputations from many counties and questioned them about affairs at home. Like other southern governors, he spent most of his time in the summer of 1865 attempting to restore order by reestablishing local government. He called local and state political leaders to Richmond to learn their views and gather information on Reconstruction. Since virtually everyone who had supported the Confederacy was disfranchised and disqualified for office by the 1864 Alexandria constitution, the governor needed to know how many consistent Unionists lived in each county. They would run the state until Reconstruction could be completed.[21]

Pierpont had other questions for these local leaders: Were the people ready to resume their allegiance to the national government? Did they accept the abolition of slavery and the repudiation of state sovereignty? For three weeks the governor probed and questioned until he came to a decision: since there were not enough men qualified under the Alexandria constitution to reorganize state and local government, the disabling clause of the constitution would have to be removed by the General Assembly. In adopting this course and thereby deciding to allow most former Confederates to hold office and vote, Pierpont followed the same path most of his counterparts in other former Confederate states would travel. As he told visitors from Hanover County, "no man's heart is more earnest [than the governor's] in the desire to restore to Virginians and all other Americans their rights."[22]

Accordingly, Pierpont called a special session of the Restored legislature to meet in the Governor's Mansion on June 19. On that day he addressed the tiny group, asking for an amendment to the constitution. There were not enough Unionists in the state to organize civil government, he informed them. Indeed, he exhorted, "it is folly to suppose that a State can be governed under a Republican form of government when a large portion of the State—nineteen-twentieths of the people—are disfranchised and cannot hold office." But there was still another reason for repealing the disabling clause—the Anglo-Saxon spirit of fair play, which forbade "humiliating terms after a fair surrender." Declaring that the nature of the Union and the status of the freedmen had been settled by the war, Pierpont also appealed for an act legalizing slave marriages, suggested that the maximum legal interest rate be increased in order to attract capital to Virginia, and urged the Assembly to provide for state and congressional elections.[23]

The legislature, still reflecting its abbreviated wartime membership, consisted of only eleven delegates and five senators.[24] But since they were the only government the Old Dominion had at the moment, they went to work and put through several measures in a whirlwind session of five days. The Assembly amended the 1864 constitution, providing that all white adult males who met the residency requirements could vote if they would take the president's May 29 amnesty oath, including those who had been worth more than $20,000 in 1860, whom the president had excluded; if they were included in any of the president's other excepted classes, they could vote only after receiving special pardon from the White House. Pardoned or not, however, both groups were still disqualified for office. Moreover, those who had held office under the Confederate national or state governments were still disfranchised and disqualified. The Assembly, in order to remove these restrictions, provided for an October referendum; at this election, to be held at the same time as state and congressional elections, the voters could decide whether to give the next legislature power to remove the remaining disabling clause. Thus, most Virginia white males were enfranchised in June 1865, and they were given the option to remove all remaining state restrictions on voting and office-holding.[25]

The legislature also passed a law providing for state and congressional elections in October, one staying the collection of debts for one year, and another raising the property tax from ten to twenty cents per hundred dollars of property. It failed to legalize slave marriages, but before adjourning, it resolved "that the general policy of the present Federal administration, and especially its policy in regard to reconstruction in Virginia, is eminently wise, just and proper, and merits the warm approbation of the loyal people of Virginia." The Richmond press was effusive in its praise of the governor and the Assembly. The ex-Confederates could hardly have hoped for easier terms or a more lenient governor.[26]

With most antebellum voters reenfranchised, the state began electing city and county officials in July and preparing for the statewide election in October. Contrary to Pierpont's expectations, men who had fought for the South only four months earlier were elected to the various local offices in almost all cases. In the Richmond city election of July 25 all except a few of the successful candidates had been prominent Confederates. In fact, this was the major issue in the campaign, for the former soldiers openly reminded the voters of their war records. Moreover, local poll officials prevented some Unionists from voting because they allegedly had lost their residence by being away in the Federal army; those Richmonders who had worn Confederate gray, however, were allowed to vote. For all these reasons, Major General John W. Turner, the military commander in the Richmond area, set aside the municipal elections and forbade all but one officer to assume their duties. Failing to find suitable Unionist replacements, however, the general was forced to restore most of the elected city officials to office within a few weeks.[27]

Governor Pierpont apparently was not greatly disturbed by the local elections, for he continued on his lenient course. When he could not ascertain exactly what the president's pardoning policy was, despite repeated inquiries at Washington, he simply signed all applications for special pardon and forwarded them to Attorney General Bates. For Joseph R. Anderson, a prominent Confederate general, he made an "urgent recommendation" for pardon. He asked men who had served in the Confederate Congress whether their home areas required the continued presence of Federal troops. And he intervened to urge clemency when General Alfred H. Terry, military commander of Virginia, suppressed the *Richmond Whig* for printing a fiery anti-Johnson editorial.[28]

The governor, whose actions stunned his wartime Republican allies, surprised them even further when he openly opposed one of the founders of the Virginia Republican party, John C. Underwood. One of the most colorful and important figures in Virginia's Reconstruction, Underwood was a New York native who had moved to northern Virginia in the 1840s to promote free labor by using white workers in a dairy-farming scheme. In 1856 Underwood had attended the Republican national convention as a delegate from Virginia and had been forced to flee the state for remarks he had made to the convention. Shuttling between New York and Virginia in the late 1850s, he had helped to organize the Virginia Republican party and had worked to provide northern funds for the establishment of Republican newspapers in western Virginia.[29]

During the war Underwood had continued his work for the state's Republican party and had been rewarded with a Federal judgeship in 1863. As judge of the eastern district of Virginia, Underwood had vigorously pursued the confiscation of rebel property under the Federal Confiscation Acts of 1861 and 1862. Indeed, his court had expropriated more property than any other single court in the nation, almost half of the national total. The judge apparently regarded confiscation not only as apt punishment for rebels but also as an opportunity for loyal men to improve their lot in life while converting the Old Dominion to free-labor principles. Numerous Republicans, some from Massachusetts and others from Virginia, hastily bought up the confiscated Virginia lands and buildings with the judge's assurance, later proved erroneous, that the property was theirs permanently.[30]

Fifty-six years old in 1865, Underwood presented a virile appearance—broad forehead, piercing dark eyes, a thin straight nose, and long black beard. Even after the Confederate surrender and the establishment of the Restored government in Richmond, Judge Underwood's court continued to confiscate property at a rapid pace. Governor Pierpont, anxious to restore good relations between North and South, protested to Attorney General Bates in Washington and had the confiscation proceedings halted. Pierpont's lenient course in this and other matters made the governor the darling of the Virginia conservatives, and they sang his praises in numerous public meetings. Indeed, it seemed that the Union war governor himself had returned the state to Confederate control only a few months after Appomattox.[31]

Republican Reaction

Virginia Republicans were furious. They could hardly believe that the man they had supported during the war, the man who had raised troops in western Virginia for the Union armies, the man who had urged them to adopt an antislavery constitution—that this man could consult Confederate governors Henry A. Wise and John Letcher, reenfranchise thousands of rebel soldiers, and sign pardon applications indiscriminately. Republicans wondered whether the state was to be controlled by the same men who had led it through rebellion. Were the freedmen and the Unionists to be left at the mercy of rebel neighbors, rebel sheriffs, and rebel courts? Were the state's newspapers again free to denounce and insult Congress and the

North? Had the war been in vain? To Virginia Republicans the fruits of victory included more than an end to slavery and state sovereignty; it also meant personal safety for Unionists and blacks, impartial courts, political leaders untainted by a secessionist past, an end to Yankee-baiting by the press, and real respect for the Federal government, not just "acceptance of the situation."

Republicans reacted in various ways to the governor's lenient policy, at first hesitating to break with him. The Unionist *Alexandria Virginia State Journal* had urged Pierpont late in May not to ask the General Assembly to amend the constitution. Virginia, it claimed, should be in the hands of loyal men, not secessionists. Other Republicans wrote to the governor pleading with him not to turn the state over to the former Confederates. One lamented that "if men who have vilified and denounced the Government, and waged war upon it for the last four years, are now to be pardoned, enfranchised, and qualified to hold the offices, upon terms of equality with the loyal men of the state, then the triumph of the Union over the late rebellion will have been in vain."[32] When local elections began returning ex-Confederates to office, a Unionist who had fled Virginia during the war complained to Pierpont that "we are even now suffering outrages and if there is not some protection given us we will be compelled to leave our homes again."[33]

But the governor refused to change his course, and Virginia Republicans began openly to criticize their erstwhile leader. Lewis McKenzie, a leading figure in Pierpont's wartime Restored government in Alexandria, described with disgust "the former enemies of the government coming in crowds to the governor." George Tucker, another veteran of the Alexandria government, called Pierpont "an apostate" and informed northern congressmen that the governor was "very unacceptable" to Union men. In mid-August the *Alexandria Virginia State Journal*, one of the mainstays of the Restored government during its Alexandria years, condemned Pierpont in an editorial: "The truly loyal population of the State are almost unanimously opposed to him, while those who have been fighting the battles of the Confederacy are just as unanimously in his favor." Nearly three weeks later the *Journal* made a prediction that would ultimately prove painfully true. "He has sold himself cheaply to his old, bitter and most deadly enemies," the editor complained, "and as soon as he has accomplished their desires they will kick him to the dogs."[34]

But the Republicans did more than write letters and editorials; they began forming local political organizations to oppose Pierpont's policy. On June 12 northern Virginia Unionists organized the Union Association of Alexandria. The officers of the new group included S. Ferguson Beach, a northern-born Alexandria lawyer who had participated in the Alexandria Restored government; Dr. Gillet F. Watson, a Virginia native and former Whig of the Eastern Shore who had served on the Union state central committee formed during the war; Westel Willoughby, a native of New York and former major in a Union volunteer regiment who in later years would be a judge on the Virginia Supreme Court of Appeals; and John Hawxhurst of Fairfax County, an 1846 immigrant from New York and one of the most radical Republicans in the Restored government during the war.[35]

The association, heavily influenced by antebellum and wartime northern immigrants, resolved that it was essential to prevent secessionists from regaining control of the state; that it seemed as if they would; and that the state constitution should grant suffrage to "loyal male citizens without regard to color." This was the first time the Virginia Republican party, or any part of it, had advocated black suffrage. It was also a time, significantly, when Unionists most needed black votes. Virginia Unionists thus joined those in Louisiana in calling for black political participation at least a year before similar requests were heard from Republicans in other southern states.[36]

Similar groups appeared in other cities. A Democratic Republican Association was formed in Norfolk, another Virginia city with numerous immigrants from the North, and its members agreed not to vote for anyone who was not in favor of black suffrage. The Unconditional Unionists of Frederick County met in Winchester on June 28 to express their dissatisfaction with Governor Pierpont, condemn the proceedings of the special session of the legislature, and compliment the forthright Unionism of John Minor Botts, the antebellum Whig had had stood firm against secession and who, after a brief imprisonment for his political beliefs, had remained on his farm, isolated from the Confederacy, for the remainder of the war. The *Richmond Whig* was not impressed. It called such meetings "the bigotted cavillings and silly censures of the hand full of insane Radicals."[37]

These Republicans, on hindsight, seem to have been clairvoyant rather than insane. Some of them urged Congress to adopt a Reconstruction policy that was far ahead of its time. The Alexandria Union Association issued an address to Congress and the North on June 30 to acquaint them with events in Virginia. The address, written primarily by northern-born Virginians, expressed surprise and disappointment at Governor Pierpont's recent Reconstruction policy, protested his appointment of ex-Confederates to state offices, complained that Unionists were now at the mercy of rebels, and predicted that Virginia would pay the debts it had contracted as a rebel state. To prevent a complete Confederate takeover, the association agreed, black suffrage was necessary. To effect this, a constitutional convention, chosen by the loyal people of the state without regard to color and excluding all who had participated in the rebellion, should amend the 1864 constitution or form a new one. Meanwhile, a military or territorial government should rule Virginia. Republicans in Norfolk echoed the request for military government. Thus, Virginia Republicans called for a policy in 1865 that Congress would adopt during "radical Reconstruction" two years later.[38]

While the startling Republican calls for black suffrage attracted a great deal of attention in Virginia in the summer of 1865, not all Virginia Unionists were ready to accept the idea. "There is already far too much ignorance and depravity existing among the voters," Lynchburg Unionists complained in July. "The servant will be almost sure to vote for the master's favorite candidate." Thus, some Virginia Republicans, primarily native-born whites, felt the idea of black voting was too radical and that it would backfire on their party. After questioning some southern Unionists, John Richard Dennett, the northern traveler in Virginia, sighed, "I found the Union men nearly or quite as unwilling to see Negroes voting as the secessionists are." Southern white Republicans in other states echoed these concerns. But these more traditional voices were barely heard above the din.[39]

Looking back on the spring and summer months of 1865, many Republicans in Virginia and in the North later agreed that the nation had lost its best opportunity to achieve sweeping reform in the Confederate South when President Johnson and southern governors restored former Confederates to power. Three northern journalists who had spent considerable time in Virginia and other southern states reported to their readers that a golden moment had passed. J. T. Trowbridge lamented the lost opportunity: "The ground was thoroughly broken; it was fresh from the harrow; and then was the time for the sowing of the new seed, before delay had given encouragement and opportunity to the old rank weeds." Expanding on the agricultural metaphor, Dennett wrote that "then, better than at any other time, the North might have reaped the fruits of the war." Whitelaw Reid agreed with his fellow travelers. "The whole body politic was as wax," he wrote. "It needed but a firm hand to apply the seal."[40]

Virginia Republicans echoed the same ideas, sometimes in virtually the same words. George S. Smith of Culpeper County, a New Hampshire native who had been living in Virginia at least since the 1840s, had been driven from his home for expressing Unionist ideas during the war. Referring to leading Confederates in the early months after Appomattox, Smith told a congressional committee that "they were very plastic indeed; you could have moulded them in any way." Jacquelin M. Wood, another Virginia Unionist, concurred: "They were very humble at first, before any pardons were granted." While not all historians agree that the moment was quite that golden, still it did seem to those who lived through the spring and summer of 1865 that a great opportunity had been lost by President Johnson and Governor Pierpont.[41]

White Unionists were not the only ones protesting Pierpont's policy in the summer of 1865, for Virginia freedmen, like those in other Confederate states, took the initiative and held numerous public meetings to express their own views. Indeed, blacks in Union-occupied Norfolk had begun agitating for change even before the end of the war, as early as February 1865. Ably led by free blacks such as William Hodges (brother of Willis A. Hodges, a member of the radical constitutional convention of 1867–68) and Thomas Bayne (one of the most radical members of the constitutional convention), these men demanded black suffrage in the winter and spring of 1865, months before white Republicans of the Old Dominion would reach that radical stage. In addition, blacks in the Norfolk area and on the Peninsula southeast of Richmond formed at least three Republican clubs in the spring of 1865. Nervous white Republicans who feared that southern blacks would be too childlike or ignorant to pursue their own interests obviously were not familiar with the ambitious and aggressive black folk of southeastern Virginia.[42]

Early in June, Petersburg blacks met publicly to advocate black suffrage. Richmond blacks sent a committee to the White House a few days later to complain that they were being subjected to insults and unjust imprisonment and to ask for more military protection. Despite anonymous death threats a large biracial meeting in Alexandria on August 2–5 called for black suffrage for three reasons: (1) the ballot would provide protection for the freedmen; (2) black Virginians were citizens entitled to all the rights of other citizens; (3) and freedmen, though not highly educated, were intelligent enough to know who should rule them. A minority report denounced Governor Pierpont and appealed to Congress for protection.[43]

Union Leagues and Loyal Associations also began springing up in other parts of the heavily black areas of eastern and central Virginia. A Loyal League was formed in Richmond soon after the fall of that city in April. This and similar groups in Petersburg, Norfolk, Hampton, and Alexandria favored black suffrage and Unionist control of the state. Secret political associations were organized among the freedmen, often with white Republican aid. The white northern-born president of Richmond's Union League told General Benjamin F. Butler that white and black groups were already cooperating by August and "not a move is made by them [the blacks] without our advice, consent or direction." While this statement somewhat exaggerated the role of whites, white Republicans often did encourage the freedmen to speak out. Federal district judge John C. Underwood, usually on the leading edge of Republican thinking, published a letter to a black Virginian in October, arguing that "without the right of suffrage there is great danger, nay, almost absolute certainty, that you will be oppressed by tyranny and gross injustice."[44]

On July 4, the first Independence Day since the end of the war, the only substantial body of Virginians who gathered in Capitol Square in Richmond to celebrate (besides a few curious street urchins) were black residents of the city and surrounding area. After a reading of the Declaration of Independence and a few speeches by army officers, the crowd quietly dispersed. But the black men and women who stood politely near George Washington's statue and Thomas Jefferson's state Capitol undoubtedly understood that this was a new kind of Independence Day for them.[45]

Letters to the governor, visits to the White House, the formation of loyal associations, and Unionist meetings were the most visible Republican activities in the summer of 1865. But behind the scenes leading white members of the party also were planning to establish Republican newspapers in the Old Dominion. Not above stretching his ethics to achieve his ends on occasion, Judge Underwood apparently suggested to General Terry that the army suppress one of the more vehement antinorthern papers in Richmond and confiscate its press for the use of a projected Republican organ, the *Nation*. General Terry believed that such action would only be reversed by higher authorities, and the plan evidently was scrapped. Underwood later tried unsuccessfully to persuade Frederick Douglass, the prominent black abolitionist, to establish a Republican paper in Alexandria.[46]

Other Republicans had more success with similar projects. James W. Lewellen, a Virginia Unionist in 1861, founded the *Richmond Republic* in July 1865. Lewellen's editorial policy was moderate, very similar, in fact, to Governor Pierpont's views. The *Republic* followed this line for several months but ultimately discovered what Governor Pierpont would also realize—that the middle ground between Virginia's white conservatives and the bulk of the state's Republicans was too weak to support a potent political movement. Twenty-five miles to the south, in the river city of Petersburg, James P. Prince, a former surgeon in the Union army and a leading member of the Loyal League, established a less conservative Republican newspaper, the *Petersburg Times*, in August.

Downriver from Richmond and Petersburg another former Union army officer established an additional Republican organ in Hampton, a city near the tip of the Peninsula. The publisher of the *Hampton True Southerner*, former colonel D. B. White of New York, was a Methodist minister, a strong defender of the freedmen, and an object of scorn among tidewater whites. He pressed on with his newspaper from November 1865 to February 1866, when he transferred his offices across the James River to Norfolk. White antipathy was even stronger in Norfolk, however, and a mob sacked his newspaper office and dumped his press into the river in April.[47] Still, for the first time, Republicans were making loud noises in eastern Virginia, mainly in the larger tidewater cities.[48]

The Conservatives Return to Power

While Governor Pierpont labored to reconstruct Virginia and his erstwhile allies tried to undo his work, the state was preparing for the October 12 elections. The voters would choose eight United States congressmen and senators and delegates for the state General Assembly and also would decide whether the legislature should be empowered to amend Article III of the 1864 constitution, which disfranchised and disqualified for office Confederate officeholders and also disqualified for office anyone who had supported the Confederacy since 1864. Since the prewar Whig and Democratic party organizations had faded away after 1860, conservative candidates ran on their own initiative. There were no statewide nominating conventions, and old party lines were blurred if not nonexistent.[49]

The only Republican statewide organization, the Union state central committee formed in 1864, had done nothing since the 1864 Republican national convention. While Alexandria-area Republicans were very vocal in 1865, none of them revived the party's state committee, and Republicans therefore campaigned as individuals without benefit of party backing. In the Second Congressional District, an area including Norfolk, two Republicans, C. W. Buttz and Lucius H. Chandler, ran for a seat in Congress. Buttz, a New Jersey native who had settled in Virginia during the war, had been a Virginia delegate to the 1864 national Union (Republican) convention in Baltimore. Chandler, a fifty-three-year-old Maine native, had moved to Norfolk in 1848. Arrested as a Union spy in 1861, he had been imprisoned in Richmond before escaping to the North. Later he had returned to Virginia and had received an appointment as the United States attorney for the eastern district of Virginia in 1863. It was Chandler who had prosecuted the numerous confiscation cases in Judge Underwood's court. In the Seventh District, fifty-four-year-old Virginia native Lewis McKenzie, an Alexandria merchant and former mayor, was the Republican candidate for Congress in a five-man race. Of the five candidates, only McKenzie could take the necessary loyalty oaths to be eligible for Congress.

In the Sixth District, an area including Rockingham County in the Shenandoah Valley, the former Whig and now Republican John F. Lewis was running against another prewar Whig, Alexander H. H. Stuart. Lewis, whose brother Charles was Governor Pierpont's secretary of state, was the scion of a pioneering Valley family. Born in Rockingham County in 1818, he had been a prosperous planter before the war and, as a delegate to the 1861 convention, had refused to sign the ordinance of secession. Like still another Whig, John Minor Botts, Lewis had lived out the war at his country home and refused to aid the Confederate war effort. Before his political career ended, he would become a United States senator from the Old Dominion. Thus, two Virginia natives and two northern immigrants carried the Republican banner in the fall congressional elections. No Republicans campaigned for the other five congressional seats.[50]

During the Second District campaign Buttz, who had been nominated by a local Republican meeting, withdrew from the race and gave his support to Chandler. The latter, despite his northern birth and confiscating background, was quite popular in southeastern Virginia. "Nervous, restless, [and] black-haired," he had been a successful Whig lawyer in Norfolk before the war and evidently was courting native white voters in 1865. Speaking to a political gathering in September, Chandler exclaimed, "I rejoice to tell you, my friends, that all confiscation is at an end. I have received orders to suspend all confiscation." Judge Underwood suspected that he was becoming too friendly with "rich rebels" and feared their influence over him, a fear that later proved groundless. In any case, Chandler received the endorsements of the conservative *Norfolk Post* and the moderate Republican *Richmond Republic*.[51]

Although a few hardy souls among the Republicans had the audacity to oppose the conservatives—the overwhelming majority of voters since the General Assembly's June session—many, perhaps most, Republicans repudiated the whole election. In the words of the *Alexandria Virginia State Journal*, "There seems to be a general disposition on the part of those about whose loyalty there has never been any question to allow this election to go by default—to put no candidates in the field, and to abstain entirely from voting. . . . There is not a county in the entire State where the Union men could elect so much as a constable if the election was contested by any one identified with the recent rebellion."[52]

Like those throughout the Confederate states, conservative whites in Virginia also seemed politically listless in October. Whitelaw Reid, on his second tour of Virginia in the fall, noted the apathy among the general population, and several newspapers made the same observation. Republicans seemed to believe that active campaigning was useless in the face of the majority's conservatism. Conservatives, preoccupied with physical and financial rebuilding, thought that Virginia was being controlled by the Federal military anyway. The vote totals on election day reflected the inertia. While 120,000 Virginians had voted in the 1860 elections, only 44,000 went to the polls in 1865, the smallest turnout in the state's history.[53]

While both political camps were relatively inactive, still the conservatives had large enough numbers to overwhelm Virginia's Republicans. On October 12 conservatives captured almost every office being contested. In the Valley, Alexander Stuart defeated John Lewis by a margin of 4,653 to 2,194. Lewis McKenzie received only 25 percent of the vote in his district around Alexandria. And despite the pleas and warnings of Governor Pierpont and several moderate newspapers, the voters elected at least two candidates to Congress who could not take the congressional test oath and sent many to the General Assembly who were disqualified by Article III of the state constitution. It seemed that Virginians had not learned as much at Appomattox as Governor Pierpont had believed.[54]

In the referendum to determine whether the General Assembly should be given power to amend Article III, the affirmative vote approached 100 percent. In Spotsylvania County the margin for the amendment was 511 to 0; in Greene County, 299 to 0; in Clarke County, 262 to 4. This meant that the remaining restrictions on voting and officeholding soon would be removed. Reflecting a trend throughout the former Confederacy, all but one of the ninety-seven delegates-elect had been Whigs before the war; many of them had been conditional Unionists, but only a handful were Republicans. No Republican was elected to the state Senate.[55]

For Republicans the only bright spots in all the gloom were the victories of three Unionist candidates for the House of Delegates and the election of Lucius H. Chandler to Congress. Elected to the General Assembly were Thomas H. Kellam of Accomack County on the Eastern Shore, Franklin Stearns of Henrico County, and Daniel W. Lewis of Fairfax County near Alexandria. Kellam was a veteran of the Alexandria Restored legislature and had served in the June 1865 special session. Stearns was the Vermont native and longtime Richmond businessman who had greeted Governor Pierpont upon his arrival in Richmond. Daniel W. Lewis would be the only state legislator who would vote for adoption of the Fourteenth Amendment. Chandler's ability to take the test oath, his prewar standing in Norfolk, and the voters' belief that his northern birth and education would make him acceptable to Congress, along with his courtship of conservatives, sent the district attorney to Washington.[56] But the presence of only 4 Republicans among 130 legislators and Virginia congressmen could hardly be comforting to the Old Dominion's Republicans, who had assumed back in April that Virginia henceforth would be in loyal hands.

The Unionists' only hope now was that Congress would refuse to seat the senators and representatives sent to Washington by Virginia and other southern states. Accordingly, the Republicans bombarded northern congressmen with letters and resolutions urging them to ignore the southern claimants. The Richmond Union League told Thaddeus Stevens that "Virginia is not yet prepared for restoration of civil rights. . . . This [rebel] spirit is as rampant with the people to-day as ever." A mass meeting of Hampton blacks on November 28 begged Congress not to seat the southern members until freedmen were given the vote. If the South was restored to Congress, the freedmen insisted, southern loyalists and blacks would surely suffer.[57]

On December 4 Whitelaw Reid, back from his recent tour through Virginia, mingled in the crowd gathered in Washington for the first convening of Congress since Appomattox. Inside the Capitol, Reid wrote, "floors and galleries, lobbies, reception-rooms, passage-ways, and all manner of approaches were crowded." Inside the House chamber, "members, pages, office-holders, office-seekers, and a miscellaneous crowd, swarmed over the new carpet and among the desks." Within an hour of the first call to order, the House, dissatisfied with President Johnson's Reconstruction governments, refused to seat the southern claimants and began preparations to investigate conditions below the Potomac River. For once, Virginia's Republicans were successful.[58]

On the same day, the General Assembly that had been elected in October convened in Richmond. With every county in the state represented, it was a far cry from the midget Restored legislature of previous years. Most of the members of this "Baldwin legislature" (named for Speaker of the House John B. Baldwin) were former Whigs whose views fell somewhere between those of unreconstructed Confederates on one side and Republicans on the other. While the unreconstructed muttered that the Baldwin legislature was too accommodating to the North, Republicans would soon have cause to curse the General Assembly for being too conservative.[59]

In a lengthy and well-informed message to the group, Governor Pierpont reviewed the state of the commonwealth, emphasizing its heavy public debt ($41,061,316.87), its inadequate assets, and the impoverishment of its taxpayers. Virginia's banks had been ruined by the war and should be liquidated; its railroads were crippled; its Literary Fund was almost exhausted. But the state should not dwell on its misfortunes; it should begin the work of recovery. Accordingly, the governor made several recommendations. The state government should sell to the highest bidder its 60 percent interest in Virginia's railroads. This would pave the way for a consolidation of the major lines into three great systems and remove these nonpaying assets from the state treasury. The taxes on the consolidated, and hence more profitable, roads would more than repay the state for its loss of securities. Tax collection should be streamlined by eliminating the commissions to the collectors and substituting per diem wages. The state should provide for public elementary education and take advantage of the 1862 Morrill Act, which encouraged the establishment of polytechnic schools.

In his suggestions regarding freedman affairs, the governor demonstrated that the conservatives had not completely captured him. He discouraged legislation to fix wages and to enforce labor contracts; loss of wages was sufficient motivation for black labor.[60] He again stressed the need for a legalization of slave marriages, suggested that black ministers be empowered to perform marriages, asked for a law making trials and punishments equal for all, and urged the passage of an act allowing all to testify equally in all state courts. Objections to the latter, he noted, "are founded more in prejudice than in reason."

Pierpont revealed once again his naive view of Reconstruction. At almost the very hour Congress was turning away southern senators and representatives in Washington, he told the General Assembly that only two issues were preventing complete harmony between the sections—the Confederate and United States debts. The 1864 constitution had repudiated the former, and the governor encouraged the Assembly to honor the latter. By implication, sectional hostility would cease if the rest of the South then followed Virginia's example. Pierpont also defended his Reconstruction policy of the last several months, insisting that the state could not function when three-fourths of the people were disfranchised and disqualified for office. He made no mention of those legislators who were present despite their disqualification by the 1864 constitution.[61]

If the October elections had not convinced Pierpont that his faith in the native white conservatives was misplaced, the General Assembly should have.[62] Its first action was to rescind the disabling clause in the constitution. In addition, it removed from office the state auditor (L. W. Webb), treasurer (W. W. Wing), and secretary (Charles H. Lewis)—longtime aides and friends of the governor and veterans of the Alexandria Restored government—and elected substitutes more to its liking. Charles H. Lewis, the ousted secretary of state, complained that "every Union man who held office by Governor Peirpont's appointment, whom the legislature could reach, was removed." The Assembly refused to approve Pierpont's nomination of his old wartime colleague Edward K. Snead for a judgeship and appointed a conservative instead. The House adopted a resolution instructing John C. Underwood to resign his seat in the United States Senate, to which he had been elected by the Restored legislature in Alexandria in early 1865.[63]

Hearing rumors of a pending black uprising and convinced that blacks would work only under pressure, the Assembly adopted a vagrancy act that outraged some northerners but in fact was very similar to military and Freedmen's Bureau regulations.[64] It provided that able-bodied persons who were unnecessarily idle should be hired out for three months on the best possible terms. If the vagrant ran away, he was required to work an extra month without wages, with ball and chain if necessary.

The state's former slaves had seen such rules before, however. The Freedmen's Bureau in Virginia required idlers to work under military guard until they found their own jobs. The military commander at Lynchburg forced unemployed freedmen to clean the streets. His counterpart at Norfolk refused to issue rations to idle families of black soldiers. As early as 1861 Union military forces at Hampton had forced freedmen to work for low, deferred wages. The Freedmen's Bureau officer in Petersburg ordered black vagrants to work under armed guard if necessary. In May and June 1865 the Federal provost guard in Richmond had rounded up hundreds of unemployed blacks, held them in old slave pens, and sent them to work on nearby plantations.[65]

General Alfred Terry, military commander in Virginia and a man who had little patience with reactionary whites, removed the subject from public contention on January 24, 1866, when he forbade state and local officials to apply the Vagrancy Act to blacks. The existence of numerous planter agreements to set low common wages, proclaimed the general, meant that any freedman who refused to work for the prevailing wage (usually five dollars per month plus room and meals) would be declared a vagrant and thus hired out. The combination of these agreements and the Vagrancy Act would reduce the freedmen to "a condition that will be slavery in all but its name." The conservative press accused Terry of interfering in state affairs while the Republicans rejoiced at his action against the "vile and brutal" law.[66]

The remainder of Virginia's comparatively mild black code included a contract law that, except for singling out blacks, was innocuous and even beneficial to the freedmen.[67] It required that labor contracts for more than two months be in writing, signed by the employer and the freedman, and witnessed by some public official or notary public and that the witness read and explain the contract to the freedman. The Freedmen's Bureau, which had erected similar safeguards for black laborers earlier, gladly cooperated with state officials in enforcing the contract law.[68] The General Assembly also allowed blacks to testify in court but prohibited their testimony in cases involving whites only, abolished the old slave laws, legalized slave marriages, and increased penalties for those crimes popularly associated with freedmen such as armed robbery, burglary, and poaching.[69]

Thus, while Virginia's black code was less onerous than others in the Deep South, legal distinctions between whites and blacks were left standing in areas relating to testimony and contracts; the General Assembly also continued the antebellum exclusion of blacks from voting and officeholding. Harsh or mild, the southern black codes seemed to be the result of efforts to find an acceptable halfway point between slavery and freedom. The legislatures' search, however, indicated that southern whites had not accepted the idea of civil equality for blacks.[70]

In other actions the General Assembly passed a law staying the collection of delinquent debts, effective until January 1868; provided for the liquidation of Virginia's failing banks; petitioned President Johnson for a general amnesty, a restoration of the writ of habeas corpus, and the release of Jefferson Davis from prison while praising Johnson's Reconstruction policy; appropriated money for the University of Virginia and Virginia Military Institute but none to common schools; and withdrew Virginia's consent to the transfer of Berkeley and Jefferson counties (in northern Virginia) to West Virginia.[71] In summary, although this Assembly was not as harsh toward the freedmen as the legislatures in some other southern states, it was very conservative, even reactionary, in several ways.

And the Republicans were aware of every action it had taken. Judge Underwood complained to a northern newspaperman that it was "with a few honorable exceptions, as thoroughly disloyal as any Richmond legislature during the last five years." Nothing short of black suffrage, he continued, could make Virginia tolerable for Union men. Another Republican told Thaddeus Stevens that "the influence of the old rotten Secession pro-slavery oligarchy prevails to such an extent, that all other interests and men must fall before it." Even the moderate *Richmond Republic* grieved over the Assembly's treatment of Governor Pierpont's officers.[72]

Thus, the year of victory proved less exhilarating than Unionists had expected. Governor Pierpont seemed to desert his old wartime allies in the summer. Former Confederates won virtually all local and county offices in July and extended their control to state and congressional offices in the October elections. Republicans drifted through these events without the benefits of strong party organization. The aggressive political stance of northern-born Unionists and more cautious attitude of native white Unionists, moreover, seemed to reveal a tiny fissure within the ranks of white Republicans that could create party disharmony in the future. In December the Baldwin legislature removed the barriers to even more conservative political power by amending Article III of the state constitution, removing Unionists from high state offices, and adopting several other reactionary measures. By these actions the General Assembly embarrassed the governor and provided little comfort to white loyalists and black freedmen. But Virginia's Unionists, like disillusioned Republicans throughout the South, could do nothing to reverse the tide unless Congress stepped in to help.[73] To see that it did, Republicans would make 1866 a year of constant agitation against the conservatives, better party organization in Virginia, and continuous complaint to Washington.

CHAPTER 3

Petitions and Protests

WHILE 1865 had been a year of disappointments for Virginia Republicans, it had not been completely fruitless. They had elected a handful of delegates to the General Assembly and one member of Congress, the first Republicans to win public office in postwar Virginia. They had begun to develop local party organizations in the northern and eastern sections of the state and had established some initial connections between white Unionists and black freedmen. And while they could not stem the conservative tide within Virginia, they did help convince Congress to reject the southern senators and representatives elected under President Johnson's plan of Reconstruction.

Indeed, the Old Dominion's Republicans, outnumbered and outvoted on virtually all fronts in 1865, were almost totally dependent on Congress if they were to reform Virginia along northern lines. President Johnson, of course, was satisfied with the course of his Reconstruction plan and therefore was unlikely to demand more change in the southern states. If Virginia Unionists hoped to gain control of the machinery of government, extend voting and officeholding privileges to the freedmen, and secure a more equitable judicial system for blacks and Republicans, only Congress could make the dream come true. And if Virginia conservatives continued to resist the will of the victorious North and the General Assembly persisted in its backward march to antebellum days, Congress would be more likely to act. Thus, ironically, the state's Republicans stood to gain more by the actions of others—Congress and the General Assembly—than by any measures they could take themselves. The most they could accomplish in the immediate future was to continue the stream of petitions to Washington and to organize themselves into a tighter unit.

Protest and Organization

The Virginia Republicans' first opportunity to express themselves came in late January 1866 when a National Equal Suffrage Convention was held in Washington to pressure Congress for black suffrage. Various northern and southern states were represented in the convention, but the meeting was dominated by Virginia blacks and white immigrants to the Old Dominion. Secretary of the meeting was Daniel M. Norton of Williamsburg, a man destined for political prominence. Born a slave in 1840, Norton and his brother had escaped to the North in the 1850s. After living in Troy, New York, for several years and acquiring some medical training, Norton had returned to Virginia in early 1864 and had become a political leader of the freedmen in Hampton. He would continue his Republican activities and later would serve in the 1867–68 constitutional convention and in the General Assembly.

Calvin Pepper, a white native of Massachusetts who had moved to Virginia in 1864 and set up a law practice in Norfolk, also attended the convention. While Pepper was regarded by all—white and black—as a friend for the freedmen, he later would be expelled from Hampton by the Freedmen's Bureau for defrauding unsuspecting blacks. D. B. White, the New York native and publisher of the *Hampton True Southerner*, and Madison Newby, a free black in Virginia before the war and postwar resident of Norfolk, also attended the Washington meeting. Before adjourning, the convention adopted resolutions calling for equal suffrage and sent a delegation to President Johnson, Congressman Thaddeus Stevens, and Senator Charles Sumner to express its views on Reconstruction.[1]

A few days later Republicans of northern Virginia gathered in Alexandria to discuss a new petition being prepared for Congress. The *Alexandria Gazette* grumbled that only about six of the thirty or forty Republicans were old residents of the town, revealing again the heavy influence of northern immigrants in the Virginia party. The petition protested that rebels were in control of Virginia; that the legislature was considering a proposal to change the residency requirement for voting from one year (in the Alexandria constitution) to five, thus disfranchising recent settlers;

that the vagrancy law was "intolerably oppressive"; that the General Assembly had applauded when House speaker Baldwin suggested Robert E. Lee for governor; that state courts were hostile to Unionists; and that loyalists would have to flee Virginia if the military was withdrawn from the state. The only solution, it continued, was a territorial government to supplant Pierpont's regime. On February 16 Senator Jacob M. Howard of Michigan presented this Alexandria petition and eleven others from the Northern Neck region of Virginia to the Senate, and they were referred to the Joint Committee on Reconstruction.[2]

This committee, created by Congress to investigate conditions in the former Confederacy, provided a national audience for southern Republicans. Taking advantage of their opportunity, Virginia Republicans indulged in an orgy of protest from late January to mid-February. The committee examined forty-nine residents of the state, thirty-eight of whom were Republicans; nine were conservatives, and two took positions midway between the two. The Unionists included army and Freedmen's Bureau officers, native Republicans, blacks, and several whites who had settled in Virginia shortly before, during, or after the war. The most prominent conservative witness was Confederate general Robert E. Lee.

The Republicans made several arguments during these three weeks. They agreed that the attitude of southern whites had been malleable and accommodating in the spring and early summer of 1865 but increasingly hostile to Unionists and the North since then. They blamed this change on President Johnson's lenient Reconstruction policy, which, they claimed, had heartened and encouraged the rebels to believe they could make demands on the North.[3] The Unionists criticized the state courts, insisting that white loyalists and blacks often were harshly handled in these tribunals. James W. Hunnicutt, a white Baptist minister whose Unionism had earned him the hatred of many Virginia whites during the war, testified that "there [in Virginia's courts] are the judges, the lawyers, and the jury against the negro, and perhaps every one of them is sniggering and laughing while the negro is giving his testimony." Judge Underwood said that various circuit and county courts had returned confiscated property to the original owners on petty and technical grounds.[4]

The Republicans also emphasized the great bitterness toward Unionists in Virginia. "There seems to be an almost total separation, socially, politically, religiously, and educationally," between local whites and northerners or Unionists, Underwood testified. George Tucker, a Union army officer during the war and practicing lawyer in Alexandria since 1863, said that many Virginia Unionists would leave the state if they could afford it in order to escape the ostracism and persecution they were suffering. Several Republicans claimed that only the presence of the United States Army provided protection for Unionists. Most of the witnesses were rational on this point, but George S. Smith of Culpeper, a New Hampshire native who had moved to Virginia in the 1840s to purchase slaves and a farm, apparently had been driven to the breaking point. If white southerners were left free to do as they wished, he exclaimed, "they would entirely extirpate him [the freedman] from the face of the earth. They would first commence with the Union men, and then would take the negro." Only continued military occupation could prevent widespread persecution.[5]

The white Virginians' attitude toward the Federal government, according to the Republicans, was far from ideal. Major General John W. Turner, commander of the Henrico district around Richmond, believed that white Richmonders hated the national government. To them the oath of allegiance was meaningless, and they would readily join a foreign invader of the North. Judge Underwood feared that southerners would demonstrate more cleverness and subtlety than Turner predicted. Defeated on the field of combat, former Confederates would try to attain their goals politically. Speaking of Virginia conservatives, Underwood said, "I think it is their expectation that there will be some split in the Union party, which will enable them, in concert with the democratic party of the north, to succeed by voting better than by fighting." Lewis McKenzie and Dr. Gillet F. Watson, both Virginia natives, agreed that southerners would ally with northern copperheads to repudiate the national debt. All believed that the ex-Confederates were unrepentant.[6]

Governor Pierpont received his share of criticism, too. George Tucker, the New Hampshire native who had left the Union army to settle in Alexandria, called Pierpont an "apostate" who had aided the election of rebels to the legislature. Lewis McKenzie recounted how ex-Confederates had swarmed over the governor in May and June to persuade him to amend the 1864 constitution. Dr. Arthur Watson, a Virginia native and a participant in the Restored government in Alexandria, emphasized the illegality of the June special session, pointing out that by the terms of the constitution, the June legislature had been too small to carry on any business. The governor, Watson protested, "in recognizing the illegal legislature of

June, 1865 . . . usurped power which was expressly prohibited to him." And the General Assembly elected in October was no better, according to Watson. "I know of but two or three members of that legislature who are considered everywhere as unconditional Union men." Watkins James, a Maryland native who had lived in Virginia since 1844 and had been forced to flee the Old Dominion during the war due to his Unionism, believed Pierpont had been duped rather than converted by the secessionists. "I regard Mr. Peirpoint as having been deceived by them. He thought his lenient course would work well; but it has only made them arrogant."[7]

Virginia Republicans favored black suffrage but were uncertain about its value to their cause. Underwood indicated that Unionists were agreed on the necessity of black voting but divided on whether it should be restricted to certain classes according to education or other criteria. Gillet Watson, a native Virginia Unionist, favored suffrage for blacks but feared that former masters would control the freedman's vote. George Tucker, the New Hampshire native and Alexandria lawyer, admitted that some blacks might be so influenced, but not many. Overall, Tucker summarized, "we do not feel afraid of the suffrage of the negroes; we do not feel afraid that they would give their votes to their old masters." John Minor Botts, one of the more conservative Republicans, believed freedmen would be ready for qualified suffrage only after some education and improvement.[8]

Senator Jacob Howard, one of the joint committee's questioners, and Judge Underwood had an interesting exchange concerning Jefferson Davis, then imprisoned at Fortress Monroe near Hampton:

> Question. Could either [Jefferson Davis or Robert E. Lee] be convicted
>   of treason in Virginia?
> Answer. Oh, no; unless you had a packed jury.
> Question. Could you manage to pack a jury there?
> Answer. I think it would be very difficult but it could be done; I could
>   pack a jury to convict him; I know very earnest, ardent Union
>   men in Virginia.[9]

The judge's burning zeal for the Union cause apparently was still dominating his judicial outlook.

The Joint Committee on Reconstruction heard testimony from some Virginia conservatives as well. Much of what these ex-Confederates said must have confirmed the fears and suspicions of the Republicans gathered in the hearing room. B. R. Grattan of Richmond, a member of the recently elected General Assembly, denied that white attitudes toward blacks could be easily changed. "You would have to change their skin before you can do it. The condition [of the freedmen] is annexed to the color. We are accustomed to see the color in the condition." As for white repugnance to the idea of black suffrage, Grattan testified that "it is the same sort of repugnance which a man feels to a snake." Another member of the new General Assembly, William T. Joynes of Petersburg, believed that political participation by blacks would be a fruitless experiment. "You cannot give him intelligence; you cannot give him a knowledge of our institutions; you cannot enable him to comprehend public questions; you cannot convert the darkness of his mind into light."[10]

While white witnesses, both conservative and Republican, occupied the bulk of the joint committee's time, several black Virginians also testified on conditions in their state, thus continuing the postwar trend of black assertiveness. In general, the picture they painted was bleak indeed. Madison Newby of Norfolk, born free in Surry County in the early 1830s, was more fortunate than most blacks since he had never been a slave and owned his own home and 150 acres of land. Still, life was hard even for him: "Six or eight dollars a month is the highest a colored man can get; of course he gets his board, but he may have a family of six to support on these wages, and of course he cannot do it." Richard R. Hill of Hampton agreed that pay for black men averaged only five to eight dollars a month. If freedmen demanded more money for their work, some whites resorted to violence and intimidation to keep wages low. "In Surrey County," Newby testified, "they are taking the colored people and tying them up by the thumbs if they do not agree to work for six dollars a month." Explaining the torture, Newby continued: "They have a string tied around the thumbs just strong enough to hold a man's weight, so that his toes just touch the ground; and they keep the man in that position until he agrees to do what they say. A man cannot endure it long."[11]

Some freedmen had received no pay at all for their work on white-owned farms, according to Daniel Norton of Yorktown. Born free in Williamsburg around 1840, Norton was serving as a physician to the thousands of blacks who had streamed to Union-occupied areas around Hampton. As Norton described the situation, "A number of persons living in the country have come into Yorktown and reported to the Freedmen's Bureau that they have not been treated well; that they worked all the year and had received no pay, and were driven off on the first of January. They say that the [land]owners with whom they had been living rented out their places, sold their crops, and told them they had no further use for them, and that they might go to the Yankees."[12]

The black Virginians agreed with their carpetbag and scalawag allies that Republicans, no matter what color, were not safe in the Old Dominion. When asked what would happen to the freedmen if the Union army and Freedmen's Bureau were withdrawn from the state, Norton replied that "they would be in danger of being hunted and killed. The spirit of the whites against the blacks is much worse than it was before the war." Alexander Dunlop, a freeborn blacksmith, testified that two white teachers in Williamsburg's black schools could be protected from local whites only by putting them "in a room over a colored family." One of the most famous black political leaders of Virginia's Reconstruction era, Thomas Bayne of Norfolk, summed up for the black witnesses: "The only hope the colored people have is in Uncle Sam's bayonets."[13]

Two other statements illustrate how clearly black Virginians understood the meaning of the war and emancipation, especially their new freedom to speak up. When asked whether the freedmen were willing to be sent "back to Africa," Richard Hill of Hampton said they were not. "They say that they have lived here all their days, and there were stringent laws made to keep them here; and that if they could live here contented as slaves, they can live here when free." Here was a "dark" mind that needed no conversion to light. Alexander Dunlop, the Williamsburg blacksmith, happily described to the joint committee how he had narrowly escaped hanging for giving scouting information to General George B. McClellan's Union army during the Peninsula campaign in 1862:

> When [Confederate general Henry A.] Wise made his raid into Williamsburg, I just had time to leave my house and make my escape. They broke up everything I had; they took their bayonets and tore my beds all to pieces. All they wanted was Aleck Dunlop; they wanted to hang him before his own door. One day, since the fall of Richmond, I met General Henry A. Wise at Norfolk. He spoke to me, and asked me how I was. I said, "I am doing a little better than could be expected." Said he, "Why?" Said I, "Them devils of yours did not catch me; I was too smart for them that morning!"[14]

Unionists from Virginia and other southern states painted a picture that could only alarm Republicans in Congress and the North. The loyalist testimony, combined with the black codes, the election of prominent Confederates to office, and the reports of some northerners traveling below the Potomac River convinced many voters and congressional leaders that the South was far from reconstructed, that additional legislation was necessary to protect white loyalists and freedmen. Accordingly, Congress passed a second Freedmen's Bureau bill on February 19, 1866, and a civil rights bill late in March. The former extended the life of the bureau and gave it increased authority to protect southern blacks; the latter bestowed citizenship on blacks and gave them equal rights before the law.

Virginia Republicans rejoiced upon learning of the reforms. James W. Hunnicutt, the South Carolina native whose Unionism had forced him to flee Virginia in 1861, exclaimed joyfully that "if we had command of one hundred guns, we'd have them all fired from the Capitol Square [in Richmond]." When President Johnson vetoed the bills, the reaction was bitter. D. B. White, the tall and heavily bearded former colonel then editing the *Norfolk True Southerner*, called the president a "deceitful wretch" and abandoned all hope of separating him from the copperheads. Fortunately for the Republicans, Congress later that year passed both bills over the president's veto. [15]

Letters to congressmen, public protest meetings, and testimony in Washington, however effective, were not enough to give adequate publicity to Republican activities and views. Virginia Unionists needed a strong core of newspapers within the state to support their party. Newspapers in Alexandria (the *Virginia State Journal*), Richmond (the moderate *Republic*), Petersburg (the *Times*), and Norfolk (the *True Southerner*) were struggling along with minimal advertising and public support. A strong radical voice in the state capital, some Republicans thought, would boost the party's prospects. Judge Underwood had made some effort in this direction during the summer of 1865, but his plan had failed. In the spring of 1866, however, the party welcomed a new newspaper to Richmond. On March 22 the *New Nation*, edited by the Reverend James W. Hunnicutt, took its place as the radical organ in the state capital. [16]

Hunnicutt, like Judge Underwood, was one of the most colorful figures in Virginia's Reconstruction politics. A native of Pendleton district, South Carolina, he had attended Randolph-Macon College in Virginia and had acquired a few slaves before the war. As editor of the *Fredericksburg Christian Banner*, he had denounced northern abolitionists and southern fire-eaters with equal fervor during the secession crisis. His outspoken Unionism had forced him to abandon his Fredericksburg home and flee to the North in 1861. This trauma seemed to radicalize the former slaveholder, and he became one of the most strident voices for black rights in Virginia during and after the war. The thin-lipped, grim-visaged Baptist minister, fittingly, had a certain physical resemblance to an earlier outspoken radical, John Brown of Harpers Ferry. [17]

Hunnicutt's weekly *New Nation*, established with the help of Union general Alfred Terry, commander of occupation forces in Virginia, had issued one number in October 1865, but inadequate financing had postponed the second until March. In the interim Hunnicutt had convinced sympathizers in New England to pay for a press and type for his venture, thus putting the project on its feet. It was still wobbly, however; lack of funds forced Hunnicutt to work, eat, and sleep in one dimly lit room for the first few months of the *New Nation*'s life. His wife helped with the newspaper, and both happily accepted small donations from sympathetic Republicans north and south. Always pressed financially, Hunnicutt would continue to appeal for contributions and subscriptions for many months. [18]

With the support of Richmond blacks and northern Republicans, Hunnicutt plunged with gusto into the journalistic world of the state capital. [19] Among other causes, he advocated equal rights before the law for all loyal citizens, public education for black and white children, the rights of Union men in the South, a color-blind political system, black suffrage, and a territorial government for Virginia. While he was doubtless sincere at the time he supported these controversial measures, Hunnicutt's steadfastness in the cause of reform was not absolute. He had been a slaveholder and bitter enemy of "black Republicans" before the war; he had denied in 1864 that racial equality was possible or desirable; and when the majority of radical Republicans ignored his quest for the governorship in 1868, he would abandon them and join the moderate wing of the party. [20]

The old minister seems to have been propelled along his zigzag political course primarily by his hatreds: when he hated abolitionists in the 1850s, he denounced them in his Fredericksburg newspaper; when secessionists chased him out of Virginia, he became a strident Unionist; and later, when fellow radicals rejected his bid for the governorship, he turned against them. Black Virginians who had known him before the war scoffed at his post-1865 professions, but many others came to regard him as their most valuable friend in the years from 1865 to 1868. Indeed, he often received letters threatening to kill him for his problack activities. His usual response was that "money can't bribe us—nor threats intimidate us—we have heard the roar of lions, the braying of asses, and the ranting of fools, for lo, these many years."[21]

While the *New Nation* was the most prominent new Republican newspaper in Virginia, primarily because of its location in the capital, at least four other party organs were established in 1866. The *Marion Record*, *Harrisonburg American Union*, *Norfolk Union Republican*, and *Winchester Journal* all followed Unionist editorial policies. These new papers were smaller and less influential than Hunnicutt's, and too few copies have survived to characterize them further.[22]

With the *New Nation*, other Republican newspapers, and an increasingly radical Congress all active in the spring of 1866, Virginia Unionists decided to organize themselves into a more efficient political unit. A state central committee had been organized in Alexandria in 1864, but it had remained silent since then and was outmoded now that the whole state was under Federal control.[23] So, after repeated calls for a statewide Unionist meeting, ninety Republicans from ten counties and cities convened in Alexandria on May 17.[24]

The great majority of those present were from the counties around Alexandria, while a few came from central and eastern Virginia. The *Alexandria Gazette*, repeating a complaint it had made earlier, groused that not more than a dozen Unionists were Virginia natives. Neither Underwood, nor Hunnicutt, nor any blacks were present.[25] Underwood, who had just begun judicial proceedings against Jefferson Davis for treason, probably stayed away to preserve an appearance of nonpartisanship; Hunnicutt may have been occupied with the *New Nation*. Why no black leaders attended is not clear. Since freedmen could not yet vote or hold office and therefore were not part of the political process, they may simply have not been invited to participate in an organization whose purpose was to wield political power.

After hearing the prominent Tennessee Unionist Horace Maynard call for harmony and unity among the various brands of Republicanism, the meeting called John Minor Botts to the chair.[26] The chairman, an antebellum Whig congressman who had opposed radical southern policies since the 1830s, had been outspoken in his opposition to secession in 1861. Like several other Virginia Unionists, Botts had been arrested and briefly imprisoned during the war for his loyalty to Washington. Anything but handsome, his large head was topped by long, wavy dark hair. Bushy eyebrows shaded a wide nose, and a double chin gave him the appearance of a well-fed bullfrog. He had just published a book, *The Great Rebellion*, which accused Democratic demagogues of plotting secession and war before Lincoln was elected. Indeed, he was present at this meeting because his hatred of secessionists and Democrats (virtually the same for him) had overcome his Whiggish conservatism.[27]

A platform committee, after considerable debate, decided that southern Unionists should "avail themselves of the negro element" to reconstruct the South. The committee's resolutions, accepted by a vote of 38 to 22, called for "impartial qualified suffrage," stressed the need for universal education through a system of free public schools, and warned that ex-rebels would try to accomplish by votes what they had failed to effect with arms.

In other actions, the meeting adopted the name "Union Republican party"; elected a state central committee composed of Lysander Hill, Burnham Wardwell, John Hawxhurst (all northern born), Botts, Lewis McKenzie (Virginia natives), and other less prominent individuals; and recommended Botts's plan of Reconstruction, which called for provisional governors, constitutional conventions composed of loyalists only, and nullification of all pardons. The tone of the debates and speeches indicates that moderate Republicans such as Botts and McKenzie were asserting themselves within the party's leadership more than previously and that the radical (usually northern-born) elements were making some grudging concessions for the sake of party unity.[28]

Press reaction to the convention was predictable. The *Richmond Whig* called it the most "ignorant, obscure and selfish gang" ever to gather in Virginia. The *Staunton Valley Virginian* refused to print the proceedings because they were "too stupid to publish." The *Fredericksburg Ledger* referred to the members as "the ferrets of Alexandria." On the other hand, Hunnicutt's *New Nation* compared the meeting to a small cloud that would eventually cover the whole state, and the *Brooklyn (N.Y.) Daily Union* called the resolutions "broad and generous and statesmanlike." E. L. Godkin's *Nation* in New York praised the delegates as "more than politicians, more than statesmen, more than patriots . . . men of singularly profound convictions, tenacity of faith, stern resolution, and heroic endurance." Although conservatives remained in control of the state government for the moment, they would have a more organized Republican party to contend with in the next political contest.[29]

A Summer of Troubles

The seven months from October 1865 to May 1866 had been a period of intense political activity for Virginians—the fall 1865 election, the convenings of Congress and the Baldwin legislature, the hearings of the Joint Committee on Reconstruction, the passage of the second Freedmen's Bureau bill and the civil rights bill, and the organization of the Virginia Republican party. These events had stirred passions across the entire spectrum of Virginia politics that would be aroused further by a series of racial and political incidents in the spring and summer of 1866.

The middle months of 1866 produced more racial clashes than any comparable period since the war. The causes of this upsurge of violence (and fears of violence) in Virginia and other states are not immediately obvious, but several factors may have been at work. President Johnson's and Governor Pierpont's lenient policies seem to have emboldened Virginia whites, encouraging them to insist on their rights as American citizens and leading them to expect that political power would return to their control. When Congress refused to accept the governments constructed under Johnson's plan, held hearings dominated by dissatisfied southern Republicans, and passed the civil rights and second Freedmen's Bureau bills, white conservatives became angry and frustrated, believing that they were being denied their right of self-government.

At the opposite end of the political continuum, Virginia Republicans were also angry and frustrated. They had expected postwar America to be completely different from what it was becoming. They had expected Unionists to control the state government and bring Virginia into line with the ideas and trends in the North. Instead, their governor apparently had been captured by rebels, their legislature was totally controlled by former Confederates, white Republicans were still objects of their neighbors' scorn, and black Virginians were still at the mercy of white employers, mayors, courts, and sheriffs. Both camps believed they had been unfairly handled, and both had become more rigid in their attitudes since Appomattox.[30]

The anger and suspicions of both groups spilled over into provocative rhetoric and violence in the spring and summer of 1866. In April,

Richmond blacks organized a celebration of the first anniversary of Richmond's fall to Union forces. For freedmen, the speeches and parade on April 3 symbolized their deliverance from slavery, but it reminded whites only of defeat and humiliation. Somehow, with the help of heavy security measures by Federal soldiers, both sides avoided violence. But some white employers retaliated by firing black workers who had participated in the festivities. Two weeks later Norfolk blacks gathered to celebrate passage of the Federal civil rights bill. This time, frayed nerves, white provocation, and poor security resulted in the deliberate killing of one white man, the apparently accidental death of a white woman, the beatings of three other whites, and the deaths of at least two blacks and injuries to several others. That night Confederate veterans attacked the Federal military commander in the city, and further bloodshed was only narrowly averted.[31]

Across the James River, in York County on the lower Peninsula, a black man named Robert Lewis was arrested in late May after he had struck a white antagonist. The next day Lewis escaped from jail and was protected from pursuing whites by 200 armed freedmen. That same month the families, friends, and admirers of Confederate veterans conducted several major commemorations in Richmond cemeteries. These emotional memorials, coming on the heels of various racial incidents, seemed to increase the unity and anger of conservative whites.[32]

Tensions were screwed even tighter in May, thanks partly to the actions of Judge Underwood in an event that captured national attention—the indictment of Jefferson Davis for treason. In July 1865 President Johnson and his cabinet had decided to try Davis for treason in a civil court. After much study Attorney General James Speed had concluded that the case should be heard in the United States circuit court that sat in Virginia, where Davis had levied war against the United States. This was the circuit presided over by Chief Justice Salmon P. Chase, and District Judge John C. Underwood normally sat with him. Chase, however, refused to hear the case in Virginia so long as the state was under military occupation. This left the matter in Underwood's hands. But Attorney General Speed and his assistants, familiar with Underwood's partiality in such cases, hesitated to prosecute without Chase on the bench.

To expedite matters, Underwood had a grand jury called in May 1866 to find an indictment against Davis. Among the jurors were several active Republicans, including the radical Maine native Burnham Wardwell and black radical Lewis Lindsay, both of Richmond. Whether Underwood had packed the jury against Davis, as he had boasted he could in his testimony before the Joint Committee on Reconstruction, is difficult to prove. But the judge, by his own admission, would have had few qualms about such a maneuver.

In his charge to the grand jury Underwood passed lightly over the case at hand and delivered a scathing denunciation of slaveholders and secessionists. The judge agreed with President Johnson that "treason is the greatest of crimes and ought to be signally punished." Turning to Virginia newspapers, he criticized "the vanity, egotism and heartlessness of our disloyal editors" and blamed them for much of the state's troubles. After an enumeration of the evils of slavery, he lost all semblance of judicial restraint and denounced "the subjection of the women of one complexion to the wild fury of [slaveholders'] unbridled licentiousness." Hardly half the South's births, he claimed, were of lawful wedlock. Indeed, "it would seem that masculine virtue must be nearly extinct in the proud circles of the chivalric aristocracy of the State." After this fiery address, the indictment found against Davis was anticlimactic.[33]

The reaction to Underwood's charge was vociferous. The *Petersburg Index* called him an "absurd, blasphemous, cowardly, devilish, empirical, fanatical, ghoulish, horrible, ignorant, jacobinical . . . yankeeish zero." The *Richmond Whig* added "dirty demagogue" and "monster" to the list. The *Norfolk Virginian* compared him to George Jeffreys, the seventeenth-century English judge known for his cruelty. When Underwood's court convened early in June to continue the case, the judge retaliated, blaming the Richmond press for "the murders, lusts, assassinations, violent and ungoverned passions" of the capital. The counterattack was as venomous as before. The *Abingdon Virginian* longed for the day when Underwood and his Yankee friends would be "silenced, banished or hung." The *Richmond Whig* called him an "ignorant blockhead" and "indisputable ass."

Even the moderate *New York Times* was shocked, and Godkin's *Nation* characterized Underwood's June 6 statement as "a violent, unbecoming harangue." If this man was to preside, the *Nation* believed, the trial "would neither shed much light on the law of treason nor have much moral weight with the public." As it turned out, the case dragged on until President Johnson dropped it in 1868. But meanwhile Underwood had generated a vast supply of bitterness against himself and his friends in Virginia.[34]

Hostility toward Republicans and their black allies flared again a few weeks later when freedmen, some with arms and some mounted, paraded through Richmond streets to celebrate the Fourth of July. Halting before the home of Burnham Wardwell, they called for a speech. Wardwell, a Maine native who had moved to Virginia before the war and served as a Union spy in Richmond for General Butler during the conflict, was an ice merchant and a well-known radical. While Wardwell's speech grated on conservative nerves, what they resented more than radical words was the presence of armed blacks in the streets of the capital.[35]

Black militia companies, privately organized and armed, were parading and drilling almost nightly in Richmond. When conservative newspapers denounced the armed companies and their drilling, Hunnicutt responded that the freedmen had a perfect right to do whatever the white citizens of Virginia could do. The controversy became so heated that General Terry finally forbade all public military drills except for those authorized by Governor Pierpont. Both conservatives and blacks were restricted by the ban, but its impartiality did nothing to remove the antagonism between local whites and the freedmen.[36]

Two other incidents in midsummer, both involving white Republicans, contributed to the tension between conservatives and Unionists. George Rye, a Maryland native who had been living in Virginia since boyhood, was one of the founding fathers of the Republican party. The Quaker saddlemaker had attended the Pittsburgh convention where the national party had been organized in 1856, and he had accompanied John C. Underwood to the party's national nominating convention in Philadelphia the same year, both claiming to be delegates from the Old Dominion. His longtime residence in Woodstock and his ability to take the necessary loyalty oaths had enabled Rye to win office as a justice of the Shenandoah County court after the war. His strong loyalty to Unionism and the Republican party would elevate him to the office of state treasurer in the late 1860s.[37]

In August 1866 he used his authority as a member of the county court to issue a proclamation against "disloyal proceedings" in Woodstock. Rye claimed that "rebel sympathizers" of both sexes were intimidating Union families. Young women "sometimes strumpeting the streets, singing rebel songs, and making insulting remarks" were particularly offensive to the justice. Continued demonstrations, he warned, would lead to arrests. The area press compared Rye's statement to General Butler's notorious "Woman's Order" in New Orleans during the war, and the *Charlottesville Chronicle* intimated that he should be punished by his neighbors. Three

Woodstock youths had the same idea and whipped Rye with a cowhide strap, much to the delight of Valley conservatives. The boys were later tried, convicted, and fined one cent each, thus adding weight to the Republicans' charge that they could not find justice in Virginia's local courts.[38]

The second event stemmed from the activities of the ever-active John C. Underwood. In July and August the judge was trying to bring before the eyes of the nation the scarred back of a small black girl, apparently beaten as a slave before the war. He sent a photograph of the girl's back to General O. O. Howard, head of the Freedmen's Bureau, and wanted to take the girl to the White House to show President Johnson. He asked Horace Greeley, editor of the powerful *New York Tribune*, to induce the famous showman P. T. Barnum to exhibit the girl "as a specimen of rebel reconstruction." In fact, he wrote, "I do not believe the sight of the true cross would produce a more thrilling effect." Virginia conservative newspapers were outraged and called Underwood's story "an atrocious lie."[39]

One of the most widely publicized racial incidents of 1866 occurred later in the year. On November 13 Dr. J. L. Watson of Rockbridge County shot and killed a black man whose wagon had collided with the doctor's carriage a few days earlier. A state court promptly acquitted Watson, but General John M. Schofield, General Terry's replacement as military commander in Virginia, had the doctor arrested and put on trial before a military commission. General Schofield cited the 1866 Freedmen's Bureau Act as authority for the trial. When the military commissioners met on December 19, they were served with a writ of habeas corpus issued by a state circuit court in Richmond. General Schofield refused to surrender Watson, but United States Attorney General Speed and President Johnson, with the Supreme Court's recent *Milligan* decision in mind, overruled him, released Watson, and discharged the commission. This series of events in Virginia and similar developments in other southern states stiffened the resolve of southern Republicans and alienated increasing numbers of northern voters from President Johnson's Reconstruction.[40]

Republican Resurgence

With the exception of the Republican convention in May, there had been no statewide political activity in Virginia since the October 1865 elections. The pace quickened in early August 1866 when the 1860 Bell, Breckinridge, and Douglas state committees met in Richmond to appoint delegates to the approaching pro-Johnson National Union Convention in Philadelphia. The antebellum political organizations had faded away during the war, making this three-way arrangement necessary. The conservatives appointed twenty delegates and twenty alternates, mostly former Whigs, to the Philadelphia meeting, the purpose of which was to form a new nationwide conservative party. Delegates from North and South met in the Pennsylvania city on August 14, but the National Union movement sputtered and died before the autumn national elections.[41]

To offset any possible impact the National Union convention might have, Republicans planned ambitious countermeasures. On July 4 fifty-eight southern Unionists—including Underwood, Hunnicutt, Burnham Wardwell, John Minor Botts, Franklin Stearns, John F. Lewis, Lewis McKenzie, and seven other Virginians—issued a public call for a meeting of southern loyalists in Philadelphia to recommend measures for the Reconstruction of the South. In preparation for the September 2 convention, Hunnicutt's *New Nation* urged Virginia Unionists to play down their differences and emphasize their points of agreement; they would need all the strength they could muster in the coming months. Displaying poor organization, the Republican state central committee appointed some delegates without their knowledge and announced that any Republican who attended the Philadelphia conclave would be given credentials. In addition, some local meetings appointed delegates. The *Alexandria Gazette* dismissed the whole idea of a southern radical convention as a "laughable political farce," and the *Charlottesville Chronicle* termed it "monstrous" and "supremely ludicrous."[42]

Several hundred Republicans from throughout the nation met in Philadelphia's Union League House for several days during the week of September 3 to suggest new terms for southern Reconstruction. There were, in fact, two conventions, one for northerners and one for southerners. The Deep South delegates were the most radical faction in either meeting. While the southern members insisted on black suffrage, many northerners feared that their promotion of such a cause would cost them votes in the upcoming 1866 congressional elections. Some of the border-state men in the southern convention also opposed black voting as too radical a step.

Virginia's sixty-one-man delegation reflected this split.[43] John Minor Botts, a vice-president of the convention, had little faith in black voters and believed they would be driven to the polls like cattle to vote for their old masters. His Republicanism stemmed mainly from his deep hatred of secessionists and his Whiggish distaste for Democrats.[44] On the other hand, Hunnicutt, George Tucker, and others berated Botts for his timidity and insisted on black suffrage. Thus, the faint outlines of factionalism within the Virginia Republican party, first evident at their organizational meeting in May, appeared again in September. These lines would continue to deepen, and eventually they would cripple the party.[45]

In the end, the southern convention adopted a platform that praised the recently passed Fourteenth Amendment but was silent on the suffrage question per se. Many delegates from the former Confederate states remained in session after most of their colleagues had gone home. By a vote of 66 to 11, they adopted resolutions calling for universal suffrage and equal rights; former rebels, however, were excepted from these rights. Among the dissenting eleven were Botts, Dr. G. K. Gilmer of Harrisonburg in the Valley, and C. W. Buttz of Norfolk.[46] If the Virginia party was to remain whole, it would have to come to some agreement on the role of blacks in its affairs.

Before returning to Richmond, Hunnicutt and Wardwell along with delegates from a few other states spent several weeks in the North and Midwest campaigning for radical Republican congressional candidates. The 1866 national elections, fought primarily on the issue of the new Fourteenth Amendment, were the first since the end of the war. If the voters of the North sent a conservative Congress to Washington, President Johnson's lenient Reconstruction policy doubtless would be continued, and Republican hopes for deeper reform would be dashed. On the other hand, if the electorate chose a more radical Congress, the prospects were excellent that Johnson's policy would be scrapped and that Republicans would be able to shape Reconstruction along their own lines.

The southern Republicans retraced President Johnson's September "Swing around the Circle," traveling from New England to St. Louis, meeting countless new Republicans, and making many speeches. Hunnicutt, whose health had deteriorated in his first few months as the *New Nation*'s editor, found the campaigning a welcome relief from the worries and labor of a newspaper office.

When the Republican party emerged from the 1866 elections with a smashing triumph, Hunnicutt was jubilant. The southern conservatives would have to take directions now: "Gentlemen the great political battle has been fought, the terrible struggle has ended in a glorious and brilliant triumph of the Radical party. Do you believe it? Can you realize it? The loyal party is in power, and they are going to remain in power for the next half century at least."[47] For Hunnicutt and other Virginia Republicans it was good to be on the winning side at last. The dozens of meetings, scores of resolutions, and numerous letters and visits to sympathetic Republicans in the North had finally borne fruit.

Before the Virginia party could taste the fruit, however, the Baldwin legislature convened for its second session on December 4. In the previous session, exactly one year earlier, the General Assembly had virtually ignored the advice of Governor Pierpont and had followed its own course, much to Pierpont's embarrassment. The governor evidently had realized early in 1866 that his confidence in the state's conservatives was bringing meager returns. They had turned out his wartime state officers and criticized him when he appointed the jobless men as his administrative assistants.[48]

In turn, Governor Pierpont had changed his ideas about Reconstruction. He now believed that President Johnson's policy was too lenient, for Confederate generals and rebel congressmen were dominating southern politics under the presidential plan. The ex-rebels, Pierpont protested, were only continuing the war by political means, an idea often expressed by another Whig-turned-Republican, John Minor Botts. Conservative former Whigs, instead of soothing the state's wounds, were pouring salt into them. The most prominent among them, Speaker of the House John B. Baldwin, was "the worst man in the state." A coalition of secessionists and copperheads, the governor believed, was ruining his attempts to construct a moderate Republican party in the Old Dominion.[49]

The governor had further alienated conservatives in August 1866 when he pardoned Edward Long, a black man who had been convicted by a state court of murder in the Norfolk riot. Four months later, just as the General Assembly was gathering in Richmond, Pierpont commissioned five companies of black militia, an intolerable insult to many Virginia whites. Despite the conflict between the governor and conservatives, Pierpont had not taken the Republicans to his bosom; many of them were too radical for his taste. Neither had the Unionists forgiven the governor. They hoped he realized the error of his ways now, but they made little effort to win him to their cause.[50]

Thus, when the legislature opened its session in December, it was ill disposed to heed the advice of a politically isolated governor. In his message to the General Assembly, he repeated some of the recommendations he had made a year earlier and called for ratification of the Fourteenth Amendment, then in circulation among the states.[51] It was useless to hope for conservative help from the North, he warned, for the recent elections had demonstrated the Republicans' great strength. Because of that power, there was no hope of easier terms for readmission into Congress. Moreover, the amendment was not particularly harsh. It provided for the restoration of political rights at some future time, it left Confederate persons and their property undisturbed, it left civil government intact, and it left the matter of suffrage to the states. If Virginia should reject the amendment, however, Congress would be asked to set aside civil government and to govern through loyal men only. Future conditions would be "much more objectionable to our people."[52]

General Schofield, anything but a radical, seconded Pierpont's argument. He advised leading members of the Assembly to ratify the amendment "as the only means of saving the State from the more 'radical' reconstruction under the act of Congress, which was then threatened." After consulting prominent Republicans in Washington, he assured the Virginia lawmakers that the state would be readmitted upon its acceptance of the amendment. The governor and Joseph Segar, a native Unionist and participant in the Alexandria Restored government, also returned from Washington during the legislative session to warn that Virginia would be "territorialized" if it refused to ratify.[53]

This was hard news for many conservatives. Their newspapers had been denouncing the amendment since its congressional passage in June. The *Staunton Valley Virginian* (September 26) called it "That Bill of Abominations"; the *Richmond Whig* (June 11) claimed that Virginia would rather stay out of the Union than ratify such a measure; the *Richmond Enquirer* (October 15) denounced it as radical and unconstitutional. The *New Nation*, on the other hand, complained on November 11 that the amendment was not stringent enough; rebels, it said, should be disfranchised forever.

The warnings by Pierpont and Schofield seemed to have some initial effect on the legislature. A Republican in the Richmond Post Office, Alexander Sharp, wrote Illinois Republican Elihu Washburne in Washington that there was some possibility of adoption. General Schofield believed the amendment's chances were good, and a Richmond correspondent of the *New York Times* reported that some legislators were undecided.[54]

When the matter came to a final vote on January 9, however, the Senate unanimously rejected the amendment. In the House vote (74 to 1 against) only Republican Daniel W. Lewis of Fairfax County voted to accept the measure. The *Richmond Dispatch* rejoiced at the General Assembly's decision. If Virginia had voluntarily ratified the amendment, "she would be disgraced and degraded till the very name 'Virginia' would be offensive to the nostrils of all intelligent and decent people." What had hardened the Assembly's attitude since December? The *New York Times* correspondent believed it was the conservative newspapers' violent response to the wavering of some legislators. General Schofield, on the other hand, identified the hardening agent as "some source in Washington (probably President Johnson)."[55]

Whatever the reason, Virginia conservatives would never know what would have happened had they ratified. Tennessee representatives had been readmitted to Congress in July shortly after that state had accepted the amendment. Both past experience and informed advice told the Virginia legislators they should adopt the measure and make the best of it. When they refused, they only confirmed the worst opinions of northern lawmakers. Those congressmen and senators who had given the South the benefit of every doubt were convinced now that they had been wrong. They now agreed with Thaddeus Stevens and Charles Sumner that the countless petitions and letters sent to Washington by southern Republicans were based on solid fact, were considerably more than carping criticism from disgruntled politicians. The congressional elections in November and the rejection of the Fourteenth Amendment in January would change the nature of Reconstruction in the Old Dominion.

While 1865 had been a year of disappointments and 1866 had not resulted in any immediate changes in the political structure of Virginia, still Republicans were in a much more favorable situation in January 1867 than at any time since Appomattox. The state's Unionists had publicized their plight in testimony before the Joint Committee on Reconstruction, reorganized their party in May, taken a leading position in the September Southern Loyalist Convention, and campaigned in the North during the fall congressional contest. They had done all in their power to forestall the southern conservative view of the future—black agricultural peonage, counties and courts dominated by the old white established order, and lily-white politics. Just as important in fending off that gloomy prospect, ironically, were events beyond the control of Virginia Republicans. The crushing victory of the northern Republican party in the autumn elections and the self-defeating rejection of the Fourteenth Amendment by the conservative General Assembly had prepared the way for a new type of Reconstruction, a more radical congressional policy that was now sure to come in the early months of 1867.

CHAPTER 4

Congressional Intervention

THE THIRD year after Appomattox would finally bring Virginia Republicans what they had been demanding for two long years—a congressionally directed Reconstruction that would truly change the Old Dominion and bring it into closer alignment with the North. The "radical" or congressional plan of Reconstruction announced in March 1867 included many of the elements Virginia Unionists had suggested as early as 1865—martial law, black suffrage, new constitutions and state governments, and the political and legal punishment of some ex-Confederates. With the military to protect them, the removal from office of hundreds of conservative whites, and the votes of tens of thousands of freedmen to elect loyal men to positions of power, Republicans would now be able to fashion a new society, one that would bring Virginia out of the old world of slavery and rebellion and into the new era of free men and free labor.

With all these advances came one potential problem—the Virginia party's uncertainty about the precise nature of Reconstruction. In May 1866, when Republicans had reorganized themselves for the postwar years, and again in September 1866, when moderates like Botts and radicals like Hunnicutt had clashed at the Southern Loyalist Convention, Virginia Republicans had displayed a fissure within their ranks. Black Virginians and some northern-born whites envisioned a future in which blacks and whites would enjoy equal rights, equal respect, and equal access to economic progress, including land ownership and good jobs. In this vision freedmen would play an active role in Republican politics, not only at the polls but in the decision-making councils of the organization.

Moreover, former Confederates would be excluded from the halls of power, not only as punishment for their rebellion but to protect the reforms that Republicans would bring to the Old Dominion.

Other whites, mostly native Unionists, had a different conception of Reconstruction. They regarded the freedmen as a means to an end; their votes would enable good Union men to replace rebels in positions of power and lead the Old Dominion into the new age. In this view, only white Republicans had the education and experience to handle the reins of government; freedmen should recognize their deficiencies and follow the advice of their white allies. While the moderates were often bitter toward those Virginians, especially Democrats, who had led the secession movement in 1860–61, they were generally more forgiving toward those, including many Whigs, who had initially opposed separation and who had joined the Confederacy only reluctantly. In the moderates' vision of Reconstruction, the Republican future would bring economic progress for all, black and white, but freedmen would inevitably remain what they had always been, an agricultural laboring class. Unless Virginia Republicans could come to some agreement on the nature of Reconstruction, how far it should really go in changing their society, the bright possibilities inherent in the new congressional plan would be wasted.

The Reconstruction Act and Reorganization

In the early months of 1867 Virginia Republicans, hoping for some dramatic action by Congress, put aside their differences to press for a more stringent Reconstruction policy. William B. Downey of Leesburg, formerly a conservative Unionist, wrote Thaddeus Stevens that Virginia Republicans were solidly behind him in his quest for a different kind of Reconstruction. "There is some small amount of squirming about the privileges extended to the recent slaves," Downey said, "but time will overcome all this as there is no Union man who does not infinitely more fear and dread the combination of the recent Rebels than that of the Recent Slaves."

Even John Minor Botts had surrendered on the suffrage question and was now ready to accept black voting. The 1866 elections and pressure from other Virginia Republicans doubtless changed his mind. On January 14 Hunnicutt joined hands with Botts, G. K. Gilmer, and 2,400 others, mostly freedmen, to petition Congress for a new state government controlled completely by loyalists. The petition, presented to Congressman William D. Kelley of Pennsylvania and to the House Committee on Reconstruction, denounced Governor Pierpont for appointing rebels to office and recommended Judge Underwood as governor of the new regime. [1]

And for the first time, Republican sounds emerged from the hills of southwest Virginia. In that corner of the state were many herdsmen and small farmers who had grown weary of the war and had turned against the Confederacy in 1862 and 1863. Their bitterness toward Confederate conscription and expropriation and the memory of their wartime skirmishes with southern troops remained with them after the war. Indeed, the battle between Confederates and southwestern deserters continued after Appomattox, in the form of fistfights, ambushes, and murders. Now, in January and February 1867, they adopted the resolutions that Hunnicutt and Botts had agreed upon in Richmond and called for Underwood as governor. Hatred for Virginia conservatives, not concern for the freedmen, had brought them into the party. [2] If Virginia Unionists could manage to mobilize southwestern mountaineers and combine them with tidewater freedmen, northern immigrants, and old-line Unionists, they would have an excellent chance to control Virginia politics.

Congress finally obliged the southern Unionists on March 2 when it passed the first Reconstruction Act. The southern states were placed under martial law, Virginia was converted into Military District No. 1, General Schofield was made military governor of the state, blacks were given the right to vote and hold office, and several thousand ex-Confederates were disfranchised and disqualified for office. In addition, Congress ordered the southern states to call conventions to adopt new constitutions embodying these reforms on a permanent basis. Finally, the new governments thus established were to ratify the Fourteenth Amendment. Only then could these ten states once again be represented in Washington. [3]

This law opened the radical, or congressional, phase of Reconstruction in the postwar South. According to Michael Perman, one of the leading historians of Reconstruction, several features of the statute were "indisputably radical": its terms were mandatory rather than voluntary, it placed the southern states under martial law, it disregarded states' rights by ignoring state boundaries and subordinating state civil governments to the rulings of Union generals, and it brought hundreds of thousands of black southerners into the political life of the nation for the first time. While the Reconstruction Act certainly did impose martial law across the old Confederacy, the weight of the Federal military machine rested more lightly on the southern states than contemporaries realized. Only about 16,000 United States soldiers were stationed in the South in 1867, and one-fourth of them were guarding the Indian frontier in Texas. Some Virginia Republicans would eventually have cause to wish for 16,000 soldiers in their state alone.[4]

The new law met the expected reception in conservative circles. The *Charlottesville Chronicle* complained that "harder—more cruel terms were never imposed upon a helpless people." The *Lynchburg Virginian* preferred a military dictatorship to "that mob at Washington." Republicans, on the other hand, were both thankful and apprehensive. Burnham Wardwell, the former Union spy, wrote Benjamin F. Butler that "we are thanking God and the 39 Congress for what has been done for us." Yet Republicans were not sure the March 2 act was enough. They wanted Congress or the military to oversee the registration of voters and election of delegates to the upcoming constitutional convention. If the registration and election machinery were left in conservative hands, they feared Unionists and freedmen would be defrauded.[5]

Governor Pierpont, however, was satisfied with the recent act. He deplored the necessity for such a measure but was grateful that it left the state and the governor some power over Virginia's Reconstruction. At least he as governor could initiate and supervise the registration of voters and election of delegates to the constitutional convention. His powers were now subordinate to General Schofield's, but they were still formidable.

When some southern states refused to initiate the Reconstruction process, however, Congress passed another act that applied to all the states not represented in Congress—even Virginia, whose legislature was then processing a bill to call a constitutional convention. The new law ordered the Military District commander, General Schofield, to direct the entire program of Reconstruction. He was authorized to establish voting districts, register voters, conduct the election, and submit the new constitution to the voters for ratification or rejection. Governor Pierpont was downcast. He believed he could have organized the state with the help of the old Unionist Whigs and freedmen. "That golden opportunity is past," he lamented, "by the folly of the new bill, and with it ability to do good on my part."[6]

The man who did enforce the Reconstruction laws was as moderate in his administration of Virginia affairs as the Reconstruction Acts allowed.

Thirty-six years old, General John M. Schofield was a West Point graduate who had risen from the rank of lieutenant to major general during the recent war. After the war he had served as President Johnson's special emissary to Napoleon III of France and had succeeded General Alfred H. Terry as commander of Virginia in August 1866. A moderate Republican, he had urged Virginia to accept the Fourteenth Amendment in order to avoid a harsher type of Reconstruction. He had serious doubts about the wisdom of removing white leaders from positions of power, and he believed the freedmen were in an "ignorant and degraded condition."

Schofield's racial views endeared him to Virginia conservatives. Shortly after the first Reconstruction Act was adopted but before a military commander was named for Virginia, the General Assembly had petitioned President Johnson to appoint Schofield, who had shown "great impartiality" in his previous dealings with the state. Conservative Virginians would have little cause to quarrel with their military governor.[7]

Soon after taking command of Military District No. 1, General Schofield ordered all officials of the existing state government to remain in office until they were removed by military order or succeeded by officers elected under the Reconstruction laws. After the second Reconstruction Act was passed on March 23, he began establishing voter registration boards throughout the state. Registrars were chosen from four groups: preference was given to Freedmen's Bureau and army officers, then to honorably discharged Union veterans, next to Unionist civilians from the local area, and finally to other loyal citizens. Of the 102 presidents of registration boards appointed in 1867, about half were Freedmen's Bureau agents or officers, and most of the rest were army officers. Fewer than one-fourth of the chairmen were civilians. In addition, the general created biracial panels of local citizens (three white and three black voters) to challenge any applicant who could not legally register to vote under the Reconstruction laws (i.e., those who had sworn formal allegiance to the United States before the war and then violated the oath by supporting the Confederacy— primarily antebellum political leaders).[8]

Although the official position of the Freedmen's Bureau was nonpartisan, Chief Commissioner Oliver O. Howard agreed with the basic aims of Reconstruction and did nothing to discourage his agents from expressing opinions sympathetic to the Republican party. Agents were instructed to register all eligible blacks in their districts or be considered derelict in their duty. Moreover, they were expected to "counteract" the influence of those whites opposed to black suffrage. While some bureau agents were certainly racist, others balanced this racism with open contempt for Virginia whites. One officer in central Virginia sniffed that "it will be some time yet before . . . the people [of Virginia] *en masse* [are] brought up to that standpoint of morality and civilization presented so gloriously in old New England." Whatever their personal opinions, the efficient bureau agents who followed their instructions inevitably would advance the fortunes of the Republican party.[9]

While General Schofield was taking command of Reconstruction in Virginia, the state's Republicans, like those in other southern states, were preparing for a convention to organize their party for the coming campaigns. On March 20 the party's state central committee, appointed at the May 1866 convention in Alexandria, issued a call for state Republicans to meet in Richmond on April 17.[10] This change in the geographical location of the party's meetings symbolized the shift in the basic makeup of the party itself. Alexandria had been home to the Virginia Republican party during the war and through 1866, when only whites could vote and hold office. Now that the great majority of Republicans were the blacks of eastern Virginia, Republican power slid southward to Richmond.

The Reconstruction Acts, by adding tens of thousands of black voters to the party, necessitated a reorganization of Virginia Republicans. And the forthcoming election of delegates to a constitutional convention demanded some unity and preparation. In the four weeks before the party convention, numerous freedmen meetings, especially in southern and eastern Virginia, appointed delegates and adopted resolutions expressing approval of the Reconstruction laws. From Lynchburg and Farmville to Petersburg and Gordonsville, black Virginians assembled, listened to speeches, and applauded speakers who urged them to support the Republican party. Darting from one gathering to another was James W. Hunnicutt, editor of the *New Nation*. Hunnicutt took a leading role in the black rallies, encouraging the freedmen to organize and damning the General Assembly for sundry sins. The old minister's close ties with Richmond freedmen soon would elevate him to the powerful position he had long sought.[11]

On April 17, 300 Republicans, three-fourths of them black, gathered in Richmond's First African Baptist Church on Broad Street two blocks from the Capitol. The meeting opened on an informal note when those in attendance agreed that everyone present who was not a known rebel could act as a delegate. Fifty counties and cities from all parts of the state were represented, but the great majority of members were from the heavily black sections of eastern and central Virginia. Hunnicutt, Wardwell, and others represented Richmond; Lewis McKenzie and Charles Whittlesey, a Connecticut native and now editor of the *Alexandria Virginia State Journal*, came with others from Alexandria; C. W. Buttz, one of Virginia's delegates to the 1864 Republican national convention, and Henry Bowden, a Williamsburg native from a strong Unionist family, were part of the Norfolk delegation; obscure Republicans from the hilly southwest joined George Rye from the Valley and E. J. Underwood, son of the judge, of the city of Alexandria. [12]

But far outnumbering these white Republicans were the newly enfranchised freedmen, anxious now to participate in the great American experiment of self-government. One of their most vocal leaders, Thomas Bayne of Norfolk, had been born a slave in North Carolina in 1824. He later escaped to Norfolk where he learned dentistry and became involved in the Underground Railroad. He used the secret route in 1855 to escape to New Bedford, Massachusetts, where he practiced dentistry and participated in local politics. He returned to Norfolk in 1865 and became one of the most radical of black Republicans. Another black radical who would achieve political prominence was Lewis Lindsay of Richmond. Born a slave in Caroline County in the 1830s, he had worked in Richmond hotels before the war and had become a prominent musician for antebellum Richmond parties and receptions. Lindsay had married a slave owned by John Minor Botts before the war and served on Judge Underwood's petit jury in 1867. Lindsay would become a popular spokesman for Richmond blacks and would serve in the constitutional convention required by the Reconstruction acts. James W. D. Bland, born free in Farmville in 1838, was a literate carpenter from Prince Edward County in southern Virginia. [13]

One of the most remarkable black leaders in Virginia, and indeed the entire South, was fifty-two-year-old Willis Augustus Hodges of Princess Anne County near Norfolk. Both his parents had been born free, and his family had acquired considerable property in the southeastern corner of the state even before the war. Hodges and his siblings were well educated and had a tradition of resistance to slavery and racial discrimination. His brother William (often confused with Willis) had been arrested for making trouble in the late 1840s, had escaped to Canada, and eventually had made his way to New York City. Willis himself moved to New York in the 1840s where he helped to organize black schools, edited his own newspaper (the *New York Ram's Horn*), and voted and held local office in upstate New York. Before the war he became close friends with the white abolitionists John Brown and Gerrit Smith.

In 1862–63 he returned to the Old Dominion where he served as a guide and pilot for Union forces in the Norfolk area. Hodges would later be elected to the Reconstruction constitutional convention in Richmond and hold various local offices in Virginia into the mid-1870s. He would remain active in black public affairs until his death at age seventy-five in 1890. His political activism stirred resentment among many whites, while his neat attire and large silver-rimmed spectacles earned him the disparaging nickname "Specs" in the conservative Richmond press. While Hodges and Bayne certainly were not typical of all black Virginians, they do demonstrate that the Old Dominion's black population included many varieties and degrees of individuals. They were not, as so many ex-Confederates seemed to believe, a faceless, ignorant, childlike, and uniform dark mass.[14]

In the election of officers for the party convention both black and white Republicans were represented. John Hawxhurst was made president, and among the vice-presidents were Lewis McKenzie, Hunnicutt, Bayne, Hodges, and R. D. Beckley of Alexandria, a black man originally from Syracuse, New York. By the time committees were finally appointed, the convention was ready to adjourn until the next day.[15]

On the second day the meeting nearly disintegrated on the question of land confiscation. J. B. Baldwin, a freedman of Prince William County, took the floor and announced that all tracts of land over 100 or 200 acres belonging to persistent rebels should be confiscated and sold at low prices and in small parcels to poor loyal men. C. W. Buttz, the white Union army veteran from New Jersey, immediately had the resolution tabled. Soon, however, another black delegate, Joseph Wilson of Norfolk, offered a resolution praising the Confiscation Act of 1862 and hinting that it should be revived. This time R. D. Beckley, the black delegate from Alexandria, opposed the resolution and moved that it be tabled. Such extreme measures, he warned, would only weaken the Republicans, who were at best a minority party even when white disfranchisement and black suffrage were taken into account. Thomas W. Conway of Massachusetts, a former Freedmen's Bureau officer in Louisiana who was then organizing Union Leagues in Virginia, agreed that the party could not carry the state with black votes alone. Fields Cook, a free black before the war and a prominent and literate Richmond minister, supported Beckley and Conway, and the confiscation talk was finally silenced.[16]

The opposition to confiscation expressed by Beckley and Cook demonstrated further that the black political community was not a single bloc of radicals. As in other southern states, moderate blacks, usually property-holding and free before the war or educated former slaves or northern immigrants, constituted a small slice of the state's Republican party. The careers of Hodges and Bayne indicate that others with similar backgrounds took very advanced ground politically. Generally, even the moderates were not as conservative as native Unionist whites. Instead, the views of these moderate blacks were very often similar to those of white northern immigrants; that is, black radicals considered them moderates and conservatives considered them radicals. In any case, in most of their dealings with local whites, black Virginians of all political and social shades forgot their differences and stood together.[17]

The convention ended with an address to the citizens of Virginia and several resolutions. The address pledged allegiance to the Republican party, which had "delivered us from the power of our ancient and life-long enemies" and which considered character, not color, as the true standard of a man's worth. The resolutions (1) thanked Congress for the Reconstruction Acts, (2) called for equal political and legal rights for all men, (3) recommended a system of free common-school education open to all classes on an equal basis, (4) emphasized the need for a more equitable financial system in which property carried the burden of taxation, and (5) assured white Virginians that "we do not desire to deprive the laboring white men of any rights or privileges which they now enjoy, but do propose to extend those rights and privileges." The would-be confiscators failed to include their resolutions in the platform.[18]

Before adjourning, the delegates appointed a state executive committee that included both radicals and moderates. Lewis McKenzie, the former mayor of Alexandria who had participated in the wartime Restored government, was joined on the committee by a few other moderates. G. K. Gilmer, another veteran of the wartime Alexandria government who was publishing the *Harrisonburg American Union* in 1867, had allied with Botts and C. W. Buttz to oppose universal manhood suffrage a few months earlier at the Southern Loyalist Convention. G. F. Watson of Accomack County on the Eastern Shore was a prewar Unionist Whig; he had served on the party's 1864 state central committee. Among the radicals named to the new executive committee were Hunnicutt, Wardwell, and Orrin E. Hine of Fairfax County. Originally from New York, Hine was a veteran of the Union army who had settled on a farm in northern Virginia. He would become one of the most radical of Republicans in the upcoming constitutional convention of 1867–68.[19]

The Richmond correspondents of the *New York Times* and *New York Tribune* agreed that most blacks present at the meeting favored confiscation. For the *Tribune* reporter this was incidental, and he called the meeting "a perfect success." The *Times* reporter, however, wrote that the convention "looked to a bystander like a hari-kari" and that the party was now "a hopeless minority." The confiscation talk, he feared, would prevent all but the most radical whites from joining the party.[20]

Several incidents after the April convention intensified the fear that white conservatives were now feeling. When Richmond blacks were prevented from riding the city's streetcars late in April, a riot ensued that necessitated intervention by General Schofield. On May 7 black and white Republicans of Richmond met to ratify the April convention's proceedings. One of the orators, a Massachusetts abolitionist named Zedekiah Haywood, called for confiscation of rebel land and received "tremendous applause." Lewis Lindsay and Burnham Wardwell echoed Haywood's confiscation demands in subsequent speeches, and Hunnicutt advised the crowd to scorn any moderate philosophy. Two days later Richmond freedmen rioted again when city police arrested one of their number for fighting. Three policemen were injured, and General Schofield had to call in a company of soldiers with fixed bayonets before the crowd would disperse.[21]

The Rise of the Moderates

Reeling from the devastating conservative defeat in the 1866 national elections, the passage of the Reconstruction Acts, and the new aggressiveness of radical whites and blacks, some Virginia whites finally began to think the unthinkable—that only by accepting radical Reconstruction and working within the Republican party could they ever bring Virginia back to normal conditions. On the night of April 18 moderate whites in Petersburg gathered at the courthouse and adopted a set of resolutions that came to be known as the Petersburg platform. The moderates agreed to "perform in good faith the terms and conditions prescribed by the Congress of the United States" in the Reconstruction Acts, accepted the reality of black political participation, and assented to the framing of a new constitution that would make no distinctions based on race.[22]

Some historians are skeptical about the degree of moderation centrist whites in the South truly represented. This is understandable, given the history of the South in the later decades of the century. Still, the fact that some antebellum Whigs, Constitutional Unionists, and conditional Unionists were willing to take a public stand in favor of cooperation with Congress and the Republican party is strong evidence that they were considerably more flexible in their thinking than the stand-fast, diehard Confederates who denounced them for their apostasy. In short, there was a segment of the native white population of Virginia whose politics fell somewhere between those of the black and white Republicans on one side and the reactionary conservatives on the other. In effect, this segment was a floating bloc of native white moderate voters. Their decision to move toward the Republicans in 1867 raised the possibility of a Republican-cooperator coalition that could tip the balance of political power in the Old Dominion toward the Republicans.[23]

Within days of the Petersburg meeting the *Richmond Whig*, always less stridently conservative than some other Richmond newspapers, took up the cause. The *Whig* proposed an alliance of southern moderates and northern Republicans, not out of any concern for the freedmen, but as a means to "*make the best bargain* we can for ourselves." By uniting with Republicans, the *Whig* insisted, the South could moderate the administration of the Reconstruction laws. The more conservative *Richmond Enquirer* blasted the *Whig*'s move toward Republicanism as a "profoundly humiliating and fatal step."[24]

Some Republicans, seeing the opportunity to bring centrist whites into their party, maneuvered throughout the spring of 1867 to welcome antebellum Unionist Whigs and the old conditional Unionists of 1861 into the fold. This had long been a dream of Governor Pierpont, and he was particularly active in the movement to forge an alliance. His first scheme was to bring in prominent northerners to encourage the marriage of moderate whites and Republicans. Fortunately for Pierpont, northern party leaders were quick to respond to his call for aid. Virginia's proximity to Washington, its large potential electoral vote, and its position of leadership among the Confederate states made the Old Dominion an object of interest to northern party officials. Indeed, northern Republicans paid more attention to Virginia than to any other southern state in 1867.[25]

The initial effort was made by radical Senator Henry Wilson of Massachusetts. At the urging of Massachusetts Republicans, the senator had visited Richmond and Petersburg before the state party convention, praising the bravery of Confederate soldiers and appealing for white support. Now that the Virginia party had flirted with confiscation, Governor Pierpont requested Wilson's return to the Old Dominion to put out the political fires. On the first leg of a tour through the southern states, Wilson swung through northern, central, and eastern Virginia late in April, speaking to blacks at Orange, Richmond, Norfolk, Portsmouth, and Hampton. His largest audience was in Richmond on April 21 when he spoke from the Capitol steps to a huge gathering of freedmen, legislators, and other public officials.

Wilson opened his address by thanking "several members of the Legislature" for inviting him to speak in Richmond. He appealed to the freedmen, old Whigs, and those Jackson Democrats who had never been seduced by Calhoun's doctrines to unite in the Republican party and carry the state in the autumn election. He reminded blacks that the Republican party had liberated them but discouraged the idea of a purely black party. There should be no black or white parties, only a party of freedom and one opposed to freedom. Every man who agreed with the aims of the Republican party, no matter what his past, should be welcomed into the fold. And talk of confiscation, he warned, was useless; Congress would never agree to such measures. Governor Pierpont, who accompanied Wilson for most of the Virginia tour, spoke next, emphasizing the dignity of labor and the necessity of economic recovery. Three rousing cheers ended the rally, then Wilson continued on to Norfolk where he repeated his plea for an alliance of moderate whites and the freedmen.[26]

Hunnicutt's *New Nation* applauded Wilson's and Pierpont's speeches, but the old editor was secretly suspicious of efforts to include former rebels in the party, no matter how reluctant they may have been to secede in 1861. At the opposite end of the political spectrum, the *Richmond Enquirer*, one of the most conservative papers in the state, believed Wilson's effort was futile. No man could unite blacks and whites, it asserted, not even General Lee himself.[27]

A few weeks after Wilson left Virginia on his way south, Horace Greeley, editor of the powerful *New York Tribune*, and Gerrit Smith, the

New York abolitionist who had helped Hunnicutt establish the *New Nation*, visited Richmond. Greeley, John Minor Botts, and others used the occasion to provide bail for Jefferson Davis in an attempt to soothe postwar hostilities. On May 14 Greeley and Smith addressed a large group of blacks and whites in the African Church. Greeley repeated Wilson's message that confiscation was not popular in Congress; only a very few men in Washington spoke of such legislation. Freedmen would do well to forget this idea; by purchasing their own land and working diligently, they would soon become self-sufficient. Gerrit Smith agreed: "The [confiscation] scheme will never be realized. It never should be." Moreover, the Reconstruction Acts had disfranchised all the rebels who needed such punishment. Proscription of southern rights, he warned, should go no further. 28

Greeley's *Tribune* had been pounding away at this line since April. It deplored Hunnicutt's "bitter and offensive" zeal. "To organize a campaign on the Hunnicutt plan," the *Tribune* protested, "is to abandon any hope of a permanent Union party in the South." Stung by the criticism, Hunnicutt replied that "Mr. Greeley has never been driven from his home and family for years for his love of country—has never had his houses burnt down, his goods all wasted." Hunnicutt also denied that he was encouraging race hatred. Fields Cook, the literate and moderate black minister from Richmond, however, remembered Hunnicutt differently. "He has tried through his whole political career to teach us, as colored men, to have no confidence in the white man of the South." Despite his attempt to answer Greeley's charges, Hunnicutt continued on his path, warning freedmen to reject a moderate party. 29

Joining Governor Pierpont in the moderate offensive was John Minor Botts. He had stayed away from the April 17–18 meeting in order to maintain his ties with white centrists. He cultivated a friendship with the moderate General Schofield and circulated a petition through the General Assembly that appealed for a biracial Republican party. With the support of northern party leaders such as James Edmunds (president of the Union League of America), Charles Gibbons (an officer of the Philadelphia Union League), and Senator Wilson, Botts approached more radical Republicans with the idea of a second convention to be held on July 4 in order to build upon the foundations laid in April. He did not ask for a repudiation of the April proceedings; he simply desired another meeting to bring in the native white moderates who were ready to cooperate with the Republican party. He hoped to enlarge party committees to include some of the new Republicans. Finally, Botts wanted to add members from the predominantly white Valley and western counties. Without a substantial influx of white voters, money, and political experience, he contended, Republicans would remain a weak minority.[30]

The radicals' response to Botts's movements was generally negative, even hostile. The *Alexandria Virginia State Journal* thought his effort to recruit Republicans from the General Assembly was "grotesque enough to make an owl laugh." After Botts had approached them with his plan for a second state convention, radicals on Judge Underwood's grand jury denounced him as a copperhead and a rebel. A Richmond radical, C. E. Moss, described the maneuvers to erect a biracial party as an ill-disguised attempt to resurrect the Whig party. Virginia radicals, he scoffed, would not "breathe the breath of life into the old, time-serving and intriguing Whig party." Hunnicutt, of course, was no more receptive. If the old Whigs would accept the April platform as Botts claimed they would, there was no need for a second convention. If former rebels were allowed into the party, he feared, the freedmen would desert it. This was a gloomy prospect for Hunnicutt, who drew virtually all his political power from the black voters. He was willing to accept the new members if they were as radical as Botts; otherwise, they were not true Republicans and should be scorned.[31]

The most powerful of the moderating maneuvers began early in May. On the same night (May 7) that Zedekiah Haywood, Wardwell, and Hawxhurst were calling for confiscation and spurning the advances of Botts, Governor Pierpont was in New York where he attended that city's Union League Club meeting. Invited to speak by his hosts, the governor gave a full account of Republican affairs in Virginia and doubtless emphasized the deep divisions in the party. The Union League Club, which wanted a unified biracial southern party, immediately adopted resolutions creating a joint committee of the New York and Philadelphia clubs "to confer at Richmond with leading men of Virginia on the best means of organizing the Republican party in that State." Apprised of the project, congressional Republicans gave their approval to the venture. Massachusetts Republicans soon joined the movement, partly for political reasons and partly because powerful businessmen in Boston, including John Murray Forbes and Edward Atkinson, wanted to cultivate a climate in Virginia favorable to economic development and cooperation. The spring of 1867 was one of the few times during Reconstruction that northern Republican party leaders intervened to settle intraparty differences in a southern state. Virginia's leading role in earlier American history, its prominence as the capital of the Confederacy, and its proximity to Washington apparently made national party leaders more sensitive to that state's Republican party than to some others.[32]

Led by John Jay, grandson of the Revolutionary era's John Jay and a founder of the New York Republican party, and Thomas B. Van Buren, a son of the Jacksonian president, the New York delegation arrived in Richmond on June 10.[33] Charles Gibbons, a prominent Keystone-state Republican, and several other members of the Philadelphia League joined the New Yorkers in Virginia. Senator Henry Wilson headed a seven-man delegation from Massachusetts. The next night the northerners met about fifty Republicans of both wings of the Virginia party in the Governor's Mansion. Judge Underwood opened the discussion and was followed by Botts, Hawxhurst, Hunnicutt, Pierpont, R. D. Beckley, Lucius H. Chandler, and others.[34]

The Botts-Pierpont faction protested that the party as organized at the April convention was too narrow, both racially and geographically. Very few whites had attended the April meeting, and eastern Virginia had been heavily overrepresented. The radical tone of the convention, moreover, had alienated those native whites who would join the party if it was more responsible. To bring these men into the party, Botts said, he had scheduled a second convention for July 4 in Charlottesville. Three hundred men of "respectability and note," mostly "old Union Whigs and land owners," had signed Botts's call. Many of the signers, according to Charles H. Lewis, Governor Pierpont's aide, were scions of pre-Revolutionary families. With their numbers, their experience, and their influence, the Republicans could become a powerful majority in Virginia.

The Hunnicutt wing replied that the April convention had been called by the state executive committee and was perfectly legitimate; that Botts's friends should have attended if they believed the meeting was too narrowly based; that to accept the Charlottesville meeting as official, the radicals would have to repudiate all they had done in April; that the old Whigs were welcome to be Republicans if they would conform strictly to the April platform, but their numbers and experience were expendable; and that the freedmen, who would never follow Botts, could carry the state without the aid of native whites.

Botts replied that blacks and white radicals, through discipline, might carry the state for a short time. But if the more numerous whites should ally on strictly racial grounds, the old Democrats would seize power and persecute the freedmen. He wanted to organize all Unionists in one party; by cutting across racial lines, the Republicans could control the state. After more than five hours of debate, the weary Republicans adjourned at 2:00 A.M., and all parties agreed to meet again the next morning. While members of the two factions shuffled out into the early morning darkness, John Jay, chairman of the meeting, worried that "reconciliation was very improbable." An "absolute and fatal division of the party" was fast approaching.

The late-night conference in Governor Pierpont's home exhibited all the features of the classic problem faced by all political parties, especially the Republicans during Reconstruction—whether to dilute the party's philosophical unity for the sake of greater numbers or to remain ideologically sound and depend upon internal unity for electoral victory. The so-called competitive approach to politics, urged by Botts and Pierpont, emphasizes practicality and moderation and attempts to lure uncommitted voters into the party. In essence, this strategy appeals to the political center, hoping thereby to secure enough support to win elections. The "Cooperators" believed the key to political power in the Old Dominion was the floating center of former Whigs, conditional Unionists, and political moderates. If Republicans could incorporate this vital center into their ranks, their party would control the state for the benefit of moderate Unionists as well as the freedmen and recently arrived northerners. If, on the other hand, the conservative whites should ever manage to gather themselves into a party organization and lure the moderate center into their lines, the Republicans would remain a weak minority for the foreseeable future and suffer the political consequences.

The expressive approach insisted upon by Hunnicutt rejects flirtations with the political center and stresses ideological purity and party discipline. Hunnicutt and his allies hoped to win elections, in short, by stressing party unity and by getting out the black vote. On the national level Republicans were committed to the competitive strategy in the late 1860s, and this doubtless explains the recommendations of Wilson, Greeley, Gerrit Smith, and the New York Union League Club during the spring.[35]

By the next morning tempers had cooled, both sides were more conciliatory, and a compromise was soon effected. The state executive committee appointed in April would join the 300 signers of Botts's call in inviting all Republicans, black and white, to a convention in Richmond on August 1 "for the purpose of extending and perfecting the organization of the Republican party." The April address, platform, and committees would remain intact, but they could be enlarged if the new meeting so decided. Warm applause and a "cordial reconciliation" ended the conference. That night at a rally in the African Church, several of the northerners hailed the reunification of the party and assured Virginia Republicans that they would carry the state in the autumn election. To make the victory as great as possible, the New Yorkers agreed to raise $1,500 for the organization of Union Leagues in Virginia.

Leaders of both wings of the party agreed that reconciliation would have been impossible without the mediation of the northern Union Leaguers. A willingness to compromise, however, had also been necessary. The Botts faction clearly surrendered more ground in the negotiations. They agreed to accept in toto the April proceedings, address, platform, and state executive committee. They abandoned their plans for a July 4 convention in Charlottesville, an old Whig stronghold, and consented to meet in Richmond, center of radical strength in Virginia. They had no guarantee that they could enlarge the April platform to include some of their own resolutions nor any assurance that the August convention would appoint some of their number to the state executive committee. They had abandoned their lifelong attachment to the control of state politics by white gentlemen, had agreed to universal manhood suffrage and political and legal equality, and pledged themselves to cooperate with radicals like Hunnicutt, Bayne, and Wardwell. Finally, the national party, like the state organization, was less conservative than the old Whigs would have preferred. Even though they wanted to restrain the more radical elements of the party and make it comfortable for moderates to live in, they entered it as a minority with little chance of controlling its affairs in the near future. [36]

The radicals, on the other hand, had surrendered little ground. They had agreed to a new convention, but they made sure it would be in Richmond, and they secured the April platform and state committee as starting points. Finally, they had made no promises to adopt new resolutions or appoint additional committee members. If this new harmony prevailed and if Unionist Whigs and western mountain whites could be incorporated into the party, Virginia Republicans would have an excellent chance to become a political majority for the first time.

Press reaction to the meeting was predictable. The *Richmond Enquirer* scoffed that "Peirpoint and Hunnicutt have hugged, Botts and the negroes have kissed." Virginia Republicans, it warned, were "caucusing and juggling" in order to prey upon the people. Greeley's *New York Tribune* and E. L. Godkin's *Nation* were pleased. For Greeley, reports of the successful conference were "cheering news," and it appeared that victory was certain. The *Tribune* appealed to recently arrived northerners in Virginia to step back and permit native Virginians to receive the party's nominations for seats in the constitutional convention.[37]

The old Whigs' response to the June agreement must have delighted Botts. On July 1 a large meeting in Charlottesville appointed delegates to the August convention. One resolution advocated cooperation with the national Republican party. A second asked Albemarle County blacks to appoint their own delegates to cooperate with those of the whites. Leaders of the meeting included some of the most prominent men in central Virginia: William F. Gordon, Jr., a lawyer and former clerk of the House of Delegates; William T. Early, for several years an important member of the House of Delegates; R. T. W. Duke, an attorney and ex-Confederate colonel; William P. Farrish, a respected Baptist clergymen; and Dr. W. C. N. Randolph, a former state senator, a grandson of Thomas Jefferson, and a brother of the Confederate secretary of war, George W. Randolph. Such men could wield heavy influence among moderate whites. Commenting on the Charlottesville meeting, the *Richmond Enquirer* predicted failure for the cooperator movement. Indeed, it asserted, "it is impossible for the people of Virginia and the South sincerely to kiss the hand that is ever smiting them."[38]

But similar rallies in the counties of Rappahannock (in the northern piedmont), Buckingham, Louisa (both in central Virginia), Amelia, Charlotte, Halifax, Pittsylvania, Prince Edward (all in the south-central region), and Smyth (in the southwestern mountains) seemed to contradict the *Enquirer*. Governor Pierpont spent several days in July addressing these meetings, always urging racial harmony and pleading for the formation of "one great harmonious organization" for all those who loved their country. Botts, meanwhile, was assuring the freedmen that they had nothing to fear from him. He promised to fight for a system of free public schools open to all, for equal political and legal rights, for northern immigration into Virginia, and for permanent exclusion from political power of those who had pushed the state into secession. If the June-July spirit of unity prevailed, the party would possess a numerical majority of voters in the state and at least as much talent and influence as the more conservative whites.[39]

The Stillborn Alliance

The bright hopes of so many Virginia centrists and national party leaders were dashed at the August convention, however. The first sign of serious cracking in the new coalition appeared when black and white radicals filled the meeting hall, leaving no room for the centrist cooperators.

Early on the warm morning of August 1, hundreds of Richmond freedmen and about fifty white radicals gathered in the streets around the African Church. In the Richmond black community the meeting was regarded as so important that the city's tobacco workers announced they would not work that day, and the tobacco manufacturers therefore shut down the tobacco factories.[40] Although the convention was not scheduled to begin until noon, the church doors were opened at 11:00, and the milling crowd poured in to fill every seat. About two thousand freedmen were left outside for lack of space. By the time the 200 to 300 white cooperators arrived just before noon, there was no room inside and very little outside. Hunnicutt later denied that he had advised the freedmen to fill the church and keep out the white Unionists, but he implied that he might have ordered such exclusion for the old conditional Unionists of 1861 who had followed Virginia into the Confederacy.[41] The Pierpont-Botts faction, however, included many such individuals, and they doubtless resented the radical snub. In any case, the convention was off to a poor start.

Someone inside the church moved that the meeting adjourn to Capitol Square, large enough to accommodate everyone. Mistaking the motion for an adopted resolution, the crowd outside walked the two blocks to the Capitol to organize the convention. Before the group inside the church left for the square, Hunnicutt warmed his audience with a fiery statement of radical views. If the Botts men wished to call themselves Republicans, he shouted, they would have to swallow the Fourteenth Amendment, the 1866 Civil Rights Act, the 1867 Reconstruction Act, "Wardwell, Hunnicutt, and the nigger, head and feet, hide and hair, tallow, bones and suet, body and soul, and then, perhaps, they might be called Republicans." Otherwise, they should leave, for they were not wanted in the convention.[42] The old preacher was willing to accept the cooperators—if they did all the cooperating.

After everyone reached Capitol Square, someone asked to hear Botts, but the request was hooted down by the crowd. A committee on organization headed by Hunnicutt recommended that the April slate of convention officers preside again, and the suggestion was overwhelmingly adopted. In an effort to prevent the introduction of moderate resolutions, the radical black leader from Norfolk, Thomas Bayne, then moved that the April resolutions be adopted once again. C. W. Buttz, the Norfolk white moderate, attempted to head the radicals off by asking for a committee on resolutions, but he was voted down, and Bayne's motion passed. James H. Platt, former colonel of a Vermont infantry regiment and in 1867 a prosperous banker and hotel owner in Petersburg, continued the radical assault on the moderates.[43] Platt received approval for his resolutions "that we deem it inexpedient to present new issues at this time" and that only those who favored the April platform should be Republicans. This, of course, was directly contrary to the understanding achieved in the northern-sponsored agreement of June. To make the radical victory complete, Bayne moved that the convention adjourn sine die, but Hunnicutt prevailed upon the crowd to hear Botts the next morning. Listening would do little harm.

On August 2, in a meeting marked by shouting, shoving, and disorder, Bayne opened the proceedings by moving that the convention adjourn sine die since it had completed its business the previous day. Hunnicutt tried once again to prevent an adjournment, but this time Bayne succeeded. The moderates could speak after the convention ended, he announced, not before. Hunnicutt surrendered, and the convention adjourned. Bayne thus skillfully maneuvered the proceedings to turn away the white cooperators. In doing so he placed himself at the head of the black radical wing of the party. Hunnicutt would continue for several months to be recognized as a radical leader, but his day as the foremost spokesman for the radicals was passing.[44]

In the mass meeting that followed, Botts, finally allowed to speak, protested that the moderates would have endorsed everything done in April if only they had been given a chance. By shutting them out, the radicals had prevented united action. He then read a prepared address that (1) declared treason a crime requiring punishment, (2) advocated free public education for all, (3) recognized the political and legal equality of all men, and (4) recommended permanent exclusion from all political power of those who had brought on the war. A handful of black listeners supported Botts's ideas, indicating that there were gradations of opinion among blacks as well as among whites. But the majority of the black listeners supported Hunnicutt and Bayne, while the greater number of whites followed Botts and Pierpont.[45]

Someone moved that the mass meeting adopt the Botts address, "but so much confusion arose and [so much] opposition [was] made thereto, the motion to adopt was withdrawn."[46] Governor Pierpont and Lucius Chandler of Norfolk then addressed the meeting, but the governor's speech was cut short by a fistfight in the crowd. It hardly mattered, however. The three moderates were speaking mainly for themselves, for most of their allies left the party in disgust. "The dissolution of the cooperationists," the conservative *Richmond Enquirer* crowed, "was remorseless and complete beyond any previous example in politics."[47]

The crippling effects of these events were not readily apparent to some observers. The appearance of Botts, Pierpont, and Chandler on the second day temporarily deceived the *New York Tribune* into believing the August meeting had been a success. The convention had "quarrelled a little," in Greeley's words, but a split had been averted, and the party was unified. Hunnicutt ignored the factionalism of the meeting and thanked God for "the glorious results of the Convention." Other politicians and newsmen saw the meeting differently. The *New York Times* reporter was deeply discouraged by the events of early August. The August meeting, he wrote, had "no competent leadership; no wise heads in authority; no steady hand at the helm; no skillful direction, watchful, prompt and energetic." The result was a party split as wide as ever.[48]

The conservative press was particularly bitter about the Republican convention. The *Charlottesville Chronicle* warned the freedmen that they were sealing their own political doom. They could never control the state alone. The *Richmond Enquirer* called the August proceedings a "disgusting and loathsome exhibition" and a "hideous Radical carnival."[49]

The rejected white moderates were disappointed and bitter. When a handful of black moderates, including Joseph Cox and Fields Cook of Richmond, asked Botts a few months later to bring the Unionist Whigs back into the party, Botts rejected their overtures. "I do not think, with the experience of last summer, that those gentlemen could be induced to come again on a similar errand, and all that I can see just now to be done, is to recommend that you act for yourselves." In fact, Botts, the veteran of so many political struggles stretching back even before the war, would gradually fade from the political scene. Two years later he was dead. Some white moderates—including James W. Lewellen, editor of the defunct *Richmond Republic*, Franklin Stearns, the wealthy Richmond businessman, and others—turned against the radicals by joining their Union Leagues and creating dissension wherever possible. "We succeeded in getting into the 'ring,' and in a few months we had them fighting each other," Lewellen later boasted.[50]

The northern Republicans who had spent their time and resources to cement the moderate-radical alliance in Virginia also were disillusioned. Senator Wilson, recalling the events of June and August 1867 a few years later, regretted "the petty ambitions of politicians" and the "palpable mistakes of our own friends there. . . . But, sir, we cannot guaranty men's wisdom; we cannot make them prefer public considerations to private or subordinate their ambition to the public good." In a newspaper interview two years after the summer of 1867, Wilson lamented the lost opportunity for the Republican party:

> There cannot be a shadow of a doubt in the minds of those acquainted with affairs in Virginia in the Spring and early Summer of 1867, that, had a wise, earnest, and unselfish effort been made at that time, a Reconstruction party could have been formed that would have framed a liberal Constitution, adopted it, sent a delegation to Congress, and given Gen. Grant last year a majority of many thousands. . . . I believed then, and I believe now, that there was a time when a liberal, just, and unselfish policy would have made Virginia a strong loyal and Republican state. . . . [But] the golden opportunity was lost, and with it was lost much than can never be retrieved.[51]

Unfortunately for Wilson and other national Republican leaders, the Virginia party split was just the first of several in the former slave states. One by one, these southern Republican organizations would crack, usually along the lines between black and white radicals on one side and native white moderates on the other.[52]

Those interested in the history of Virginia and the South and the Republican party may well wonder whether compromise with former Confederates was a course even to be considered by black and white Republicans. After all, the subject of discussion at the Virginia Governor's

Mansion that hot summer evening involved fundamentals, not just details or mere tactics. Perhaps fundamentals should not be diluted or compromised. Certainly that was the opinion of Hunnicutt, Bayne, Wardwell, and other radical participants that night. On the other hand, men of equal intelligence and concern for reform—men with solid radical credentials like John Jay, Henry Wilson, and other northern Republicans—went to extraordinary lengths because they believed that inclusiveness was necessary to control the politics of the Old Dominion. Purity of motive may soothe the soul, but it seldom wins elections or gains control of the levers of government. This was especially true in Reconstruction Virginia when Republicans had so many handicaps to overcome and needed every ounce of strength they could muster to stay competitive. While Senator Wilson and the other northern Union Leaguers would never know for certain that their strategy would have succeeded, the next two years would demonstrate clearly and painfully that the exclusionary approach favored by the radicals would result, eventually, in defeat for Virginia Republicans.

Thus, the August convention, which was expected to produce a more powerful and more unified party, ended in failure. The moderates bear some responsibility for not overcoming the opposition and obstacles placed in their way. They might have marched into the African Church, stood in the aisles, and refused to be silenced. Their delicate sense of etiquette and perhaps some distaste for mingling with the freedmen and radical whites kept them in the background. The conduct of the radicals, however, was even more damaging. They ignored the spirit of the June agreement, refused to consider additional resolutions of a moderate nature, reelected the officers of the April convention with no effort to add moderate members, and shouted down the few moderates who dared to speak. Bayne, Platt, and Hunnicutt (despite his attempts to let Botts speak) contributed most to the intolerance, but the rank-and-file radicals supported their every move.

What had happened to produce such a state of affairs? Hunnicutt, who had his eye on the Republican nomination for governor in 1868, doubtless feared that the moderates would seize control of the party and choose their own nominee. His strength lay with the freedmen and white radicals, and he was loath to give it up. The July reports of so many ex-Confederates calling themselves Republicans may have disturbed the freedmen and white radicals, who remembered the cooperators as slaveholders and rebels, not colleagues. Old emotions were not easily controlled in a new party.

Finally, the radicals lacked hardheaded political professionals, men who were accustomed to adjusting political differences and arranging face-saving compromises, who were ever searching for new recruits, who knew how to organize conventions and arrange party affairs. Stirring speakers and men who believed deeply were in abundance in the African Church and in Capitol Square. But the type of leader who could direct the party along the competitive line of politics, who could put together winning coalitions—those were the men who had been turned away. The party had not had time to develop such managers. Most leaders of the antebellum Republican organization had left the Virginia party in 1863 when they became citizens of West Virginia. The wartime captains, in the absence of any political opposition in the Restored government, had let the party machinery rust after the 1864 Republican national convention. From then until May 1866, when the Unionists reorganized, there were no formally recognized Republican leaders and no central direction of their party. The experience, money, political talents, and respectability the Republicans could have gained by cooperating with the native moderates were lost, ironically, partly because the party needed them so badly.[53]

The August convention was the Virginia Republican party's best opportunity to forge a powerful political weapon during the Reconstruction years. If the friends of Governor Pierpont and Botts had been welcomed into the party, thereby securing their votes, wealth, experience, and social standing, the Republican party would have gained a type of respect it had never enjoyed before. It had always been denied legitimacy by most white Virginians as a symbol of Yankee rule, as a refuge for radicals and outsiders, as a fringe group hardly worth noticing. With descendants of Thomas Jefferson, veterans of Confederate service, and men of long political experience and wealth in its ranks, however, the Republican party could have become a much more formidable force in the Old Dominion.

Moreover, with such men beside them, Virginia Republicans may have made a stronger effort to expand geographically beyond the heavily black counties of eastern Virginia. Botts himself had stressed how beneficial such an expansion would be for the party. Prominent white politicians would have had a greater tendency and a better chance than Hunnicutt or Bayne or Platt to mobilize the discontented poorer whites of the western mountain counties, a segment of the population that strongly supported the Republican party in other southern states. And if the party had enjoyed the support of all three groups—black and white radicals, antebellum Unionist Whigs, and the herdsmen and small farmers of the western hills—they might have controlled Virginia politics well into the 1870s and 1880s.[54]

Some historians doubt that Republican incorporation of the old Unionist Whig element would have benefited the freedmen and radical whites.[55] Certainly it is possible, even probable, that the addition of this group would have diluted the reform program of the more radical element of the party. On the other hand, the cooperators in Virginia would have entered the party as a definite minority. They would have owed any success or power they might have gained to black voters since the freedmen would have comprised well over half the party's strength, even with the centrist whites' numbers added to the Republican column.

Furthermore, these were no cringing freedmen who could be easily duped. They were organized, politically sensitive, and very aware of their own interests. Any Unionist-Whig attempt to turn the party away from its basic reform program or to pursue policies harmful to black interests would have been met with stern resistance, by blacks as well as by white radicals. In short, the centrist whites would have had to move further away from other native whites and toward the radical Republican view of Reconstruction if they had joined the party. Since the radicals rejected the cooperator overtures, however, Botts, Pierpont, Senator Wilson, and the northern Union Leagues would never know whether their strategy would have succeeded in the Old Dominion. They would discover, however, that the exclusionist approach, while temporarily successful, would ultimately bring defeat to the Virginia Republican party.

Congressional Reconstruction, then, did not solve all the problems faced by the Virginia Republican party. The new Reconstruction plan did enfranchise tens of thousands of black voters, thereby transforming the Republican party overnight into a serious contender for political power in the Old Dominion. But within five months of the March 1867 Reconstruction Act, Virginia Republicans had squandered their best opportunity to become a majority party. If radical leaders could maintain strict party discipline and get all potential Republican voters to the polls, and if white conservatives continued to drift without any type of party organization, Virginia Republicans would still have a chance to win a majority of seats in the upcoming constitutional convention. The fall political campaign would tell the story.

CHAPTER 5

Black Republicans

THE 1867 political campaign was the first in the Old Dominion's history to include the mass of black Virginians. This revolution in state politics, spawned by the congressional Reconstruction Acts of March, would have far-reaching consequences in the lives of the freedmen and in the future of the state. In order better to understand the political emergence of Virginia blacks, an investigation of their place in the Old Dominion at the outset of congressional Reconstruction is in order.

Who were the black voters of Virginia? Where did they live, and what occupations did they follow? Residence patterns of the antebellum period persisted to a great degree after Appomattox, and black political power would be strongest where slavery had been most dominant. How did the slaves react to the war and emancipation? Were they the faceless, docile, and dull-witted servants so many slaveholding whites had described in their letters and diaries before the war? Or, as historians in the second half of the twentieth century have taken pains to demonstrate, were they very aware of their places in southern society and of the potential that freedom held for them?

What steps did Virginia freedmen take to realize their freedom after the war? How and when did they organize themselves politically? In the Old Dominion blacks were highly sensitive to their new status and took the initiative very early, even before Appomattox in some cases, to arrange political meetings and rallies and even attempt to vote. How much success did Virginia freedmen enjoy in these early efforts? And what vision of the future did black leaders have after emancipation? The answers to all these questions should reveal much about the black Republicans of Virginia.

The Black Population

The United States census of 1860 counted 1,219,630 people of all races in the 102 counties and cities that would constitute the Old Dominion after the separation of West Virginia in 1863. About 56.7 percent (or 691,773) of that total were white, while blacks numbered 43.2 percent (527,763). Thus, black Virginians were a clear minority of the state's population at the beginning of the war and, despite wartime disruptions, continued to be a minority when the war ended four years later. [1]

Slaves accounted for nearly 90 percent (472,494) of all black Virginians in 1860; free blacks, slightly over 10 percent (55,269). Despite their small share of the total, those who were free before the war would dominate positions of political leadership in the black community during the Reconstruction years. Free blacks, like bondsmen, were primarily rural, agricultural people, but a higher proportion of free blacks tended to live in urban areas than did slaves. While 22.2 percent (12,258) of the Old Dominion's free blacks lived in towns and cities in 1860, only 7.4 percent (35,144) of the slaves lived in such urban zones. [2]

Slavery had existed in Virginia for roughly two hundred years before it was swept away by the Civil War in the 1860s. In those two centuries certain areas of the Old Dominion had depended on slave labor to a far greater extent than others. In general, the tidewater counties along the eastern edge of the state and the central and southern piedmont in the middle of Virginia contained most of the Old Dominion's slave plantations and farms, and therefore most of the state's black bondsmen (see map 1). While the disruption of normal living patterns caused by the war allowed black individuals and families to move about more freely than ever before, and while many of the freedmen took advantage of this freedom to seek lost family members and better economic opportunities, still, the majority of black Virginians remained in the same eastern and central sections after the war where they had toiled as slaves before Fort Sumter (see map 2).

One significant population shift had occurred during and immediately after the war—the movement of thousands of freedmen from rural counties to towns and cities, especially those occupied by the Union army during the conflict. Beginning as early as the summer of 1861, slaves by the dozens, then hundreds, and eventually thousands, streamed toward the tip of the Peninsula in eastern Virginia, the area around Fortress Monroe held by the Union army throughout the war. Many of the able-

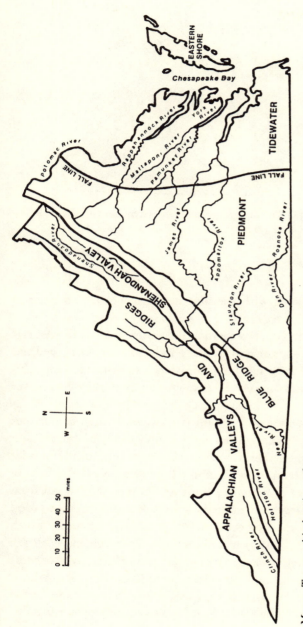

Map 1. Topographical regions of Virginia. From *State Maps on File: Southeast* (Copyright © 1984 by Martin Greenwald Associates; reprinted with the permission of Facts on File, Inc., New York).

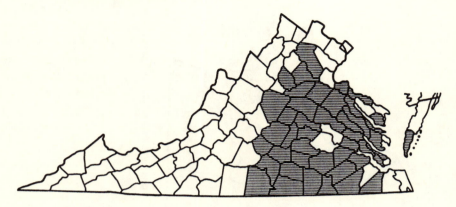

Map 2. Counties with black population in majority, 1860. From United States, Bureau of the Census, *Population of the United States in 1860; Compiled from the Original Returns of the Eighth Census* (Washington, D.C.: GPO, 1864), 516–20.

bodied refugees found work with the blue army as cooks, personal servants, stevedores, and trench diggers. Some also served as scouts and spies for the Federal military forces. Northern aid societies, such as the American Missionary Association, donated clothing and books for the ragged and mostly illiterate blacks. Some northern ministers also married many refugee couples, giving their unions a religious sanction they had never enjoyed before.[3]

These black refugees often took the initiative to build their own homes and villages within the protecting lines of the Union army. "Slabtown" and "Acreville" sprang up near Yorktown on the Peninsula, while similar villages were built in Hampton and near Alexandria. With the help of Union soldiers, fugitives at Slabtown built 400 cabins with wood from nearby forests. Their village also boasted a store and church. About 7,000 refugees in the Alexandria area constructed 700 to 800 houses, worth approximately $30,000, and organized and raised ten schools with the help of northern aid societies. The most famous and longest-lived of these freedmen's villages was built on land belonging to Robert E. Lee's Arlington estate, just across the Potomac River from Washington. Established in the summer of 1863, when the land's owner was on his way to Gettysburg, the Arlington village included well-planned streets and parks. A map of the settlement shows a Lincoln Park, a Seward Park, a Hamlin Circle (named for Lincoln's first vice-president, Hannibal Hamlin), and an Underwood Row (obviously honoring Judge John C. Underwood). Arlington's Freedmen's Village remained a black community until 1900.[4]

One result of these wartime and early postwar migrations was a swelling of the black populations on the Peninsula, near Norfolk, around Alexandria and Arlington, and even in Richmond. The number of blacks in Alexandria ballooned from 2,800 in 1860 to 8,000 in 1866. In the general area near Washington (including Alexandria and surrounding towns), freedmen's camps included probably 10,000 refugees. The black population of Richmond, capital of the Confederacy, increased from 14,000 to 25,000.[5]

These wartime population movements continued in the months after Lee's surrender at Appomattox. John Richard Dennett, the northern journalist touring the Old Dominion in the spring and summer of 1865, interviewed an Amelia County white farmer about the tendency of former slaves to leave their old homes. "Well, sir," the farmer lamented, "today, out of more than a hundred servants that were on my place on the first of April, I haven't six left, and those are mostly infirm old people." Dennett noted the large numbers of freedmen walking along the roads of Virginia: "Impelled by various motives, many were wandering about without regular occupation or fixed abode." Some were seeking work, others looking for relatives, some seeking "employment in labor which they understood better than that which they were leaving." Towns and cities held many attractions for newly freed slaves—safety in numbers, the services of the Freedmen's Bureau, black churches and schools, emerging black political organizations, and the protection of the Union army.[6]

Many local whites interpreted these migrations as black reluctance to work for a living. Dennett, on the other hand, was struck by the numbers who were searching for jobs. "At no time, I think, has anything like a majority of the Negroes thought that freedom meant exemption from labor," Dennett observed. He noted the common white opinion in Lynchburg that the freedmen would inevitably remain paupers, but he wrote that the black Virginians he saw in southern Virginia were "orderly, industrious, and self-supporting." Another northern writer, describing the manual labor performed by Richmond blacks in the "burnt district" in September 1865, contrasted their hard work with white complaints that the freedmen were not willing to labor: "They drove the teams, made the mortar, carried the hods, excavated the old cellars or dug new ones, and, sitting down amid the ruins, broke the mortar from the old bricks and put them up in neat piles ready for use. There were also colored masons and carpenters employed on the new buildings."[7]

Indeed, one other motive for the black flow to urban areas may well have been the freedmen's search for higher incomes. Wages for city workers tended to be significantly higher than for farmhands in the aftermath of war. Dennett reported that farm workers in Virginia's rural counties received only five dollars per month, plus room and board; some, in fact, received no cash wages at all, only their food and lodgings. White farmers in Albemarle County combined to fix wages at five dollars a month plus board. Union colonel Orlando Brown, assistant commissioner for the Freedmen's Bureau in Virginia, testified before Congress that farm wages were very low. But, Brown believed, the landowners "have not the means to allow them what would be considered living wages." Even their friends had not always paid the freedmen higher wages. The northern missionary Lucy Chase wrote home in 1864 that Union general Benjamin Butler "does not wish them to remain helpless paupers upon Government farms, so he gives (or allows Superintendents to give) but $10. a month to the men laborers and $5. to the women, obliging them to pay, from their wages, for their rations."[8]

Whether the reason for such low wages was the shortage of liquid capital, the landowners' greed, or a paternalistic desire to encourage them to work harder, Virginia's black families were forced to struggle if they lived on farms. Dennett described the freedmen's dilemma: " 'What kin we do, sah?' they say; 'dey kin give us jes what dey choose. Man couldn't starve, nohow; got no place to go; we 'bleege to take what dey give us.' "[9]

While wages for urban labor were not high compared with those in the North, some city workers in Virginia did earn considerably more than farm laborers. Whitelaw Reid, another northern journalist traveling through the Old Dominion at about the same time as Dennett, noted that Lynchburg hotels paid black employees twenty dollars a month, not including tips, and that Richmond freedmen received fifteen dollars per month for the same work. One black common laborer in Richmond told still another northern traveler, J. T. Trowbridge, that he was making $1.50 per day clearing rubble from the burned district. Workers in Richmond's tobacco factories, the elite among Virginia's black urban laborers, also earned $1.50 per day. The lure of higher wages doubtless attracted many former field hands to Virginia's cities after emancipation.[10]

While thousands of black Virginians did trudge down farm lanes toward towns and cities during and immediately after the war, most former bondsmen remained in the countryside, working at the jobs they and their ancestors had always performed in the Old Dominion—plowing fields in the spring, working the tobacco, corn, and wheat crops in the summer, and harvesting in the late summer and fall. Squeezed between these major jobs were the innumerable smaller tasks that black agricultural laborers were expected to carry out—mending fences, caring for livestock, maintaining farm equipment, raising their own children, planting small garden plots.[11]

These rural freedmen, isolated as they were from fellow blacks and from black political and social organizations in cities and towns, were generally less politically active than their urban counterparts. Physical isolation was not the only force muting their political voices, however. Freedmen in rural areas were under the more direct observation and control of white Virginians. A black farm worker would find it much more difficult to speak out and organize his fellow freedmen for political action than a black minister in Richmond or a tobacco worker in Manchester. While they generally did not provide political leadership for Virginia's black population during the late 1860s, these rural freedmen did understand their new status and longed as much as other blacks for the freedom that the Union victory had promised. Some white Republicans in both the North and the South expressed the fear that rural blacks would be cowed by their former masters and would vote as their white employers directed them. But their voting patterns in 1867 and 1869 would demonstrate black Virginians' allegiance to the party of Lincoln, Stevens, and Sumner.[12]

The Response to Emancipation

The moment of freedom—the instant Virginia's slaves realized they were free—remained one of the most vivid memories of their lives, even into old age. The slaves' deep longing to be free finally came to the surface in the spring of 1865. Even when white masters attempted to frighten them about the vicious nature of the invading Yankees, the state's bondsmen seemed to realize that the soldiers in blue promised a brighter future for them and their children. One tidewater woman remembered the stories that whites told about the Union army: "they said that the yankees had horns and said that the yankees was Goin to kill us and somthing told me not to Believe them and somthing told me not to Be afraid."[13]

All across the Old Dominion the scenes in the slave quarters when freedom came were similar. In Pamplin, just a few miles from Appomattox where General Lee's gray army surrendered on April 9, 1865, Fanny Berry described the joy. "Never was no time like 'em befo' or since. Niggers shoutin' an' clappin' hands and singin'! Chillun runnin' all over de place beatin' tins an' yellin'. Ev'ybody happy. Sho' did some celebratin'." If anything, slaves in the larger cities, especially Richmond, understood the implications of emancipation even more clearly than those in the countryside. One black resident of the capital exulted that "we'uns kin go jist anywhar, don't keer for no pass—go when yer want'er. Golly! de kingdom hab kim dis time for sure—dat ar what am promised in de generations to dem dat goes up tru great tribulations." Farther east, on the Peninsula near Yorktown, another black woman celebrated when she learned of the fall of Richmond. Running down to a spring where water was taken for the white household, she made sure no one else was around, then jumped and shouted out her happiness. "An' I got sort o' scared, afeared somebody hear me, an' I takes another good look, an' fall on de groun', an' roll over, an' kiss de groun' fo' de Lord's sake, I's so full o' praise to Masser Jesus."[14]

These individual and spontaneous expressions soon were joined by more organized celebrations. On Friday, April 7, two days before Lee's surrender but four days after Union forces marched into Richmond, 1,500 black civilians and soldiers held a "Jubilee Meeting" in the capital's First African Baptist Church on Broad Street, singing hymns and praising God for their emancipation. Such demonstrations were repeated wherever the blue columns of the Union army replaced the ragged remnants of the Confederacy.[15]

The joyful displays of the first moments of freedom soon gave way to the disheartening realization that white Virginians, despite their defeat, were determined to maintain control of their former bondsmen. This attitude portended trouble for ex-slaves who looked forward to enjoying their new independence. Virginia whites, like their counterparts throughout the Confederacy, believed that the freedmen were lazy and shiftless and needed white direction. Even those blacks who had been free before the war were considered fit only for white-directed manual labor. An Amelia County farmer told visiting journalist John Richard Dennett that free blacks "have been always perfectly worthless and lived in wretchedness." As for the slaves, the farmer said, "When I look at my servants, I feel weighing upon me all the responsibilities of a parent." Some white Virginians doubted that blacks could survive even with white paternalism. A Norfolk resident told Dennett that "unless the colored people were removed to Texas, or some South American country, they would surely die out by reason of their laziness and shiftlessness."[16]

While some whites saw themselves as gentle parents to their irresponsible servants, other former Confederates emphasized the necessity of force when dealing with the former slaves. These men, the northern traveler Whitelaw Reid observed, "have no sort of conception of free labor. They do not comprehend any law for controlling laborers, save the law of force." Reid's fellow journalist Dennett quoted another white Virginian: "A good many of the masters forget pretty often that their niggers are free, and take a stick to them, or give them a cuff with the fist, though they don't attempt to administer a regular flogging."[17]

Although former Confederates were compelled to concede that blacks were no longer slaves, they did not believe that freedom for their former bondsmen was quite the same as freedom for themselves. The end of slavery, to most Virginia whites, meant only that they no longer legally owned their chattels. It did not mean that the ex-slaves could behave as though they were equal to whites. The humiliation and shame that white Virginians felt as a result of their military defeat frequently boiled over into violence when the freedmen did speak and act as free men.

A revealing example of this took place in Prince William County in January 1866. James Cook, a black veteran of the Union army, made the dangerous mistake of saying in the presence of whites that he was proud of his service in the Federal army. For this remark a local white man, John Cornwell, chased Cook through the streets of Brentsville, shot at him, and beat him over the head with a pistol, opening "a deep cut over the eye." Cook did not draw his own pistol but instead ran to the local Freedmen's Bureau officer, Lieutenant Marcus Hopkins, who investigated the affair and confirmed Cook's story. During the inquiry a local physician angrily informed Lieutenant Hopkins that "subdued and miserable as we are, we will not allow niggers to come among us and brag about having been in the yankee army. It is as much as we can do to tolerate it in white men." Hopkins sadly concluded that many whites "hold an insane malice against the freedman, from which he must be protected, or he is worse off than when he was a slave." The full exercise of their new freedom would require considerable courage on the part of black Virginians, especially those who assumed positions of leadership and openly expressed their opinions.[18]

White resistance to the new order of things was not entirely surprising to the freedmen, of course. They had grown up and lived among the Old Dominion's white people for generations and knew their deeply ingrained attitudes about black inferiority. More disappointing was the realization that even their white friends from the North often harbored ideas that could only retard the march toward full equality. Whitelaw Reid, a solid Union man from the North and fully in sympathy with the freedmen, still regretted the special efforts being made in Virginia for the former slaves. Black Virginians would never learn to fend for themselves, he wrote, unless they learned that freedom meant work. "To teach them this, do not gather them in colonies at military posts, and feed them on Government rations; but throw them in the water and have them learn to swim by finding the necessity of swimming." Another true Union man and journalist from the North, touring the state at about the same time as Reid, was critical of the ex-slaves' deference to whites: "So far as concerns the Negro's manners, it seems to me that he has by no means removed all traces of his former servility of demeanor." In summarizing his findings after his tour of the postwar South, Reid concluded that the former slaves "are not such material as, under ordinary circumstances, one would now choose for the duties of American citizenship." Blacks would need far more than lukewarm and condescending acceptance by their northern allies if they were to overcome the obstacles that Virginia whites were putting in their way. [19]

More important to the freedmen than the opinions of touring journalists were the policies of the Union army. While Federal forces had fought since 1863 to liberate southern bondsmen, and while many northern soldiers befriended the former slaves out of feelings of common humanity, not all Federal officers and men displayed enlightened attitudes in postwar Virginia. In the first months after Appomattox, Union military officials set curfews for black Virginians, required passes (as in antebellum slavery days) if they were away from their jobs, and arrested them for insulting local whites. In a policy that anticipated by several months the actions of the conservative General Assembly of 1865, some Federal officers arrested freedmen who could not produce passes and invited local planters to bid for their labor. General Alfred Terry, who would void the General Assembly's Vagrancy Act in early 1866, took the same action with regard to his own army's regulations in June 1865. Not realizing the irony of his remarks, a less enlightened officer, the Federal military commander in Lynchburg, said that the Old Dominion's freedmen had "all the rights at present that free people of color have heretofore had in Virginia." This was certainly not the conception of freedom that most of the state's black people embraced.[20]

An incident in Richmond two months after Lee's surrender must have given local blacks reason to question the commitment of the Federal army to the new freedom promised by the war. A black man, Ned Scott, and his wife were walking down Main Street when they were accused, apparently wrongly, of crowding two local white men on the sidewalk. During the ensuing argument the white men pushed and hit Scott and his wife, whereupon Scott threatened them with a knife. Three Union soldiers, observing the encounter, quickly intervened on the side of the white men and assaulted Scott. By this time Scott was reacting with more than words, and he cut two of the soldiers with his knife before escaping down the street with his wife. The next night Union soldiers arrested him and brought him before a military court which gave him a thirty-day jail term. To compound Scott's misery, the army publicly humiliated him by tieing him up, marching him through the streets, and placing him in a partly open coffin with meal on his face to attract flies.[21]

The army's relations with Unionists and freedmen depended to a great degree on the attitudes of commanding officers. Men like General Terry did not tolerate mistreatment of the former slaves. Other military officials, however, especially some of those in command at the end of hostilities, regarded Virginia's ex-bondsmen as nuisances to be controlled, not free people whose rights had to be protected. Referring to the policies of the Federal army in Richmond in the spring of 1865, one white Richmond Unionist summed up the frustration felt by white and black Republicans: "The Union men were insulted and bullied by them [Union officers], the colored people were treated worse under their rule than they had ever been by the Rebels, and the secessionists were coaxed and petted." It is a tribute to the patriotism of black Virginians that they continued to regard the North and its army as their friends and protectors despite the actions of some Federal officers in the early postwar months.[22]

The sometimes repressive policies of the occupying Federal army, coming at the same time as Governor Pierpont's restoration of many former Confederates to their antebellum positions of power and influence, no doubt dampened the enthusiasm that Virginia freedmen had expressed at their first moments of liberty. Black Virginians' response to emancipation, nevertheless, was hopeful and optimistic. In many ways they understood the meaning of the war better than did their emancipators and their former masters. They followed numerous avenues to exploit and broaden their new freedom in the first two years after the war.

One of the new liberties that freedmen most valued was control over their own families. No longer subject to forced separations and sales away from other family members, Virginia's freedmen took steps to shore up family ties wherever possible. In order to protect wives and children by assuring them that they would inherit any property that might be accumulated after emancipation, hundreds, perhaps thousands, of freedmen took the initiative to approach northern missionaries and Union army chaplains to ask for marriage ceremonies that would legally record their unions. As early as September 1861 in occupied counties of the Old Dominion, hundreds of black couples joined hands and exchanged vows, giving their antebellum slave marriages a new sanction. Further strengthening family bonds, many ex-slave women withdrew their labor from the fields and kitchens of white families in order to cook and sew for their husbands and nurture their children. Their husbands even began to negotiate restrictions on female labor in their annual labor contracts after Appomattox. The removal of outside, white control of their family relations was one of the most satisfying rewards of emancipation.[23]

Taking advantage of their new status, Virginia's freedmen also began to assert more control over their religious lives. For two hundred years they had been required to worship under white supervision. Even when urban blacks, many of them free, had organized their own churches before the war, they had been forced to follow the lead of white ministers. With the end of slavery, however, the Old Dominion's freedmen, especially in the larger cities, began to take control of their own churches. In Richmond alone five black churches dismissed or pressured white clergymen to resign and replaced them with black preachers in the first three months after the Confederate surrender. The former slaves lost no time in pushing the boundaries of freedom as far as possible in every area of their lives.[24]

Almost as important to the freedmen as their families and churches was education for themselves and their children. They responded immediately and enthusiastically to every opportunity for schooling. Only two weeks after Confederate columns abandoned Richmond, northern missionary Sarah Chase could write home from the Virginia capital that "we have already enrolled over two thousand [black] pupils and expect to nearly double the number before long." Two days later Chase's sister and fellow missionary informed a correspondent that within a few days "we shall go to Petersburg, in accordance with an urgent request from its Col'd citizens to open schools." John Richard Dennett, the northern journalist traveling through the state in 1865, remarked upon the thirst for formal education among black children and parents. The children, he wrote, "were docile pupils, regular in their attendance, more laborious in application and more rapid in their progress than white children accustomed to the regular routine of school life. I think the parents are anxious to have their children taught, and may be expected to make sacrifices for the sake of educating them."[25]

All across the Old Dominion black children and adults filed into classrooms wherever space and teachers could be found. In Lynchburg about 130 students, ranging in age from three to twenty, met in an empty tobacco warehouse to hear lessons taught by two Union soldiers. In Hampton convalescent Union soldiers introduced nearly 400 students to the mysteries of the alphabet and to arithmetic. One of the most ironic settings for a freedmen's school was a former jail in Richmond where a slave trader had housed bondsmen before putting them on the auction block. The slave trader's wife, a black woman, allowed a Massachusetts clergyman to renovate the building for a school in early 1867. By early 1866 nearly 13,000 pupils were attending classes in 90 schools, hearing their lessons from about 200 teachers, most of them northern missionaries or Union soldiers. Between 1862 and 1870 more than 200 northern teachers served in freedmen's schools in Virginia. Over half of these immigrant instructors were from the New England states. They conducted classes in 222 different towns or cities in the state, but three-fourths of the missionaries served in three areas—the Norfolk-Peninsula region in southeast Virginia, Alexandria and Arlington near Washington, D.C., and the region around Richmond and Petersburg.[26] Like those in other parts of the old Confederacy, Virginia freedmen responded immediately to the educational opportunities provided by northern missionaries and the Freedmen's Bureau.

The chance to become self-supporting and independent economic beings was one of the most exciting prospects for the Old Dominion's black folk after the war. Anxious to be free of white control and supervision, freedmen followed every avenue of economic opportunity they could find. Some black women sold homemade snacks to hungry train passengers traveling between Richmond and Lynchburg. Rural freedmen, no longer limited to the supplies doled out by their former masters, now purchased whatever they could afford from country merchants. And if by some chance a black farmer or urban laborer managed to save a few dollars for the future, he often took advantage of the new Freedman's Savings and Trust Company (the Freedman's Savings Bank) to deposit his money and have his own account. A forerunner to the Freedman's Savings Bank was established by Union general Benjamin Butler in Norfolk in the fall of 1864. By mid-1865 this institution had almost $8,000 in deposits from 180 black depositors. Soon the more famous Freedman's Savings Bank was operating in southeastern Virginia, opening its first branch in Norfolk in June 1865. The bank's third branch began operating in Richmond four months later, receiving deposits from hundreds of the capital's freedmen—typically male urban laborers between the ages of twenty and forty-nine. The Freedman's Savings Bank was doubtless even more attractive to Virginia blacks because some of their own people served as cashiers and board members.[27]

When black farmhands negotiated labor contracts with white landowners, the former bondsmen used their new status to pressure whites into granting them more independence and new rights. Farm workers bargained with landlords for the right to keep garden crops for themselves, better food and clothing, more time off for meals and holidays, and the right to participate in the selection of overseers. Freedmen also pressed white farmers to abolish the old gang system of labor so reminiscent of slavery and to replace it with some form of rent arrangement that would allow black families more autonomy. Indeed, contrabands near Norfolk had voted as early as the spring of 1863 to abandon the gang system in favor of individual plots when given the choice by Union occupation officials. If the farm operator balked at these new conditions, the freedmen could (and often did) take their labor elsewhere. As the Old Dominion's black population gained more confidence and experience in dealing with whites, their demands for increased autonomy and rights expanded. For example, labor contracts for 1866 and 1867 were generally more favorable to the freedmen than those negotiated at the end of the war for the 1865 crop year.[28]

Urban workers were at least as zealous as farmhands in asserting their new rights in their dealings with white employers. On the day the Union army marched into Richmond, the servants in one of the capital's households appointed a delegation of three to inform the master that they expected to receive cash wages in the future. Similar confrontations took place in Fredericksburg (and probably all over the state) at about the same time. The tobacco factory workers of Richmond and Manchester, some of the highest-paid black laborers in the state, complained in September 1865 that even their wages were too low to support a family.[29]

While farmhands used their new status to negotiate better conditions for themselves and their families, their eyes were on an even more exciting prospect, the chance to become independent, landowning yeoman farmers. The desire to own their own land and operate their own family farms was a powerful drive among the newly freed class. Whitelaw Reid and John Richard Dennett, the perceptive touring journalists, noticed this urge as early as the summer after Appomattox, in eastern as well as southwest Virginia. In some cases, the freedmen formed cooperatives to buy land. Approximately 3,000 black Virginians in the area around Fortress Monroe on the tip of the Peninsula in eastern Virginia pooled $30,000 to buy a large estate near Hampton in 1866. When their efforts to buy a farm confiscated by Union officials during the war were frustrated by President Johnson's pardon of the owner after the conflict, Norfolk County freedmen drove off the sheriff and Union army officers who had come to remove them from the land. Reminded that the president and Freedmen's Bureau would look after their needs, their spokesman shouted back, "We don't care for the President nor the Freedmen's Bureau. We have suffered long enough; let the white man suffer now." After further fighting with county officials, the homesteading black families were finally driven off the farm, and it was returned to its antebellum owner. Similar incidents took place in Hampton and Yorktown on the Peninsula, shattering the hopes of thousands of freedmen.[30]

One black farmer, evicted by the army from a farm near Yorktown, demonstrated a keen grasp of economics (if not the law) in his cry of protest:

> We has a right to the land where we are located. For why? I tell you. Our wives, our children, our husbands, has been sold over and over again to purchase the lands we now located upon; for that reason we have a divine right to the land. . . . And den didn't we cleare the land, and raise de crops ob corn, ob cotton, ob tobacco, ob rice, ob sugar, ob everything. And den didn't dem large cities in de North grow up on de cotton and de sugars and de rice dat we made? . . . I say dey has grown rich, and my people is poor.[31]

Far from the cringing and ignorant lump of humanity that many white southerners perceived when they regarded the freedmen, postwar Virginia blacks were generally perceptive, clever, ambitious, and anxious to exercise and extend their new rights as members of American society.[32]

Political Activities

While educational achievement and economic advancement were high priorities for the newly freed bondsmen in the Old Dominion, they looked forward to participation in the political process even more. The ballot, they believed, would be the umbrella that would protect and advance their interests and those of their children and grandchildren. Moreover, the right to vote was a badge of respectability that had been denied them when they were slaves. Now that they were free, they would wear that badge with pride. It would be a sign that the old days of bondage had indeed been swept away and that black folk were full and equal members of a new America.

Some black Virginians edged into the state's political picture even before the war was over. As early as February 1865 former slaves and free blacks in Norfolk (occupied by Federal forces since May 1862) met in Mechanics' Hall to protest the changeover from military government in Union-occupied southeastern Virginia to civil government under the Pierpont Restored regime headquartered in Alexandria. The black Virginians complained that the Restored government "contemplated no representation of their rights and interests" and demanded that any new civil government must be created on a "loyal and equal basis," meaning, of course, the establishment of black voting and officeholding. Copies of the adopted resolutions were sent to Union army officials and to President Lincoln in Washington. At the same time a Union Monitor Club (similar to the Union Leagues established after the war) was set up to stress "the important subject of the right of *universal* suffrage to *all* loyal men, without distinction of color." This club organized several "large and enthusiastic public meetings of the colored citizens of Norfolk" in April and May, emphasizing always the subject of "Negro suffrage."[33]

At about the same time black Virginians in Hampton and Williamsburg were also organizing themselves into Union League clubs to campaign for universal suffrage. The movement to form black political clubs soon swept over other cities and towns in eastern, central, and northern

Virginia. In some cases white Unionists were central figures in the calling of such meetings, but in others black men both initiated and conducted the proceedings from start to finish. These conventions generally expressed gratitude to heaven and to the Federal government for the deliverance of the slaves from bondage, stressed the need for education and equal rights, and always put equal suffrage first in their list of priorities. A mass meeting in Norfolk on May 11 summed up the message that black clubs and organizations stressed in 1865: "That personal servitude having been abolished in Virginia, it behooves us, and is demanded of us, by every consideration of right and duty, to speak and act as freemen, and as such to claim and insist upon equality before the law, and equal rights of suffrage at the 'ballot box.'" To the former slaves and free blacks of Virginia a middle ground between bondage and equal citizenship did not exist. If they were not slaves, then they must necessarily be full and equal citizens of the state and nation, with all the rights of other citizens, especially the right to vote.[34]

Not satisfied with meetings and resolutions alone, Norfolk blacks actually voted in the state elections of May 25, 1865. Adopting as their own the three white candidates for the General Assembly earlier nominated by local white Unionists, more than 5,000 black residents of Norfolk assembled at the Bute Street Methodist Church on election day. From the church marched four committees, one to each of the city's four wards, to test the poll officials and attempt to vote. Officials in wards 1, 3, and 4 rejected the black committees, but those in ward 2 recorded their votes "upon a separate list, as of voters whose disqualifications were a matter of dispute." When word reached the church that some of their fellow freedmen had voted, "the whole assembly rose, and, at the instance of the chairman, sang the hymn 'Praise God, from whom all blessings flow.'" Having apparently breached the wall of political separation, other black residents of ward 2 then proceeded to the polls in groups of ten and cast 354 votes for each of the three Union candidates. Residents of the other wards recorded their votes at the church, giving the three Unionists 712 votes each. The local white vote for the same three candidates was only 89, 83, and 102. The results of this first attempt at political participation, according to the black leaders of the movement, filled "every patriotic heart with wonder and gratitude at the astounding progress" that had been made.[35]

When the local sheriff posted the election results the next day without any mention of the black votes in ward 2 or those offered in wards 1, 3, and 4, Norfolk Union League officers vowed to appeal to the state legislature for recognition of their votes. They would base this claim, they said, on the state constitution's Declaration of Rights and on the United States Constitution, both of which demonstrated "that color alone affords no constitutional or legal ground for the imposition of any civil disability" on black citizens. They were not naive, however: "It would be improper to conceal our expectation, that but little hope can be entertained of any redress at the hands of the present Virginia legislature, but behind these are the President and Congress of the United States, to which higher tribunal we intend to appeal."[36]

The Norfolk leaders were correct in their prediction that the Restored legislature would not recognize their votes in the election. To publicize their appeal beyond the boundaries of the Old Dominion, they arranged another mass meeting on June 5 in the Catherine Street Baptist Church. Led by Thomas Bayne, a forceful black leader and future member of the 1867–68 constitutional convention, the gathering adopted and published in pamphlet form *An Address from the Colored Citizens of Norfolk, Va., to the People of the United States*. The pamphlet listed numerous reasons for extending the franchise to the black population. Black men had played a prominent role in the building of the nation. "Every school-boy knows that within twelve years of the foundation of the first settlement at Jamestown, our fathers as well as yours were toiling in the plantations of James River." Moreover, "the first blood shed in the Revolutionary war was that of a colored man, Crispus Attucks." The discriminatory legislation that had always oppressed blacks in the slave states would simply be continued after the war unless the freedmen had some means of protecting themselves. Indeed, "so far as legal safeguards of our rights are concerned, we are defenceless before our enemies."

Equal suffrage would afford the nation a less expensive and less controversial means of protecting white Unionists and former slaves than continued military occupation. In the absence of universal manhood suffrage, the white aristocracy of the South would wield even more power than previously through the insidious workings of the three-fifths clause of the Constitution. National honor was at stake, the address continued, "but is that honor advanced, in the eyes of the Christian world, when America alone, of all Christian nations, sustains an unjust distinction . . . on the senseless ground of a difference in color?" Black political participation would bring millions of Americans into the mainstream of the political system and thereby avoid the possibility of future "Negro agitation" and civil disturbances. The spirit of the national Constitution and the Virginia Declaration of Rights both called for equal suffrage. Shorter sections of the address urged rural freedmen to form "labor associations" to demand higher farm wages and thus counteract the wage-depressing associations of white landowners and to create "land associations" by which freedmen could pool their meager resources to buy their own land.[37]

While several "colored conventions" had been held before the war, none had dared to meet south of Maryland. But in the first few months after Confederate surrender, courageous freedmen in several former slave states arranged assemblies to express their hopes and fears. Perhaps inspired by the early efforts of their fellow blacks in Norfolk, those in Richmond began organizing along the same lines in early June. A mass meeting on June 10 in the First African Baptist Church, led principally by free black ministers like Fields Cook (a cashier in the Freedman's Savings Bank), included more than 3,000 black residents of the capital. Following the practice of most other such conventions, the Richmond meeting drew up a memorial to be published and presented to Federal authorities. This address reminded readers that Virginia freedmen had been peaceful and loyal throughout the recent war; that some Richmond blacks were respectable property owners and that two or three thousand were literate; that the state's black population had prayed for and sometimes aided the Union army in its struggle against the Confederacy; that the mayor of Richmond had been and still was rebellious and cruel to blacks; that the mayor's police force "who are now hunting us through the streets, are the men who relentlessly applied the lash to our quivering flesh, and . . . appear to take special pleasure in persecuting and oppressing us."[38]

A delegation from the June 10 meeting took the memorial with them to Washington one week later to present it to President Johnson himself. The president listened politely to Richmond's black leaders and promised to protect them. In fact, the meetings and protests that had preceded this visit had already had some positive effects in the Virginia capital. Governor Pierpont had removed Mayor Joseph Mayo, target of so much black criticism, from office only days earlier; one Union general in charge of Richmond resigned his post; two other such generals were reassigned to other duties; and General Terry, a man known for his sympathy for the freedmen, was appointed military commander of Virginia. The June protest seemed to catalyze black political activity in the capital, and Richmond blacks thenceforth took the lead in the politicization of Virginia's freedmen.[39]

This politicization took a more advanced form in early August 1865 when a statewide convention assembled in Alexandria. Several dozen black Virginians from towns and counties scattered across southern, eastern, and northern sections of the Old Dominion made their way to Lyceum Hall on August 2–5 "to act and advise what is thought best to be done for the interests of the colored people of the State, and to give expression of our feelings and desires." The Alexandria convention adopted numerous resolutions and three major addresses to the public. One of these documents was also directed to members of Congress. Like their white counterparts in the summer of 1865, the black Unionists of Virginia appealed to Governor Pierpont to reorient himself away from former rebels and toward his true friends. But while white Unionists urged the governor only to appoint white Unionists to office and extend the vote to black Virginians, the Alexandria convention went further. In addition to those reforms, the black convention asked for "the repeal of all the black laws of Virginia which oppress and degrade us." Unless Pierpont complied, the convention resolved, "we cannot regard him as our friend."

Turning to those white leaders for whom black Virginians had the greatest respect, the convention thanked senators Charles Sumner of Massachusetts, Benjamin Wade of Ohio, and Henry Wilson of Massachusetts and Union generals Terry and John W. Turner for their efforts to protect the black folk of the Old Dominion. And then, in a thrust that must have stung conservative white Unionists and former Confederates alike, the meeting proclaimed that "none have a greater share of our love and respect than General B. F. Butler, who first decided the fate of slavery." The praise for Butler referred to his wartime decision to regard runaway slaves as "contraband of war" rather than fugitives to be returned to their masters.[40]

Like other black conventions, the Alexandria meeting discussed a wide array of reforms, but all of them revolved around equal rights and equal suffrage. Nearly a year before Congress adopted the Fourteenth Amendment and its provision for equal protection of the laws, the freedmen of the Old Dominion demanded that "the laws of the Commonwealth shall give to all men equal protection; that each and every man may appeal to the law for his equal rights without regard to the color of his skin." This could only be done, however, if the franchise was extended to include black men.

Federal intervention into the state's political process was necessary to bring about these changes, the convention asserted, because President Johnson had left southern blacks "entirely at the mercy of . . . subjugated but unconverted rebels." As they pointed out, "we know these men—know them *well*—and we assure you that, with the majority of them, loyalty is only 'lip deep,' and that their professions of loyalty are used as a cover to the cherished design of getting restored to their former relations with the Federal government, and then, by all sorts of 'unfriendly legislation,' to render the freedom you have given us more intolerable than the slavery they intended for us."[41]

Anticipating Congress's military Reconstruction plan of 1867, the convention resolved that the only safe course for Congress to follow was to keep the southern states "under Governors of the *military persuasion* until you have so amended the Federal Constitution that it will prohibit the States from making any distinction between citizens on account of race or color. In one word, the only salvation for us besides the power of the Government, is in the *possession of the ballot*. Give us this, and we will protect ourselves."[42]

The delegates at Lyceum Hall understood that they were being watched by the white population of Virginia and by the country as a whole. S. H. Lee of Fairfax County in northern Virginia pointed out that the convention's addresses were "the production of our own people, and not the work of our northern friends. He knew this charge would be made, and it was well to forestall it." On the last day of the meeting an anonymous letter addressed to Fields Cook and other delegates warned of white retaliation: "Beware! beware! Fields Cook, you and other negroes will die before the autumn leaves fall upon the unavenged graves of the many Southerners who are buried through our land. You are never to be on an equality with the whites, though superior to many of them; but you, many of you will die soon if this Freedmen's Convention, &c., &c., continues, particularly here in Virginia. So beware! The South must and shall be avenged!" Such threats deterred no one in the Alexandria convention, however. Henry Highland Garnet, a prominent black preacher from Washington and an honorary member of the meeting, denounced the writer as "a mean, contemptible coward." Rather than being tabled, "on motion, the letter was thrown under the table by a unanimous vote."[43]

The black conventions in Norfolk, Richmond, and Alexandria attracted considerable attention, but they were not the only meetings of

Virginia freedmen in the summer and fall of 1865. A similar assemblage in Fredericksburg struck out at the common white notion that blacks were lazy and shiftless: "we scorn and treat with contempt the allegation made against us that we understand Freedom to mean idleness and indolence . . . we do understand Freedom to mean industry and the legitimate fruits thereof." Led by Daniel Norton, a future member of the 1867–68 constitutional convention, former bondsmen on the Peninsula in southeast Virginia held two conventions in the First Baptist Church of Hampton. In August they urged Congress to allow them to remain on abandoned white-owned lands they had worked during the war since, they insisted, the land was more productive under free labor than it had been under slavery. Three months later they pleaded with Congress to refuse seats to the representatives and senators elected from Virginia under the Restored government. These white men should not be seated, the Hampton convention said, "until the colored men of Virginia are allowed the privilege of voting." Black Virginians even sent delegates to conventions outside the Old Dominion. At least two Virginians served as officers of the first annual meeting of the National Equal Rights League that met in Cleveland, Ohio, in October 1865. In Cleveland, Robert W. Johnson of Richmond urged the league to extend its efforts into the rural areas of the Old Dominion. "It is there, said the speaker, much work was to be performed, owing to the oppressive and degrading influence to which slavery has subjected the colored Virginian." Johnson, like other urban blacks, recognized how difficult it was for rural freedmen to organize and express themselves politically.[44]

The new political assertiveness that filled blacks with such pride and whites with such loathing in 1865 seemed to feed on itself and increase in strength as the months and early years of Reconstruction passed. In January 1866 black southerners and some white northerners from thirteen former slave and free states gathered in Washington's Fifteenth Street Methodist Church to publicize their views on Reconstruction and to meet with President Johnson. Several prominent black Virginians, including Thomas Bayne from Norfolk and Daniel Norton of Hampton, took leading roles in the convention. At the same time several of the black Virginians, including Bayne and Norton, testified before the congressional Joint Committee on Reconstruction meeting a few blocks away in the national capitol. Their testimony painted a dismal picture of life in the Old Dominion—low wages for black farm laborers, widespread fraud in the way whites dealt with black labor contracts, physical torture of freedmen who demanded their rights, eviction of farm families from their rented cabins without notice and often without payment for their labor, intimidation and threats directed at black leaders. One year after their first tentative meetings in Norfolk, black Virginians were speaking in louder and clearer tones before larger and more powerful audiences.[45]

The black activism that so frightened and disgusted former Confederates was not confined to the educated leaders of the freedman community. Common laborers and women joined in the new assertiveness to expand the limits of black freedom and rights. When the Richmond black community learned in April 1867 that their counterparts in Charleston, South Carolina, had gained access to the city's streetcars, the Virginia freedmen organized to gain the same rights. They took seats on all-white streetcars and refused to leave when so ordered. When city policemen arrived to arrest the trespassers, crowds of freedmen surrounded the streetcars, shouting and demanding the right to use public transportation. The streetcar company finally yielded to this pressure from below and allowed blacks to ride in four of the company's six cars; two others were reserved for white women and children. At about the same time, the black Stevedore Society of Laboring Men of the City of Richmond struck the city's docks, demanding higher wages for their work. Within days black coopers in Richmond followed suit. While both strikes ultimately failed due to a surplus of labor and willing strikebreakers of both races, the strikes demonstrated that the demand for a new Virginia was coming from all segments of the black community, especially in urban centers. Even black women joined in the crusade. Saddled with all the burdens of other blacks in addition to their traditional roles outside the political process, they nevertheless joined secret societies affiliated with the Union Leagues, conducted fund-raising activities to support black organizations, encouraged their men to vote, and used their influence to pressure wavering black men to stay solid for black rights.[46]

At about the same time as the streetcar controversy and the strikes in Richmond, the Old Dominion's freedmen became deeply involved in electoral politics for the first time in their history, thanks to the congressional Reconstruction Acts of 1867 and to their own demands for change. They continued to participate in national "colored conventions" that called for reform of race relations in the United States. At the height of Virginia's Reconstruction turmoil in January 1869, another major convention representing delegates from twenty states met in Washington's Union League Hall. This meeting, too, included prominent members of Virginia's black political leadership—Lewis Lindsay, a radical Richmond resident who served in the 1867–68 constitutional convention; Samuel F. Kelso, a school teacher from Campbell County who joined Lindsay in the 1867–68 Underwood convention; and Fields Cook of Richmond. Cook, indeed, was so focused on extending black rights that he apparently lost sight of other wrongs when he objected to the seating of a woman from Pennsylvania since the meeting was supposedly for men only.[47]

Those white Virginians who continued after 1865 to describe all blacks as lazy, shiftless, ignorant, and bewildered or frightened by their freedom simply had not been paying attention to what had happened all around them in the months and years since Appomattox. Indeed, even before General Lee's surrender freedmen in Norfolk had organized themselves politically. Within weeks or a few months at most, the black populations in Richmond, Hampton, Yorktown, Alexandria, Fredericksburg, and other parts of southern, eastern, and northern Virginia had joined their friends in Norfolk, expressing their hopes and fears, demanding to be treated as equal citizens, and demonstrating considerable organizational and speaking skills. These black folk showed no bewilderment or fear of liberty. On the contrary, they pushed and pulled at the new definitions of their freedom, always attempting to extend their autonomy and to take their places as equal citizens of a new America. This enthusiastic embrace of the new order of things would stand the Republican party of Virginia in good stead in the upcoming contest to elect the congressionally mandated constitutional convention of 1867–68.

CHAPTER 6

The Underwood
Constitutional Convention

WHILE a promising alliance with native white moderates had been stillborn during the heat of summer, the immediate future still held great promise for Virginia Republicans. The March 1867 congressional Reconstruction Act, by enfranchising more than 100,000 former slaves and requiring the creation of a new state constitution, had raised the possibility of genuine reform of old Virginia's laws and customs.

If Republicans could gain control of a majority of the constitutional convention's seats, they could alter the life of the Old Dominion, perhaps for generations to come. The state's tax system, which had favored the propertied classes at the expense of small farmers, artisans, and the poor, could be rearranged to benefit the newly freed blacks and urban mechanics. Education, limited primarily to the children of the well-to-do before the war, could be extended to a whole new generation of Virginians, black as well as white. Local and county government, dominated for generations by rural white elites, could be opened to Unionist whites and the sons of slaves. And state politics, for generations the preserve of the older and more prominent families of Virginia, could become a clearinghouse for the ideas and aspirations of the formerly silent classes of the Old Dominion.

But none of these changes would sweep over the state unless the Republican party could gain control of the engine of reform, the constitutional convention required by Congress. The party's prospects seemed to dim in August when the northern-engineered cooperator movement broke down amid the shouting and shoving of the Richmond convention. On the other hand, radicals such as James W. Hunnicutt and James H. Platt believed their party could grab the levers of power not by embracing antebellum Whigs but by hard work, discipline within the ranks, and getting out the vote. This approach, which would later be adopted by the national party as well, promised victory without compromise. But it would succeed in Virginia only as long as the majority conservative whites remained listless and unorganized. How long the former Confederates would remain idle in the face of radical Republican success was an issue beyond the radicals' control—and one that they chose to ignore.

The 1867 Election

During the hot summer months of 1867, while the Republicans caucused, compromised, and then split, General Schofield's boards of registration were signing up long lines of voters, including thousands of former slaves, in ninety-nine counties and three cities. By September 1, 114,700 whites and 101,512 blacks had registered. By election day the white and black totals would increase to 120,101 and 105,832 respectively. On September 12 General Schofield issued the order for an election. Voters would decide on October 22 whether to hold a constitutional convention, and at the same time they would elect delegates to the proposed convention.

Schofield had also established the voting districts that would be represented at the meeting. Although whites were a majority of the state's population, had preponderant numbers in fifty-two of the state's 102 counties and cities, and had a clear majority in total registered voters, they were distributed across the state in such a way that Virginia's blacks actually held an advantage in the election (see map 3). The fifty counties controlled by the freedmen were some of the most populous in the state; thousands of whites lived in these black eastern counties while relatively few blacks lived in the western white counties. Indeed, black majorities existed in districts that would elect fifty-nine convention members, while whites controlled districts that would send only forty-six delegates. If representation had been proportionally allocated along racial lines, native whites could have controlled the election. But as long as geography determined the districts and so many whites lived in black areas, the freedmen held the advantage. Some conservatives charged General Schofield with political favoritism, but his main concern seems to have been the necessity of exact and equal population-based representation in the con-

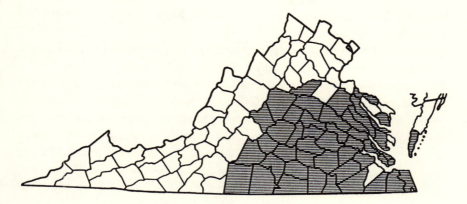

Map 3. Counties with registered black voters in majority, 1867. The cities of Richmond, Petersburg, and Norfolk also had black majorities. From *Documents of the Constitutional Convention of the State of Virginia* (Richmond: Office of the New Nation, 1867 [1868]), 51–52.

vention. Moreover, any of the other commonly accepted systems of representation, such as congressional districts or counties, would have given the freedmen an even greater advantage. And the politically moderate Schofield realized this.[1]

In some ways the 1867 campaign was much like the 1865 contest. Conservatives were generally apathetic; some preferred military control to a black-dominated convention, and others were disgusted with the whole Reconstruction process and simply refused to participate in it. More highly motivated conservatives attempted to rouse the former Confederates, but to little effect. The conservative *Petersburg Daily Index* warned that "this sleeping away of political rights will bring its own bitter reward." Another resident of the city observed wearily that "by tacit consent, the political field has been relinquished entirely to the Republicans." This listless disinterest stirred the *Charlottesville Chronicle* to chastise those who refused to register because they preferred military government to black suffrage. Thousands of whites, however, refused to heed such calls. In Richmond, for example, roughly 1,800 whites failed to register, giving blacks a majority on the city's voting rolls. Statewide, 16,343 whites who were on the tax rolls did not show up on the voting rolls. That number does not include other white Virginians, possibly thousands, who were not on the tax lists but who may have been eligible to register and vote.[2]

Republicans, by contrast, were better organized and much more numerous in 1867 than in 1865, thanks largely to the Reconstruction Acts. Even those moderates who had remained with the party after the August convention were active. Gilbert C. Walker, a moderate carpetbagger from New York and future governor of the state, ran for a convention seat in Norfolk.[3] Alexander Rives, scion of a distinguished Virginia family and a judge of the state Supreme Court of Appeals, was a candidate in Albemarle County.[4] Governor Pierpont was the moderate Republican nominee in Richmond. And the *Richmond Whig* continued to stress the need for cooperation with northern Republicans.[5]

An influential ally of the moderates was the Freedmen's Bureau. Although regulations discouraged their participation in political affairs, some bureau officers joined the Union League, and many tried to influence the freedmen's votes. Thomas W. Conway, the Massachusetts radical who had addressed the state Republican convention in April, wrote General O. O. Howard, head of the Freedmen's Bureau, that he had "organized a fine state [Union League] Council in Va, some of the officers of the Bureau being officers thereof."[6]

The bureau agents, however, were seldom as radical as Conway. Bureau officers, like many other northern visitors in the Old Dominion, tended to regard the freedmen as simple and childlike, needing the guidance of friendly whites to lead them in the correct path—the path toward the northern virtues of diligence, thrift, and pious Christianity. According to this view, Virginia freedmen should take advantage of their new political rights but leave leadership to better-equipped white Republicans.

General Orlando Brown, assistant commissioner of the bureau in the Old Dominion, had applauded the Republicans' June compromise and told General Howard shortly thereafter that "if no new trouble arises we can carry the state on an out and out Republican ticket by twenty thousand majority." Native moderates praised the bureau officers for urging the blacks to vote for the "ablest and most worthy Republicans"—that is, the educated white Unionists such as Rives and Pierpont. The officer in Charlottesville publicly supported Rives against the head of the local Union League. Seeing the antiradical tint of the bureau, Virginia radicals complained that military and bureau officers were too conservative.[7] Thus, southern charges that the bureau interfered in state politics in the interest of radicalism were only half true in Virginia; it interfered, but usually for moderate Republicans.[8]

The most active of all political factions in the 1867 campaign was the radical wing of the Republican party. It sent speakers throughout the state to address black and radical white audiences. D. B. White, the New York colonel who had established the *Hampton True Southerner* in 1865, ranged through the Valley in late August, urging freedmen and white Unionists to support the party. John W. Langston, a less prominent Republican, covered central Virginia at the same time. Charles H. Porter, one of the more zealous radicals of the August convention, spent several days in the piedmont region late in September.[9] Hunnicutt was particularly effective among the freedmen.[10]

The *New Nation* painted horrible pictures of what would happen to the freedmen if they failed to elect a radical convention. They would be skinned alive; their wives and daughters would be "tied up to the whipping-post, and thrashed for every little offense"; their children would be "bound out to task masters, to be whipped, worked and driven like dogs." Every black man who supported the conservatives, Hunnicutt advised, should be "forever discountenanced by every colored man." With the *New Nation*, the *Alexandria Virginia State Journal*, the smaller Republican papers, the itinerant speakers, and the Union Leagues all pressuring Virginia blacks to register and vote and with their own self-interest at stake, the freedmen were almost sure to turn out in large numbers on election day. Hunnicutt later recalled that "the armies were well drilled—the discipline had been rigid."[11]

Although physical violence was never so great a problem in the Reconstruction politics of the Old Dominion as in some other southern states and although the Ku Klux Klan and similar organizations were never so powerful as in the lower South, still the frightening possibility of a Republican victory in 1867 stirred some Virginia whites to countermeasures.[12] Beating drums and blowing horns, conservatives marched around the homes of northern schoolteachers; the native whites burned the schoolmarms in effigy and pledged themselves to rid Virginia of its Yankee teachers. Because these women often taught politics and "northern virtues" as well as grammar in their schoolrooms, they were especially offensive to conservatives.[13]

Hunnicutt received mysterious letters promising that he would die before sunset on election day. White employers exerted pressure of a different sort: they vowed to fire all black employees who joined the Union Leagues or voted radical on election day. Charles H. Lewis, secretary of state in the old Restored government, told Senator Henry Wilson in November that these threats had kept many freedmen from voting. Conservative white newspapers provided further evidence that blacks often suffered for their political views. "We are gratified to learn," crowed the *Lynchburg News*, "that one hundred and fifty negroes employed at the Wythe Iron Mines, all of whom voted the straight out radical ticket, were discharged on Tuesday by the owner of the works."[14]

Despite the threats and intimidation, election day passed in relative quiet. "Considering the exciting character of the contest," General Schofield wrote, "remarkably good order prevailed throughout the State during the election." Wagonloads of meat, bread, and coffee sustained long lines of black voters in Richmond. They were participating in an election for the first time in Virginia's long history. Their zeal, in fact, led them to chase from the polls those few freedmen who dared to vote for the conservatives. Indeed, of 6,021 registered black voters in the city, only twenty-two voted for any but radical candidates. Bloc voting was not limited to the freedmen, however, for only thirty-four of the 5,060 registered whites cast their ballots for radicals.[15]

The combination of intense radical activity, conservative apathy, and the concentration of freedmen in eastern Virginia districts produced a radical Republican victory, the party's first triumph in state politics since President Johnson had recognized the Restored government and the 1864 constitution immediately after Appomattox (see map 4). The number of voters who stayed home told a large part of the story. While 63 percent (76,084) of the whites went to the polls, 88 percent (93,145) of the freedmen voted. On the question of whether to hold a constitutional convention, blacks voted 92,507 to 638 for it, while whites opposed it by a margin of 61,249 to 14,835. The convention was thus approved by a margin of 107,342 to 61,887. The large turnout of black voters and their near unanimity on the convention question testify to the effectiveness of the Union Leagues and the itinerant radical speakers. Most important, these developments also indicate that the freedmen, illiterate and inexperienced though most of them may have been, were well aware of where their interests lay—in a new constitution guaranteeing them equal political, legal, and civil rights. To further that aim, they elected sixty-eight of

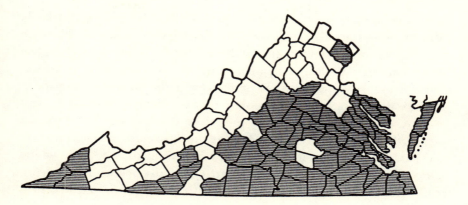

Map 4. Counties voting Republican in 1867. Some counties were part of larger districts, and some districts elected both Republican and Conservative candidates. Amelia and Nottoway counties (the two unshaded counties surrounded by shaded counties) elected delegates who campaigned as Republicans but voted with the Conservatives in the convention (S. R. Seay in Amelia County and W. H. Robertson in Nottoway County). From *Senate Executive Documents*, 40th Cong., 2d sess., no. 53, p. 2.

the 105 convention members, and twenty-four of the Republicans were black.[16]

The extension of suffrage and officeholding rights to black Virginians by the 1867 Reconstruction Acts changed the whole face of state politics. The Old Dominion's Republican party, so weak and dependent on northern protection before 1867, swept into power on a sea of black votes. Of the sixty-eight men who won seats as professed Republicans, sixty were elected from districts with black voting majorities—all twenty-four black delegates, twenty-one of the twenty-three immigrants from the North, Europe, and Canada (or carpetbaggers), and fifteen of the twenty-one white natives of Virginia (or scalawags). Four of the remaining eight Republicans were elected from districts with large black minorities and some carpetbagger and/or scalawag strength—three from south of the James River, Gaston G. Curtiss and David Staley of Bedford County and C. Y. Thomas of Henry County, and Orrin E. Hine from Fairfax County near Washington, D.C.

The other four Republicans came from the primarily white mountainous counties of southwest Virginia—William R. Dickey and F. A. Winston from Carroll, Floyd, and Grayson counties; Adam H. Flanagan from Montgomery County; and Andrew Milbourn from Lee, Scott, and Wise counties. While mountainous areas of other southern states frequently elected Republicans to state offices, the eighteen counties in southwest Virginia selected Republicans for only four of their twelve seats in the constitutional convention, indicating that the state's Republican party had only limited impact among the small farmers and stock raisers in that part of the Old Dominion. Southwest Virginians, like other whites across the commonwealth, were motivated primarily by their racial identification rather than by class interests. The party's protection of and dependence on black citizens alienated enough men of the southwest to keep that section securely within conservative ranks. One white Republican from that area, Jacquelin M. Wood, testified before Congress that "there are quite a number of men in the western part of the State who have never had anything to do with the rebellion, and, for all practical purposes, were probably loyal. . . . But they are not loyal according to our standard. They do not believe that a colored man is fit to vote or to be a citizen."[17]

The October 1867 election was the greatest victory in the party's eleven-year history. But as Governor Pierpont and John Minor Botts had predicted, the party's flirtation with confiscation schemes and radical ideas had frightened away most white voters. Only 12 percent of the registered whites voted Republican, an ominous sign for the future. Although some moderate Republicans such as Edward K. Snead were elected, the most prominent of that group were defeated. Governor Pierpont lost to James Morrissey, a former British soldier, Richmond saloon keeper, and close ally of Hunnicutt. Judge Rives was defeated by the Union Leaguer C. L. Thompson. Gilbert C. Walker met a similar fate in Norfolk. This future Republican governor complained that "a d——d Nigger" (Thomas Bayne) had won the seat he was seeking. According to Walker, the whites had not supported him because he was a northerner or simply because they did not vote; the freedmen backed his black opponent under pressure from "secret society men" (Union Leaguers). The radical Republicans, profiting from conservative inactivity and the advantageous system of representation, carried the day. Horace Greeley put the best face on the election and rejoiced that "the Mother of States records her verdict in favor of loyal Reconstruction on the basis prescribed by Congress!"[18]

Virginia conservatives were stunned. The *Richmond Enquirer* contended that the elevation of ignorant blacks over white men was "so horrible and loathsome" that military domination was preferable. "We unfurl the standard of resistance to the wretched creatures who are soon to meet to complete the work of Africanizing Virginia," the *Enquirer* thundered, "and tell them that there are no chains which they can forge in the shape of a mongrel organic law which can bind the giant limbs of the Old Dominion." The *Charlottesville Chronicle* complained that the freedmen were "drilled like an army, maneuvered like a body of disciplined troops." The freedmen, it fumed, had sealed their political doom; it was now a question of who should rule, blacks or whites.[19]

The shock of the radical victory finally stirred conservative whites from their long postwar slumber. Within days after the election the Democratic and Constitutional Union state committees of 1860 met in Richmond and called for a convention to establish a new Conservative party. This new organization would include every Virginian—Democrat, Whig, or Constitutional Unionist—opposed to Republican Reconstruction. On December 11 and 12, 800 whites from all sections of the state met in the capital to form the Virginia Conservative party. The new organization cut across old party lines. Leading Whigs like Alexander H. H. Stuart and John B. Baldwin of Staunton stood shoulder to shoulder with their antebellum Democratic foes Robert M. T. Hunter and John Letcher. The new party devised elaborate state and local organizations to combat the Republicans' vaunted discipline. Their resolutions declared the radical program "abhorrent to the civilization of mankind," insisted on white control of the state, recognized the end of slavery and secession, and asked for prompt readmission into the Union with all the rights and privileges guaranteed to citizens by the United States Constitution. The aroused Conservatives were determined now to oppose the state's outnumbered Republicans for every inch of political ground.[20]

The Underwood Convention

In early December 1867, a few days before the nervous Conservatives gathered in Richmond, other Virginians began streaming into the capital for the opening of the constitutional convention mandated by Congress. Capitol Square, the pleasant park surrounding Jefferson's Capitol and the equestrian statue of Washington, was strewn with tables and stands selling lemonade, whiskey, and peanuts. Richmond residents, drawn by curiosity to a convention featuring freedmen and transplanted Yankees, strolled through the square and into the Capitol to observe the proceedings. Former Confederates and their sympathizers found the sayings and doings of black delegates especially amusing, and the convention was the subject of many conversations and newspaper reports.[21]

Receiving much more respect from local white observers was the small band of Conservative delegates to the convention. Outnumbered roughly two to one, the thirty-odd Conservatives represented a long arc of white counties, beginning with Caroline and King George counties in northeastern Virginia, stretching northwestward to the West Virginia border, then southward through the Shenandoah Valley and mountains into the extreme southwest. Most of them were young, inexperienced Virginia natives from Whig backgrounds, and many were graduates of that institution so hated by abolitionists and radical Republicans, the University of Virginia. In general, the Conservative members were noticeably wealthier than their Republican opponents, averaging twice as much property as white Republican delegates and twenty times as much as black representatives. With only thirty-six votes they could hardly expect to compete with the sixty-eight Republicans. (Another Conservative delegate, Robert S. Beazley of Madison and Greene counties, never took his seat in the convention.) But their constant badgering and unending resistance to the Republicans modified some of the more radical proposals put forth in the convention.[22]

The convention's Republicans included twenty-four blacks, twenty-one white native-born Virginians (sometimes called "scalawags" by the white Conservatives), and twenty-three immigrants to the state. The latter group, referred to as "carpetbaggers" by the state's Conservatives, comprised a larger portion of the convention's delegates than their counterparts did in most other Confederate states. Few of them, however, fit the image of the carpetbagger that survived well into the twentieth century— shiftless and ignorant opportunists who came south after the 1867 Reconstruction Acts to use the newly enfranchised blacks to their own political and economic advantage.[23]

The Conservative delegates claimed that the Republicans included thirteen carpetbaggers from New York; one each from Pennsylvania, Ohio, Maine, Vermont, Connecticut, South Carolina, Maryland, and the District of Columbia; two from England; and one each from Ireland, Scotland, Nova Scotia, and Canada. Technically this was correct, but some of these

Republicans had been citizens of Virginia for a decade or more. John C. Underwood and John Hawxhurst were included among the New Yorkers even though they had first settled in Virginia in the 1840s. Charles H. Porter, a New Yorker by birth, had served in Pierpont's Restored government during the war. Hunnicutt, who was often called a carpetbagger even though he was from South Carolina, was an alumnus of Virginia's Randolph-Macon College, had been in Virginia since the 1840s, and had edited a newspaper in Fredericksburg before the war. James H. Platt, originally from Canada, had settled in Petersburg three days before General Lee surrendered at Appomattox—two years before black suffrage and radical Reconstruction made him a powerful political figure. James Morrissey had been in the state at least as early as March 1866 and possibly earlier. In short, many of the carpetbaggers were residents of the Old Dominion before they knew black voting was coming to the South. Some, indeed, had moved to the state while slavery was in full flower.

Nor were the carpetbaggers shiftless. Their average property holding was nearly $4,000, placing them in the state's middle class. In the South as a whole, more than one-third of them were engaged in the professions, and nearly one-fourth had bought or rented land for farming. They had planted crops, opened law offices, and established newspapers in Virginia; they had a stake in society. A few, such as Samuel F. Maddex of Chesterfield and Sanford M. Dodge of Mecklenburg, had been in the state only a few months, but they were exceptions. The convention's carpetbaggers were unpopular among Conservative whites not because of their places of birth or allegedly late arrival but because of their politics. Most of them were radical Republicans, they wielded a disproportionate share of political power among Republicans, they held up the constitutions of their native states as models for Virginia, and they usually represented heavily black districts in the constitutional convention.[24]

Neither were the carpetbaggers an ignorant lot in general. Some may have been poorly educated, but others, such as Underwood, Porter, Platt, and David B. White, were college graduates. The majority probably fell somewhere between the two extremes. Several of the carpetbaggers ran afoul of the law in Virginia. William James of Hanover County, a native of England, had recently been removed from his post as collector of internal revenue in Richmond because of his involvement in some whiskey frauds. James C. Toy, an immigrant from Maryland, "was tried last summer for stealing a hog and was acquitted although some fresh pork was found in his house." Sanford Dodge of Mecklenburg, originally from New York, was a Methodist minister and distiller of spirits. His distillery was seized after he had engaged in some profitable swindling. Judge Underwood, who apparently considered his 1865 election by the Restored legislature to the United States Senate valid even though he had never been seated, had been using the senatorial frank on his mail ever since 1865. The Conservatives, led by Jacob N. Liggitt of Rockingham County, exposed the thrifty judge's little vice, and the post office thenceforth refused to honor the Underwood frank. Except for these mostly minor transgressions, the transplanted Yankees seem to have been law-abiding citizens.[25]

The native white Republicans in the convention, like scalawags throughout the upper South, were mainly Unionist Whigs such as Dr. John B. Eastham of Louisa County and Pierpont's wartime ally, Edward K. Snead of the Eastern Shore. A smaller number, F. A. Winston of Carroll, Floyd, and Grayson counties, for example, were veterans of the wars between southwest Virginia deserters and their erstwhile colleagues in the Confederate army. Unfortunately for the Virginia Republican party, it did not tap deeply enough into this discontent in the far southwestern counties to build a strong Republican organization during Reconstruction. Only in the early 1880s would the mountain farmers and herders join the party in significant numbers. The average property holdings of the scalawags, about $3,400, approximated those of the middle-class carpetbaggers. Thus, these native whites were of the middling sort financially—less prosperous than the white Conservative delegates but about ten times as wealthy as the freedmen. In the convention debates they would vote Republican on most issues but were less radical than most of the freedmen and carpetbaggers.[26]

Although Conservatives complained bitterly about illiterate black rule, blacks in fact held less than one-quarter of the seats in the constitutional convention. Furthermore, at least nineteen of the twenty-four were literate, although doubtless in varying degrees. While only 13 percent of the South's black population were mulattoes, roughly half the identifiable delegates in Virginia were of mixed parentage. And although the huge majority of southern blacks had been slaves until the war, more than half of the Virginia convention members either had been free before the war or had escaped to the North while slaves. Thus, the typical black delegate in the Old Dominion was a member of the black elite—free before the war, a mulatto, and literate. Like their counterparts in other southern states,

Virginia's black delegates almost invariably represented heavily black districts, in either the old plantation areas or urban centers.[27]

While the black delegates generally deferred to the white Republicans in the early weeks of the convention, they gradually assumed increasingly prominent roles in the proceedings. They used their new power and status to advance proposals aiming to expand the limits of their freedom, even when their white allies, especially the less radical scalawags, refused to go along with them. Lewis Lindsay of Richmond was a century ahead of his time when he proposed that all public institutions, companies, and public places "shall be accessible to all persons alike." James W. D. Bland of Prince Edward County introduced one measure guaranteeing the right of "every person to enter any college, seminary, or other public institution of learning, as students, upon equal terms with any other, regardless of race, color, or previous condition." James T. S. Taylor of Charlottesville demanded that "all voting shall be by ballot," rather than viva voce, in order to ensure truly free elections.

While the black spokesmen emphasized political and civil equality, they did not ignore the need for economic reform. George Teamoh of Norfolk, like fellow black leaders in North and South Carolina, proposed stiff taxes on uncultivated land in order to force owners to sell acreage to freedmen or at least hire them to work the land. David Canada of Halifax County suggested the appointments of a state geologist "to discover . . . and develop . . . the mineral wealth of the state" and a state chemist for agricultural research. Willis A. Hodges of Princess Anne County, like fellow Republicans all across the South, attempted to restructure the tax system by shifting the burden away from regressive levies on individuals to taxes on property, both real and personal. If Virginia's black political leaders had been as ignorant and savage as white newspapers charged, they could not have proposed such enlightened reforms.[28]

Despite the progressive and beneficial nature of many of the reforms proposed by the black delegates, white delegates and newspapers belittled and ridiculed them at every opportunity. The convention was frequently referred to in the white press as the "Convention of Kangaroos," the "Mongrel Convention," or the "Black Crook Convention." Some Richmond papers reported each day's proceedings, printing the remarks of black delegates in a heavy slave dialect. One of the more outspoken and clever Conservatives, Eustace Gibson of Pulaski and Giles counties, even attempted to force the convention stenographer to record the proceedings with all accents and grammatical errors included. Such ridicule in the press and in the convention was too much for Thomas Bayne, the equally outspoken black leader from Norfolk: "Do not the proprietors of those papers know that it is them and their people who have robbed the black man of his education, who have taken the money and labor of the black man to support themselves in grandeur, and now they curse the black man because he is not a grammarian?" Even white radicals struck back at the Conservative press. Hunnicutt complained that "all we say here is represented each morning as a set of absurdities." Northern newspaper reporters agreed. The correspondent of the *New York Times* wrote that "the Conservatives look upon the whole thing as a farce, and act with the greatest levity, treating the proceedings with much contempt."[29]

Indeed, a quick wit became a weapon to belittle the opposition. When radicals proposed to disfranchise large numbers of white Virginians, Eustace Gibson countered with an obviously absurd amendment, "No white man shall vote or be eligible to any office within this State." In a later debate on officeholding requirements, Joseph T. Campbell, Conservative delegate from Washington County, proposed that the oath for state office should include the words "and that I am not a native born white Virginian." Another Conservative, Jacob Liggitt of Rockingham County, responded to a long speech by Hunnicutt by declaring that "this place is about equal to a Turkish tavern."[30] When Republicans attempted to discourage amendments to the new constitution, fearing that white Conservatives would strip it of its reforms, Moses Walton, Conservative from Page and Shenandoah counties, offered an amendment: "Disavowing and ignoring the doctrines set forth in the Bill of Rights . . . and thoroughly convinced that this Constitution . . . is the perfection of human wisdom . . . we hereby declare the same to be perpetual, like the laws of the Medes and Persians."[31]

While Conservatives aimed their barbs at all Republicans, they were especially galled by the increasingly prominent role played by the black delegates. "It was the subject of remark among us during the progress of the Convention," some Conservatives later remembered, "that the negroes grew more and more impracticable. The reported debates of the Convention will show how active they gradually became in the proceedings of the body." The most powerful black leader in the convention, the Norfolk dentist Thomas Bayne, naturally became the target of Conservative wrath. White newspapers especially grabbed at any opportunity to belittle him.

When Bayne returned to Norfolk at the end of the convention, the *Richmond Enquirer* gave him one last slap: "Our people will learn with profound regret that the distinguished statesman, sage, philosopher, logician, debater, elocutionist, and tooth-puller . . . will leave Richmond tomorrow per James River steamer. . . . We bid the Doctor an affectionate farewell; wish him a safe and prosperous voyage and trust that he will never more be a conventionist for Virginia."[32]

Black delegates occasionally displayed their own wit at the expense of Conservatives. When Eustace Gibson, a leading Conservative, proposed separate schools for blacks and whites, with white poll taxes supporting white schools and black poll taxes supporting black schools, Lewis Lindsay of Richmond had had enough. He immediately suggested an amendment to point up the absurdity of Gibson's plan: "And there shall also be a separate Legislature, for the convenience of all classes."[33]

From beginning to end, the convention was controlled by the radical Republicans. They elected Judge Underwood president of the convention and George Rye, another antebellum Virginia Republican, secretary. They gave the radical editor Hunnicutt the contract to print the convention's proceedings. They set the per diem at eight dollars despite the protests of Conservatives, who thought that sum was too high. And the radicals controlled most of the standing committees. The moderates usually cooperated with them, opposing them only on such issues as disfranchisement and qualifications for officeholding. The outnumbered Conservatives dug in their heels and opposed almost every Republican proposal, but with only limited effect.

Most of December was spent organizing and drawing up committee reports. Serious work began after the Christmas recess when the convention debated the bill of rights. J. W. D. Bland, the moderate black delegate from Farmville, attempted to specify that all men, "irrespective of race or color," are equally free and independent, but both black and white members objected. Thomas Bayne, the outspoken black radical who had defeated Gilbert C. Walker for the seat from Norfolk, said he had promised to frame a constitution with no reference to race, and Bland's amendment was rejected. The Republicans, so long the victims of mobs and political coercion, included a strong freedom-of-expression clause in the bill of rights on January 19.[34]

One of the radicals' favorite projects was tax revision. In previous constitutions property owners, especially slaveholders, had escaped with a relatively light tax burden. The 1867–68 convention placed an ad valorem tax on capital stock for the first time, taxed all other property according to value, approved a tax on incomes of over $600 (the only such tax in the former Confederacy), and standardized the poll tax at one dollar. Proceeds from this last source were to be used for support of a system of free schools. The expenses entailed by the new school system, the debt service on antebellum bonds, and the decreased property values after the war inevitably resulted in higher taxes. While Virginians paid only about 77.1 cents per capita in state taxes in 1850, the figure leaped to $1.66 by 1870. The net effect of the various changes was to increase the tax burden for the propertied classes (mainly white Conservatives), a reform common in other southern state conventions. The Republicans were reaping the rewards of their electoral victory in October.[35]

Virginia's huge public debt, over forty million dollars, occasioned in part by a vast program of internal improvements before the war, led the convention to limit the state's power to contract debts. After 1868 the state could issue bonds only "to meet casual deficits in the revenue, to redeem a previous liability of the State," or to defend Virginia in time of war, insurrection, or invasion. Moreover, the state's credit was not to be granted to any person, private association, or corporation. Contrary to occasional Conservative charges that the Republicans were racing forward in a feverish spending frenzy, Virginia Republicans, like those in some other seaboard states, attempted to put state finances on a stronger foundation than that provided by their antebellum white predecessors.[36]

The most controversial subjects of discussion were the requirements for voting and officeholding. Fearing the influence of Hunnicutt and other radicals, leading northern Republicans such as Schuyler Colfax (Speaker of the House in Washington) and Elihu Washburne (member of the national House Committee on Reconstruction) had been urging moderation and responsibility on the subject of political participation. Despite Hunnicutt's wish for more severe restrictions, his Committee on Electoral Franchise recommended universal manhood suffrage except for those disfranchised by the Reconstruction Acts (i.e., antebellum political, military, and judicial officials who had supported the Confederacy).[37] Orrin E. Hine, a particularly proscriptive carpetbagger from New York who was representing Fairfax County, tried to extend disfranchisement to those affected by the Reconstruction Acts plus all who had served in the Confederate army or navy above the rank of lieutenant or master, a proposal that would have increased the numbers of the disfranchised significantly.

J. W. D. Bland, the thirty-year-old black moderate, opposed proscription further than that provided for in the Federal Reconstruction Acts and said that Massachusetts senator Charles Sumner and Pennsylvania congressman Thaddeus Stevens had supported his position in personal letters. Bland, born free before the war and educated as a child by his mother's former master, was a representative of that class of Virginia blacks who demanded real and significant reform during Reconstruction but were less radical than some carpetbaggers and many former slaves who had not enjoyed the same advantages. While many Conservatives regarded blacks as a single bloc of extreme radicals, men such as J. W. D. Bland, Fields Cook, and Joseph Cox demonstrated that black political life included more shades of opinion than untrained white eyes could discern.[38]

Hunnicutt, who was more radical than his committee, objected to Bland's statements, claiming that Sumner and Stevens had nothing to do with Virginia affairs. The uncompromising editor wanted to disfranchise thirty thousand more whites in order to give Republicans a majority on the registration rolls. Proscription of numerous classes of former Confederates was a tactic frequently used by Republicans in the upper South where black votes alone were not sufficient to carry the state for their party. The convention, however, rejected the extreme radical approach and adopted the committee's recommendations.[39]

The radicals, led by Hine, had more success barring Conservatives from office. They managed finally to add a provision that would bar from office every man who had participated in or supported the Confederacy in any way. In effect, the test-oath clause would make state government an almost exclusive preserve for carpetbaggers, scalawags, and freedmen. This provision, anathema to Conservatives, was adopted by a vote of 40 to 32 (with 32 delegates not voting) on March 24. Almost one-third of the Republicans failed or refused to vote on the roll call. All eighteen black delegates present supported the proposal; James T. S. Taylor, Frank Moses, James D. Barrett, William H. Andrews, John Brown, and James W. D. Bland were absent and did not vote. Carpetbaggers voted 13 to 2 (with 8 not voting) and scalawags 9 to 5 (with 7 not voting) for Hine's measure. Conservatives, of course, voted solidly against the disqualification (25 to 0 against, with 11 not voting). Virginia thus joined four states of the Deep

South (Alabama, Mississippi, Louisiana, and Arkansas) in removing significant numbers of whites from the political process. These and other proscriptive measures would ultimately come back to haunt the radical Republicans.[40]

The convention gave Virginia its first public school system. While free public education was the goal of many black families and white northerners in the Old Dominion, the specific shape of the Virginia school system was doubtless influenced by the Peabody Education Fund, a northern philanthropy of two million dollars established to promote elementary education in the depressed postwar South. The trustees of the fund met in Richmond in January 1868, probably to pressure the convention for action. Barnas Sears, general agent of the fund, addressed the convention and argued for a full-scale system of free public schools. Observers of the convention believed that Sears actually helped to write the school section of the new constitution.[41]

Other than some Conservative carping about the cost of public education, the only major disagreement in the debate on schools was whether classrooms should be integrated or segregated according to race. Conservative delegates attempted to specify that all schools would be segregated, but radical blacks led by Thomas Bayne and Willis Hodges successfully opposed them. On the other hand, Edgar ("Yankee") Allen, a native of England, Union army veteran, and head of the Virginia Union League, contended that mixed schools would be harmful to both races. James H. Clements, a native of the District of Columbia and moderate Republican delegate from Portsmouth, agreed. When the key vote came on April 8, only the black delegates supported mandatory integration, and then by only a narrow margin (12 to 10, with 2 not voting). Carpetbaggers and scalawags voted by margins of three to one against mandatory integration (15 to 5 against, with 3 not voting among carpetbaggers; 12 to 4 against, with 5 not voting among scalawags). Conservatives voted overwhelmingly against integration, of course (30 to 0 against, with 6 not voting). The issue was compromised by omitting all mention of race, thus leaving the way open for a segregated system but not mandating separation.[42]

Segregated schools were not as objectionable to some blacks as might be expected. In general, blacks were willing to accept segregation in order to promote recently established all-black schools and to allay white opposition to the whole idea of public education. Moreover, some black Virginians—teachers and principals especially—had a stake in a separate system.

In Petersburg, for example, public schools would be segregated even though Republicans dominated the local school board. Even the northern-controlled Peabody Fund accepted segregated schools as an inevitable fact of life.[43]

In another controversial action the convention subdivided Virginia's counties into townships, provided numerous officers for each township, and specified that most local officials be elected rather than appointed. Republicans adopted this new system partly in order to break up old patterns of local officeholding by established white families. Used extensively in the northern states, this transplanted township system was not well suited to Virginia's counties, which were of widely varying sizes, shapes, and population densities. The Conservatives bitterly opposed this change, not only because it seemed impracticable, but because so many blacks would be elected to local offices and so many whites would be displaced. "The result most feared" by local whites, wrote one military official, "is, that in counties where the colored population is in excess, ignorant, incompetent, or vicious men will be elected to fill the minor county and township offices." The township system, effectively dismantled by Conservatives after Reconstruction, never fully achieved its goal of encouraging more local participation in government.[44]

In other reforms, the convention gave the governor more power to reprieve and pardon, an authority Conservatives feared would be used to pardon black criminals; provided for an executive veto over legislation; and replaced the hoary county courts with a new system of district courts. Legislative control over the judiciary was increased by empowering the General Assembly to elect all judges for twelve-year terms. By wiping the judicial slate clean every dozen years, the General Assembly could exert considerable pressure on the judges. Like the Reconstruction conventions in most other southern states, the Virginia body reacted to the postwar depression by adopting a homestead-exemption clause that prevented creditors from seizing the homes of delinquent debtors.[45]

Taking advantage of their new power, members of the Republican majority also redrew the boundaries for state legislative districts. The lines were arranged in such a way that they would benefit the Republican party. Open and frank about this, Republicans expected the test-oath and disfranchisement clauses to combine with the new districts to give their party control over the General Assembly.[46]

Convention proceedings were generally orderly, but several fistfights were only narrowly averted, discussion sometimes degenerated into rude shouting matches, and parliamentary procedure was occasionally lost among numerous motions, countermotions, amendments, and points of order. Even the Conservatives, who claimed superior experience in such matters, confessed that they sometimes floundered in the swirl of debate. "I would like to know what I am voting upon," J. C. Gibson pleaded on December 6, "and so many resolutions are before the Convention that I cannot grasp them all at once." On another occasion the radical Orrin Hine and the Conservative Gibson adjourned to the corridors to settle one of the finer points of constitution making with their knuckles. Neither would strike first, and the fight remained purely verbal. Republican delegates were particularly hard on each other. Edward K. Snead and Henry Bowden, moderate Republicans and longtime friends, actually raised chairs to smash each other to the floor, but they calmed themselves before delivering their blows. James H. Platt, the carpetbagger from Vermont and Canada, called Thomas Bayne an "impudent scoundrel" and told James Morrissey, the carpetbagger saloon keeper from Richmond, that anyone who owned "a barrel of bad whiskey" could get what he wanted from black voters. Platt protested that the disorderly debate on the bill of rights was "disgraceful." The convention thus generated considerable intraparty bitterness.[47]

One of the most disruptive incidents occurred in mid-January when the radicals invited former Union general and prominent Massachusetts radical Benjamin F. Butler to address the convention. Despite Butler's plan to call for amnesty for former Confederates and to warn against confiscation schemes, Conservative delegates found the New England general's presence in Virginia unbearable. After attempting unsuccessfully to prevent the hated Butler's appearance, the Conservatives walked out of the convention hall. Before leaving, Jacob N. Liggett of Rockingham County offered a resolution warning citizens of Richmond "to observe more than ordinary vigilance in the preservation of their plate and silverware," referring to Butler's alleged theft of silver spoons during the Union army's occupation of New Orleans during the war. When one carpetbagger explained that he had voted against Butler's appearance as a matter of principle rather than out of any disrespect to the general, Conservative J. C. Gibson could not resist the opening to insult a Union general: "I voted no in disrespect to General Butler, as well as from . . . principle." The Conservative *Lynchburg Virginian* joined in the taunting: "With hands on their pocket books and watches, they [the Conservative bolters] incontinently fled from the presence of the great soldier, leaving old Spooney master of the field."[48]

The Republicans dealt themselves another blow late in March when John Hawxhurst charged convention president Underwood with attempted bribery. Hawxhurst, a supporter of Benjamin F. Wade of Ohio for the upcoming Republican presidential nomination, claimed that Underwood, an old friend of Chief Justice Salmon P. Chase, had offered to obtain $100,000 for the Virginia Republican party if it would back Chase for the Republican nomination. Certain that Chase knew nothing about the incident, Hawxhurst laid the blame solely on Underwood. The judge replied that he had offered no bribe; he had simply said the Virginia party would not want for money in an election year. Distracting from the substantive reforms accomplished by the convention, such fratricidal clashes did little to enhance long-term Republican prospects.[49]

Not only were they suffering from their own attacks on one another; the Ku Klux Klan soon joined in the assault. The Klan was not very active in Virginia during Reconstruction. But it did mount an offensive during the convention when whites feared that the new constitution would soon be adopted. Although the Virginia Klan used threats and scare tactics more than violence, it was sufficiently abusive to alienate some Conservative newspapers. The Klan once promised to hang Hunnicutt from the tail of Washington's horse on the Capitol Square monument and to clip Thomas Bayne's "superfluous tongue and ears." This was all bluster, however, and Klan activity died away when the constitutional referendum was postponed a few weeks later.[50]

A New Governor

Tax laws, homestead exemptions, and threats of violence were not the Republicans' only concern during the convention. They were looking ahead to the state elections that would be held under the new constitution. Moderate and radical Republican delegates alike (except for Hunnicutt and Hawxhurst) apparently agreed on a candidate for governor, Henry H. Wells of Alexandria. A carpetbagger from Michigan, Wells had been born in New York in 1823. While still a child, he moved with his family to Michigan where he became a lawyer in 1846 and served a term in the state legislature. Joining the army in 1862, he was soon provost marshal general in Alexandria, home of Pierpont's Restored government. While stationed in Virginia, Wells became a close friend of Judge Underwood. After the war he settled in Alexandria and frequently pleaded cases in Underwood's Federal court. In politics he was generally regarded as a moderate Republican.[51] His friendship with radicals such as Underwood and his reputation as a moderate doubtless enabled both factions to unite upon him for the gubernatorial nomination.[52]

To strengthen their position as much as possible, the Republicans asked Governor Pierpont to step aside so that Wells could be appointed his successor and thus have the added prestige of being an incumbent on election day. Furthermore, they told the governor, by nominating the moderate Wells, the party could widen its base of support, a tactic long favored by Pierpont. Otherwise, the radicals Hunnicutt and Hawxhurst, both longing to live in the Governor's Mansion, would battle each other for party leadership and alienate many moderate Republicans. Pierpont, who had been in the governor's chair for almost seven years, was reluctant to leave it. He had labored hard since 1861 to bring Virginia back to its normal position in the Union, and he was determined to continue as governor until that job was finished. And even though his official term had ended on December 31, 1867, the state Supreme Court had ruled early in 1868 that state officials could remain in office until succeeded. With a desire to stay and a court decision to support him, Pierpont spurned the Republican suggestion.[53]

Frustrated by the governor's obstinance, the Republicans went over Pierpont's head and appealed to General Schofield and probably to members of Congress. H. G. Bond, a wealthy carpetbagger from New York, register in bankruptcy in Richmond, and a close friend of Wells, had personal connections with General Grant and Chief Justice Chase in Washington. One of his subordinates, a behind-the-scenes political activist named R. F. Walker, said that it was Bond "who mainly secured the removal of Pierpont and the appointment of Wells."[54]

The convention Republicans asked General Schofield late in March to appoint Wells governor. Schofield liked the idea for several reasons. The thought of violating Virginia's constitution unnecessarily by letting Pierpont remain in the governor's chair beyond his term of office disturbed the general. Moreover, Pierpont and Schofield had been quarreling over appointments to state offices, the governor accusing the general of placing rebels in power. Pierpont, still resentful of Conservative attacks on him and reading the political winds within his state party, had become increasingly radical since the August convention; this may have intensified Schofield's desire to remove him. The governor, who now claimed to be a member of "the Republican party, the mean white man's party—the negro party," had become a hero to Richmond freedmen in recent months. The alliance of moderate and radical Republicans behind Wells and the Alexandria carpetbagger's reputation for moderate Republicanism convinced Schofield that Wells's inauguration was "the last hope of harmonious action among the friends of reconstruction and of the success of that measure this year."[55] Wells could unite the party; Pierpont, who had managed to alienate every faction at one time or another in his three years in Richmond, would weaken the party.

When General Grant left the matter for Schofield to settle on April 3, Schofield made his decision. The next day he issued an order relieving Pierpont and appointing Wells governor.[56] Pierpont appealed to Grant, charging Schofield with favoring rebels in his appointments. But Grant, familiar with Schofield's war record and personal background, ignored the former governor's arguments and approved Schofield's action.[57]

Hunnicutt, realizing that the Wells appointment was a blow to his own gubernatorial ambitions, was downcast. Pierpont was as good an executive and as firm a Republican as Wells, he groused; there was no need for the appointment. Hunnicutt may have expected such a move, however, for radical and moderate Republicans alike had chipped away at his political base during the convention. His close association with the freedmen and his reputation for extreme statements had convinced his fellow party members that he would prove a weak candidate for governor. Congressional Republicans were backing away from the fiery old preacher, too, depriving his newspaper of its Federal printing contract in early 1868. Conservatives were pleased that Wells had forged ahead of Hunnicutt in the race for the Republican nomination. Wells, at least, had a reputation for moderation.[58]

One of the new governor's first acts was to secure the appointment of George Rye, the antebellum Virginia Republican from the Shenandoah Valley and an associate of Judge Underwood, as state treasurer. The incumbent treasurer, John S. Calvert, was removed for alleged corruption. Wells also addressed the constitutional convention, appealing for "certain fundamental, radical, organic changes" in Virginia's laws—equal rights for all men, financial reform so that taxes would fall "principally on property and not on heads," and public education for all. A call for party unity ended his speech. Few of his listeners raised an eyebrow at this moderate's demand for "fundamental, radical, organic changes."[59]

On the last day of its session, April 17, the convention had another important visitor, General Schofield. He asked the delegates to repeal the test-oath qualification for officeholding because the oath would severely cripple the state government. In some counties only two or three men were both literate and eligible under the test oath. If this provision was retained, he warned, local and state offices would be filled with ignorant and inexperienced men. Although he stressed the oath in his address, Schofield privately opposed the township system, the disfranchisement of former officeholders, and the homestead exemption. "My impression," he told General Grant, "is that the wisest course would be to let the thing fall and die where it is—not submit it to the people at all." At the very least, the test oath should be submitted separately in the constitutional referendum; this would allow the state to swallow the body of the constitution and spit out the oath.[60]

Despite moderate Republican opposition and Schofield's advice, the majority radicals adopted the constitution as it was and adjourned on April 17.[61] Except for the excessively proscriptive disabling clauses, the new charter was an admirable document. It gave the Old Dominion its first general system of education, distributed taxes more equally among the various economic classes, enacted universal manhood suffrage (except for those disfranchised), reduced residency requirements for voting, forbade discrimination in jury selection, protected debtors in a time of economic depression, made more offices elective, and increased the governor's powers vis-à-vis the legislature. And the township system, though ill suited to Virginia, was at least created with a laudable motive—to increase popular participation in local government. Like its sister southern states, Virginia "made a sweeping extension of political democracy" in its constitutional convention.[62]

Even some Conservatives admitted the value of the new charter. The *Richmond Enquirer-Examiner* lauded the improvements in the state judicial system and said that "we are happy to find that much in it is free from censure." After the passions of Reconstruction had cooled, Conservatives would find most of the so-called Underwood constitution very satisfactory. No land had been confiscated and redistributed to freedmen; no white children would be seated next to black children in schools; and some reforms unrelated to politics actually streamlined state government.[63]

Despite the positive features in the new document, some moderate Republicans and virtually all Conservatives opposed it passionately. For these Virginians, the main flaws in the Underwood constitution—the disfranchising and test-oath clauses—far outweighed its good points. For a few veteran Virginia Republicans such as Underwood and Hawxhurst—men who had suffered for their political beliefs before and during the war—the motive behind the two controversial sections may have been to fill state offices with men who would not persecute an individual for his political philosophy. And of course, freedmen, long accustomed to holding their tongues and hiding their opinions, were anxious to have friends in positions of power. For Orrin Hine and many of the forty radicals who voted for it, however, the test oath was a key to political power. The oath would bar virtually all white Virginians from office. With it the Republican party could control the state government for years to come.

Quite apart from the question of ethics, the disabling clauses were politically unwise. Any hardheaded politician should have known that the October 1867 Republican victory was not likely to be repeated. The Republicans had won then because the Conservatives were unorganized and apathetic. But that situation no longer prevailed. Native whites had organized their own political party in December, and now that a proscriptive constitution was hanging over their heads, they were vitally interested in state politics. They would not waste their 15,000–vote majority next time. Instead of trying to divide the more numerous Conservatives by appealing to their moderates, the Republicans gave them every reason to unite and forget past differences.

The Conservative attitude toward the new constitution was adequately summarized on April 20 when the Conservative delegates published an address to the people of Virginia. They complained that their small numbers had prevented them from devising a respectable constitution, that suffrage in the Underwood charter would be universal rather than qualified, that the township system would put many freedmen in office, that the test oath and new legislative districts "give the State absolutely to the negroes," that taxes would fall mainly on propertied whites, that the school system was expensive and of no benefit to the whites since they would not send their children to potentially integrated schools, and that blacks would serve on juries. The Conservative delegates ended with a warning: "We contemplate the fact of the entire black population consolidated against us, enrolled in one compact, oath-bound organization, acting with the precision and discipline of an army."[64]

The Republicans were facing an aroused and angry foe this time. Their only hope of carrying the state lay in splitting the Conservative vote and presenting a less frightening appearance to the native whites. Their first opportunity to do so would come in a few weeks when the party would nominate candidates for the governorship and other state offices, to be filled on the same date as the referendum on the constitution and according to the guidelines in that charter. The gubernatorial nominee would have to be a moderate Republican, capable of attracting the old Whigs and Unionists and determined to keep intraparty affairs quiet and harmonious. In short, he would have to be a master politician. Virginia Republicans had produced few such leaders in the past. The question was whether they could do it now.

CHAPTER 7

A Year of Drift

B Y THE spring of 1868 Virginia had completed about half the congressional requirements for restoration to its normal position within
the Union. The Old Dominion had consented to a constitutional convention, elected delegates, and framed a new charter including equal suffrage.
The commonwealth had only to ratify the new constitution, elect state
officers according to its guidelines, adopt the Fourteenth Amendment, and
receive the approval of Congress before resuming its former status as a full
and equal state in the Union.

Most other southern states completed this process during 1868 and
were therefore able to participate for the first time since 1860 in a national
presidential election. The Old Dominion, however, would find 1868 to be
a year of drift. The military governor of the state, General Schofield, was
not happy with some of the features in the Underwood constitution and
attempted to delay its ratification. When Republican governor Wells
appealed over the general's head to Washington for a quick referendum on
the new charter, Congress, preoccupied with the presidential election, also
delayed. Preparations for the referendum and statewide elections, at first
lively and loud, were therefore put aside, and politics in the Old Dominion
entered a state of suspended animation. Meanwhile, the nation elected a
president while Virginia watched and waited.

The only significant movement in this general state of drift was
organized late in the year when moderates of both parties mounted assaults
on the Underwood constitution. If Republicans could maintain their hold
on their own centrist group and entice non-Republican moderates into

their camp, they might have a chance to install a Republican governor and General Assembly in Richmond. If the party refused to try or bungled the attempt, moderates from both sides might drift over to the Conservative camp, and the fear long expressed by Republican centrists like Botts and Pierpont would finally be realized—the Republicans would be outnumbered, outvoted, and ousted from political power.

The 1868 Campaign

The Underwood convention had scheduled a referendum on the new constitution for June 2. General Schofield, however, postponed the referendum indefinitely on April 24. The convention had spent the $100,000 appropriated for it and more, he explained, and there were no state funds available for an election.[1] As soon as Congress would provide money for the registration of new voters and election expenses, he concluded, the referendum could be held. The general was correct; the convention had surpassed the $100,000 mark in March, leaving no funds available for ratification.[2] For Schofield, however, this was mainly an excuse for postponement. He feared that the radicals would ratify the constitution before Republican moderates and the Conservatives had time to gather their wits and launch a full-scale attack. And ratification of the document as it stood was the last thing he wanted. Consequently, he postponed the referendum and referred the matter to Congress with a recommendation for a separate vote on the test oath. This would allow the people to accept the new charter and still reject the disabling clause.[3]

Believing Congress would provide funds for an election soon, Virginia Republicans scheduled a nominating convention for May 6. The leading candidate for the gubernatorial nomination, of course, was Governor Henry H. Wells. He had the approval of General Schofield and virtually all the Republican convention delegates and had made fewer enemies than Hunnicutt or Hawxhurst, the two radical hopefuls. Furthermore, many Freedmen's Bureau officers preferred the moderate northerner, Wells, to the radical South Carolinian, Hunnicutt. R. M. Manly, the bureau superintendent of schools, corresponded with numerous officers who agreed with him that Wells was the better man. "I want intelligence & integrity as well as loyalty in office," wrote one bureau agent. An officer in Lynchburg revealed that he and his colleagues were "working in harmony and we hope to send no Hunnicutt delegate from either Bedford[,] Campbell[,]

Appomottox or Nelson and Botetourt [counties]. Rest assured that we will do everything in our power to nominate Wells for Gov."[4]

Hunnicutt knew long before the convention that Wells was likely to win the nomination. As early as April 1 the *New Nation* was printing letters and articles from other papers that claimed Wells had done very little for the party compared to Hunnicutt. In an effort to shed his extremist trappings, the editor addressed a crowd at Capitol Square on April 24. The constitution's disfranchisement clause was a bit too harsh for him, Hunnicutt said, backing away from his earlier demands for more extensive disfranchisement. Still, the legislature could soften the clause when circumstances required. The test oath, thanks to the malignant spirit of some Conservatives, had been adopted in self-defense. It too could be waived by the General Assembly, however, and was not necessarily permanent. Hunnicutt's listeners were surprised by his softened tone, but the maneuver failed to slow the Wells juggernaut.

On May 1 the *New Nation* publicized rumors that Hunnicutt would be "crushed out" at the forthcoming convention. Hunnicutt dared his enemies to try it. He had done more for the party than anyone in the state, he protested. His opponents wanted to destroy him in order to gather the loaves and fishes of office for themselves. By the morning of the convention Hunnicutt fully expected to be sacrificed to "intrigue and political wire working"; the people, he lamented, had been "sold out to a few political aspirants." No matter what happened, however, he would not split the party by bolting. He would support the party's candidate.[5]

The expected happened on May 6. Wells received the gubernatorial nomination, and James H. Clements, the Portsmouth carpetbagger from Washington, D.C., was selected for the post of lieutenant governor. L. H. Chandler, the Norfolk veteran of the Restored government; A. M. Crane, editor of the Republican *Winchester Journal*; and Charles H. Porter, the radical from Richmond, were the party's nominees for Congress. Additional candidates for Congress and other offices would be named later. For electors-at-large the convention named Hunnicutt and former governor Pierpont, consolation, perhaps, for their disappointed ambitions. The ticket was obviously devised with an eye to party harmony. Chandler and Pierpont, two prominent moderates, were placed alongside Hunnicutt and Porter, both of whom had scorned the Botts Republicans in August 1867. Wells and Clements fell somewhere between the two wings. If the Republicans could maintain intraparty unity until the election and attract a few thousand supporters of the Chandler and Pierpont stripe, they might have a fighting chance.

Parts of the meeting's platform, too, were designed for the eyes of moderate whites. The delegates resolved (1) that Virginia should be restored to its rightful place in the Union with all its rights as soon as possible; (2) that all men were free and equal and deserved the same rights and privileges; (3) that the constitution, though not perfect, was the best the state had ever had; (4) that Virginia needed free public schools supported by public taxes; (5) that the party would cooperate in removing the political disabilities of those who helped to reconstruct the state; (6) that Congress deserved thanks for the impeachment of Andrew Johnson; and (7) that U. S. Grant and Henry Wilson should head the Republican national ticket in 1868.[6]

The Conservatives were scheduled to meet in Richmond on May 7 to nominate their own slate of officers. Considerable backstage maneuvering preceded the convention, however. One of the most proficient political wire-pullers in the state (though not so proficient or omnipresent as sometimes portrayed) was William Mahone of Petersburg, a Confederate military hero and postwar railroad magnate. In 1868 Mahone was in the midst of a crucial battle with northern railroad interests, particularly the Baltimore and Ohio line. Mahone was president of three Virginia railroads—the Norfolk and Petersburg, the South Side, and the Virginia and Tennessee. The first connected the port of Norfolk in the southeast corner of Virginia to Petersburg, twenty miles south of Richmond; the second ran from Petersburg westward to Lynchburg in south central Virginia; the last continued the line from Lynchburg westward to Bristol, Tennessee. Thus, Mahone's three roads funneled freight and passengers from all of southern and southwestern Virginia and parts of Tennessee eastward to Norfolk.

The slender little general had secured legislative permission in March 1867 to consolidate all three roads into one line, the Atlantic, Mississippi and Ohio Railroad Company. The act required that the stockholders of the three companies effect the consolidation by May 1, 1868, or legislative permission would expire. Mahone had failed to meet the deadline in 1868 and was still president of three short lines rather than one long one. To compound his troubles, the Baltimore and Ohio Railroad and its ally, the Orange and Alexandria, were trying to gain control of the Virginia and Tennessee road.[7] If Mahone could keep the presidency of the Virginia and Tennessee, his lines would receive all the trade from southwestern Virginia, eastern Tennessee, and beyond. If John S. Barbour, president of the Orange and Alexandria, gained control of the contested road, the southwestern traffic would be diverted from Norfolk and directed northward to Alexandria and Baltimore. Thus, it was a question of which way traffic, and therefore profits, would flow from Lynchburg—eastward to Norfolk or northward to Baltimore.

The key to the situation was the state government, which owned 60 percent of the Virginia and Tennessee line. The Board of Public Works—consisting of the governor, treasurer, and auditor—annually appointed proxies for the state's interest. Thus, if the governor was friendly to Mahone, Norfolk would retain command of the southwestern road. If Barbour could get the ear of the governor, however, Baltimore would profit. Mahone therefore had two objects in mind. He had to get another consolidation bill through the General Assembly the next time it met; this would eliminate the annual scrambling for proxies by Mahone and Barbour. Until then, however, he had to remain on friendly terms with whoever happened to be governor.[8]

In May 1868 he was searching the state for a Conservative friendly to his consolidation scheme. If such a man received the Conservative gubernatorial nomination, Mahone's railroad interests would be safe, for it was generally understood that the Republican nominee, Wells, favored consolidation. With both candidates on his side, he could not lose.[9]

On May 7, however, Mahone's plans received another setback. The Conservatives nominated an outspoken anticonsolidationist, Robert E. Withers of Lynchburg, a graduate of the University of Virginia, a physician, Confederate colonel, and editor of the *Lynchburg News*. Withers had opposed Mahone's railroad scheme in his editorials for over two years. He believed consolidation would create a dangerous monopoly that would control the economic life of Lynchburg. His running mate was John L. Marye, Jr., member of a prominent Fredericksburg family, Withers's college classmate, and a member of the constitutional convention. James A. Walker of Pulaski, an ex-Confederate general from southwestern Virginia, ran for attorney general.

That night the party's executive committee met to devise a campaign strategy. Some moderates preferred a policy of conciliation and friendship with the freedmen, believing the blacks would heed the advice of, and vote with, their former masters. Withers, however, scotched such plans and "insisted that the only chance for a successful fight lay in making the race issue." Conservatives must hammer away at the theme of black domination inherent in the test-oath and disfranchisement clauses. Thus, the railroad question was only a minor concern to the Conservative party in the spring of 1868. Far more important were the issues of race and "outside" control of state politics. [10]

While the Virginia campaign was in its first stages, the Republican national nominating convention met in Chicago's Crosby Opera House on May 20. The Virginia Republican meeting of May 6 had appointed twelve delegates to the Chicago convention, but since party leaders were needed at home, few prominent Republicans were sent to nominate a presidential candidate. John Hawxhurst, the Fairfax County radical who had longed for the governorship, was joined in Chicago by Lysander Hill, a Maine native, Union army veteran, and radical Alexandria lawyer. Other delegates included New Yorker Sanford M. Dodge, a member of the recent constitutional convention; Edgar Allen, the English native, Union army veteran, and chief of the Virginia Union League; and George S. Smith, originally from New Hampshire but a Culpeper County farmer since the 1840s. The other Virginia delegates—Henry A. Pierce, Stephen R. Harrington, John Burke, Frederick M. Kimball, John M. Thacher, Thomas L. Tullock, and Minor Goodell—were obscure men who never became prominent in Virginia politics.

The only suspense at the Chicago convention was who would receive the vice-presidential nomination. General Ulysses S. Grant, the overwhelming favorite for president, had virtually no opposition. On the first day, May 20, the convention once again faced the southern problem: should delegations from unreconstructed states be seated with full privileges, including the right to vote? In 1864 the Virginia delegation had been seated without the right to vote, even though the Restored government had been recognized by all branches of the Federal government. In 1868, when the Old Dominion had only a provisional government subordinate to the military, its Republicans were seated and given full privileges. [11]

On the second day the delegates adopted a platform that had caused considerable debate in committee. While a minority favored a forthright call for equal suffrage, most northern Republicans opposed it; their constituents would not stand for it, they claimed. The compromise plank endorsed black suffrage in the South but left the matter for loyal states to decide for themselves. The tariff question aroused so much conflict that it was completely ignored in the interest of harmony. The monetary issue was likewise smoothed over. While some Republicans believed the national debt should be paid in greenbacks, others insisted on gold. The money plank called for payment according to the spirit and letter of the law— which was sufficiently ambiguous to satisfy everyone. The other resolutions congratulated the country on the success of congressional Reconstruction, called for the equalization and reduction of taxes, asked for an extension of the national debt, spoke for honesty and economy in government, applauded the impeachment of Andrew Johnson, and reaffirmed the need for pensions for "widows and orphans of the gallant dead."[12]

Shortly thereafter Grant was unanimously nominated for the presidency. Immediately, a large curtain at the rear of the stage dropped to reveal a giant portrait of the general, white doves were released in the large hall, and the band blared out "Hail to the Chief" and "Yankee Doodle." "Then," a New York reporter wrote, "the Opera House rang from floor to ceiling, from balcony to curtain, and from stage to gallery, with the wildest cheers ever heard in response to any nomination since 1860."[13] As soon as the celebration ended, Henry Pierce of Virginia nominated Henry Wilson of Massachusetts for vice-president. Delegates from other states nominated Schuyler Colfax of Indiana, Senator Benjamin F. Wade of Ohio, Governor Reuben Fenton of New York, and several lesser figures.

Because Grant refused to indicate a preference, the convention took five ballots to select his running mate. On the first tally Virginia gave eighteen votes to Wilson and two to Wade. One of the Wade votes came from Hawxhurst, who had promised the Ohio senator his support two weeks earlier. In the remaining ballots Virginia, like most other states, gradually moved into the Colfax column. When the Indiana congressman took a commanding lead on the fifth round, the Virginians and nearly all other delegates gave him their support, and he won the nomination. Shortly before adjourning, the convention named a national executive committee. The Virginia delegation selected Franklin Stearns, the wealthy Richmond businessman, to represent the Old Dominion.[14]

Back in Virginia, meanwhile, the Republican and Conservative parties were locked in combat. Hunnicutt, though he resented his defeat at the Richmond meeting, agreed to support the Wells ticket. The *New Nation* warned blacks that if the Conservatives won, they would call another constitutional convention within three years to disfranchise the freedmen; they would reduce blacks to a condition worse than the bondage they had known before the war. In mid-May, Charles Porter spoke in central and southeastern Virginia before crossing Chesapeake Bay to address Republicans of the Eastern Shore. Accompanied by W. H. Samuel, Governor Wells attended a rally in Charlottesville on May 20 and then headed for other parts of the state. The party had some disciplinary problems in the campaign. In Norfolk the independent-minded radical black leader Thomas Bayne was opposing the regularly nominated white moderate L. H. Chandler for Congress.[15]

The Conservatives were as busy as the Republicans. Withers men urged native whites to crush the constitution beneath their feet and deny employment to blacks who belonged to the Union League or supported Republican candidates. Colonel Withers embarked on a backbreaking speaking tour, covering the state by rail, horseback, carriage, and sailboat. Several newspapers supported the economic attack on black Republicans. The *Richmond Enquirer* said that white men should not allow freedmen to eat the whites' bread and then vote against the Conservative party.[16]

All the speeches, editorials, and meetings produced by both parties in the spring of 1868 ultimately proved futile, however, for Congress refused to provide for a new election. In June, Governor Wells traveled to Washington and appealed to the House Committee on Reconstruction to set a date for the election. The committee reported a referendum bill on July 9, and the House passed it the same day. But the bill died in the Senate on July 22 when the Judiciary Committee recommended that it be tabled. Since Congress adjourned a few days later, the referendum question was deferred until December.[17]

Why had Congress postponed the matter? Governor Wells may have angered some Republicans when he testified before the House Committee on Reconstruction. He asked for money to conduct an election but also specified that the bill should not provide for further registration of voters. There were 25,000 Conservatives in Virginia who had not registered in 1867 but who could and would in 1868. If they were kept off the rolls, he explained, the Republicans might carry the state. Representative James Beck of Kentucky, a Democratic member of the committee, was outraged at Wells's proposal to prevent eligible voters from participating in the election. As he told the House on July 24, the committee had ignored the governor's suggestion and included in its bill a clause opening the rolls to those who had failed to register in 1867. Wells's proposition, Beck fumed, was an "outrage too monstrous to be tolerated."[18]

This could not have been the only reason for postponement, however, for the House went on to pass the election bill after Wells testified. A more important factor may have been the timing of the referendum. This was an election year, after all. If Virginia approved its constitution and reentered Congress before autumn, it would be entitled to vote in the 1868 presidential election. Few expected the Old Dominion, with a sizable white majority, to support the party of Sumner, Stevens, and Butler. Even if Virginia could not resume its status as a regular state in time to vote for presidential candidates, congressional approval of the state's proscriptive constitution during the campaign might antagonize many moderate Republicans and neutrals. The safest course was to elect Grant first and consider Virginia later.

Politics and Governor Wells

For the next several months Virginia sat becalmed while the rest of the nation was caught up in the whirlwind of a presidential contest. Even in the hotbed of state politics, Richmond, black and white Republicans held no Fourth of July parade and celebration, the first time since the war that Independence Day had passed so quietly in the capital. [19] The only significant political developments in the Old Dominion were those connected with the administration of Governor Wells. During the summer and autumn of 1868 Wells managed to antagonize four powerful elements of Republican strength. The man who was expected to keep radicals in the fold and attract the votes of moderate Conservatives failed, like Governor Pierpont before him, to hold his party together.

Some of the governor's problems stemmed from the state party's failure to adopt a single, widely accepted strategy for electoral success. This failure doubtless stemmed from the deep political and philosophic divisions among Virginia's Republicans. Some followed the approach long championed by Hunnicutt—ideological consistency, the maintenance of party discipline, and getting out the vote. This plan spurned appeals to middle-of-the-road moderates and depended instead on the internal strength of the party. Governor Wells seemed to switch back and forth between the Hunnicutt approach and the strategy urged by John Minor Botts, Governor Pierpont, and northern party leaders. This latter scheme sought victory through appeals to the swing vote, the moderate whites of both parties. The antebellum Whigs and Unionists of 1861 were a potential source of strength and could be the balance of power in Virginia. Appeals to this middling group required the downplaying of extremist speeches and less visibility for radicals of both races. Since former Confederates were a clear majority of Virginia's voting population, hardheaded politics seemed to indicate the second approach for the state's Republicans. The problem for the Virginia party was that neither plan had been formally or widely adopted, and the state's Republicans were lurching from one to the other, depending on the circumstances and personalities involved. Either strategy would have been better than none at all.[20]

The governor's first conflict began two days after the May 1868 state convention when a group of Wells supporters led by James H. Clements attempted to buy Hunnicutt out of the *New Nation*. Although Wells had defeated Hunnicutt in the race for the nomination and Hunnicutt had agreed to support the party's ticket, the governor's friends were determined to weaken the editor still further. Hunnicutt, realizing that he would have to sell out or be starved out, agreed to sell and set a price. The prospective buyers let the matter drop for a few weeks and then circulated the story that the *Alexandria Virginia State Journal* would move to Richmond and become the official party paper. Feeling the pressure, Hunnicutt lowered his price. But the Wells men stalled again, meanwhile transferring the public patronage to the *State Journal*. This process continued until October when the *State Journal* finally did move to Richmond. It was only a matter of time before the *New Nation*, which had always operated barely above costs, would have to cease publishing.[21]

Hunnicutt did not go meekly. He brought considerable grief to the governor's camp before he was defeated. The *New Nation* charged that a small clique was governing Virginia without the aid or advice of the rest of the party. Men who had worked for the party and withstood Conservative vituperation, Hunnicutt warned, would not be "ground to dust and crushed and starved out." When his foes had come to Richmond to destroy him, he complained, they had found him established and working for the party; he was the veteran, they were the recruits.

He also painted the governor's supporters as a pack of carpetbaggers, running the state party to their own advantage. Virginia affairs, Hunnicutt protested, should be controlled by Virginians, not by ambitious northerners. This was only a tactic, however. Many of the men behind Wells were carpetbaggers, but most native Republicans also joined the governor's ranks. This duality was graphically illustrated at a Grant-Colfax rally in Richmond on August 24. Among the Republican speakers were Wells, the Michigan carpetbagger, and Williams C. Wickham, a Virginia patrician and a former Confederate general and congressman.[22]

Hunnicutt became so troublesome that L. E. Dudley, chairman of the state executive committee, secretly asked congressional Republicans to invite the old preacher to campaign for Grant in the North. Hunnicutt, Dudley complained, feels "a little chagrined that another received the honor which he coveted, and is making us some trouble by giving expression to his dissatisfaction." If he could be occupied somewhere away from Virginia for a while, the party would appreciate it. The scheme failed, and Hunnicutt remained in Richmond throughout the summer. By December, however, the Wells offensive had done its work: Hunnicutt issued the last number of the *New Nation* on December 18. He clearly had been crippled in the struggle. But he was still a hero to thousands of Virginia freedmen, and he was not yet finished with H. H. Wells.[23]

The governor also managed to antagonize many black Virginians. Wishing, perhaps, to shed the image of a black man's party, the Republicans, led by Governor Wells, severely reduced the number of black speakers at Republican rallies in the late summer. In protest, many freedmen met in Richmond on September 21 to vent their anger. Present, of course, was Hunnicutt, who castigated the governor for ignoring blacks in his appointments and in political meetings. This so angered the city's Republican leadership that they read Hunnicutt out of the party a few days later. That only produced more dissatisfaction among the freedmen, who held several additional rallies to express their support for Hunnicutt. The fabric of the party's popular base in the capital was unraveling.[24]

Wells dealt the party another blow in the summer and autumn of 1868 when he stepped between William Mahone and the ambitious general's goal of consolidation. Mahone had heard several rumors in August and September that Wells was now opposing consolidation.[25] The governor confirmed Mahone's suspicions late in October. R. T. Wilson, an agent for the Baltimore and Ohio Railroad, suggested to Wells that the state sell its stock in the Virginia and Tennessee line to the B&O. This, of course, would have ended Mahone's struggle for the inclusion of that crucial road in his consolidated company. Wells promised to sell the stock if he could get the Board of Public Works to agree. He approached state Treasurer George Rye, a member of the board, and the new military commander of Virginia, General George Stoneman, with his plan. Rye and Stoneman rejected the proposal, and public opinion turned even more decidedly against the Republican governor. The attempt to sell a Virginia railroad to an out-of-state northern company alarmed thousands of Virginians who normally paid no attention to corporate feuds.[26]

Why did Governor Wells bring Mahone and public opinion down on his neck? He certainly knew that native Virginians, especially the wealthy and powerful Mahone, would oppose a sale of the Virginia and Tennessee line to Baltimore. There was no political profit in this venture. Being from Alexandria, a city through which the B&O's ally, the Orange and Alexandria Railroad, passed and a city opposed to a Norfolk monopoly of the southwestern trade, Wells may have seen the Baltimore offer as a way to benefit Alexandria and his friends there. A reporter for the *New York Herald* discovered another possible motive. The B&O in 1868 was planning to build a railroad along the Georgetown Canal near Washington. This line would connect the B&O to the Orange and Alexandria road. Every ton of traffic from southwestern Virginia would have to pass over the canal section to reach Baltimore. Thus, the owners of the canal would receive a percentage on every passenger and every ton of freight coming up from the south. One of the owners of the canal was Henry H. Wells.[27] Whatever the motive behind Wells's action, he succeeded only in weakening himself and his party further.

The governor was not through yet, for he also antagonized General Stoneman. Stoneman, a veteran of the war and a moderate Republican like his predecessor Schofield, had assumed command in Virginia on June 2, 1868, when Schofield became Andrew Johnson's secretary of war. One of Stoneman's most vexing problems in Virginia was finding qualified men to fill state offices. The Fourteenth Amendment had turned out of office all men who had taken an oath of allegiance to the Federal government and subsequently supported the Confederacy. This group included thousands of Virginia's local and state political leaders. The July 1867 Reconstruction Act had complicated the problem by requiring all men appointed to office in unreconstructed states to take the congressional test oath, which disqualified anyone who had aided the southern war effort. This had eliminated virtually all white Virginians, for nearly everyone had voluntarily supported the Confederacy in some small way.

Even after generals Schofield and Stoneman and their subordinates had spent countless hours locating and appointing 2,504 men to office, more than half the state's 5,446 offices still were unfilled in the spring of 1869 "owing to the difficulty in finding men able to take the test-oath." Stoneman's task was to comb the state and search out men who could take the test oath and also read and write. Since most freedmen had been denied an education as slaves, the problem was serious. Instead of relying on the state's Republican party to supply him with names of men eligible for office, the general established a military screening board. This board, which received names from the various military officers scattered across the state, suggested appointments independently of the Republican party.[28]

This system, of course, angered Governor Wells, who had wielded some power over appointments during Schofield's tenure. When the time came to cooperate with the military, he was particularly headstrong. He used his pardoning power to free numerous offenders convicted in General Stoneman's military courts. Because many of those released were black, the governor's pardons were generally regarded by military men as politically inspired. Stoneman, whose military courts were complaining of Wells's allegedly indiscriminate pardoning, returned the governor's dislike in equal portions. Judge Alexander Rives, the moderate Republican on the state supreme court, asked Secretary of War Schofield to mediate, but Stoneman and Wells remained suspicious of each other.[29]

Besides being a poor politician, Wells also had a reputation for questionable business practices. While serving as governor he appeared in court as the lawyer for the defense in a whiskey fraud case. Even more damaging, he served as counsel for the plaintiff in a suit against the Petersburg and Weldon Railroad, 40 percent of which was owned by the state of Virginia.[30] Even the governor's closest supporters must have winced when these actions were denounced in the Virginia conservative press. Certainly, no governor who lost the support of Hunnicutt and some freedmen on his left and General Stoneman and General Mahone on his right could lead the minority Republicans very far toward victory.

Revolt of the Moderates

When Congress reassembled in December 1868, it received a petition from the Virginia Republican executive committee asking for a referendum on the Underwood constitution. Signers of the document included Governor Wells, Judge Underwood, Botts, General Wickham, Franklin Stearns, and others. On December 9 the House Committee on Reconstruction reported a bill providing money for an election of state officers and a referendum on the constitution as a whole. After a few minor amendments were added, the House passed the bill the same day. It was referred to the Senate Judiciary Committee on December 10, but Congress recessed for the Christmas holidays before the bill reached the Senate floor.[31]

At this point, Alexander H. H. Stuart of Staunton, a prominent Whig, former congressman, and secretary of the interior under President Millard Fillmore, began a movement to delete from the constitution the disabling clauses so hated by Conservatives and many moderate Republicans. Realizing that the Senate would pass the House bill unless Virginians publicized their objections to it, Stuart composed a long letter outlining his plan of action. He argued that black suffrage was inevitable now that the Republicans had elected Grant and Colfax by such a wide margin. The Republican party was in full control of the national government; it was useless to resist universal suffrage. If Virginia could secure universal amnesty (meaning the elimination of the disfranchising and test-oath clauses in the Underwood constitution) in exchange for universal suffrage, Stuart continued, "it would be so much substantial gain for a merely nominal concession!"[32] Stuart suggested that the Conservative party devise another constitution without the disabling clauses and present it to Congress as an example of what Virginia was ready and willing to ratify. He signed the letter "Senex" and had it published in the Richmond newspapers on Christmas Day.[33]

Many Conservatives viewed the Senex letter's acceptance of the idea of black political participation with horror. "I can never *consent* to negro suffrage," one Conservative wrote to former Confederate general and future governor James L. Kemper. "If we are to have it let it be *forced* upon us." Former governor Henry A. Wise, also a Confederate general and the chief executive who had overseen the hanging of John Brown in 1859, joined other staunch Conservatives in blistering Stuart and his allies. Virginians should "take death rather than dishonor," he fumed. Acceptance of black suffrage was a "disgrace to the Confederate living," a "living lie," a "base hypocrisy." Any Conservative who could contemplate such foolishness was nothing more than a "submissionist."[34]

Despite the thunder from the right, numerous moderates agreed that Stuart's plan was wise and practical. About thirty of the centrist Virginians met in Richmond on December 31 and January 1 to settle upon a plan of action. The meeting appointed a Committee of Nine, headed by Stuart, to go to Washington and present Virginia's objections to the constitution's more unpopular clauses. Also on the committee were John L. Marye, Jr., of Fredericksburg, the Conservative nominee for lieutenant governor, and John B. Baldwin of Augusta, Stuart's relative and a political veteran. Some members of the meeting visited General Stoneman, who gave his support to the committee and hoped for its success.[35]

At the suggestion of Marye, Stuart invited Gilbert C. Walker, the Republican carpetbagger of Norfolk and the man who had been defeated by Thomas Bayne for a seat in the Underwood convention, to aid the committee in Washington. Walker, a relative of Senator William Stewart of Nevada, was personally acquainted with several northern Republicans and proved particularly valuable. Even Horace Greeley's powerful *New York Tribune* soon joined the campaign, which "had great effect in mollifying the prejudices and moulding the sentiment of members of Congress."[36] The Committee of Nine along with Walker and other sympathizers spent about two weeks in Washington, appearing before House and Senate committees, cornering various congressmen, and visiting President-elect Grant, who assured them of his sympathy.[37]

The Virginia Republican party, which had split in August 1867 and weakened its ties to important elements of strength in the summer and autumn of 1868, split once again in the early months of the new year. The intense factionalism that plagued so many southern Republican organizations in the late 1860s and 1870s continued to rend the fabric of the Old Dominion's party. Those Republicans who had been grumbling ever since the constitutional convention joined the Committee of Nine in Washington in January to pressure Congress for a separate vote in the referendum on the test-oath and disfranchising provisions.[38] The leaders of this group included Franklin Stearns, L. H. Chandler, and Edgar Allen. While the efforts of the Committee of Nine received widespread publicity, the activities of these moderate Republicans may have had more impact than those of Stuart's centrist Conservatives. Stearns, Chandler, Allen, Walker, and the other Republicans were, after all, members of the party that controlled a majority of seats in Congress. Men of power in Washington were much more likely to listen intently to the arguments of fellow Republicans than they were to those of Conservatives and former Confederates.[39]

Worried Virginia radicals led by Governor Wells followed the Stearns Republicans and Committee of Nine around the national capital, warning senators and representatives that Unionists would not be safe in Virginia if political disabilities were removed. The referendum, Wells insisted, should be on the constitution as it was adopted in 1868; a separate vote would lead to Conservative domination of the state. The radicals scurrying around Washington were primarily the men surrounding Wells as governor—H. G. Bond, the wealthy carpetbagger from New York; Charles Whittlesey, editor of the *Richmond State Journal*; L. E. Dudley, chairman of the state executive committee; and J. M. Humphreys, collector of customs in Richmond and an outspoken critic of Hunnicutt. George Rye accompanied the Wells committee to Washington but soon deserted to the moderates.[40]

Close cooperation between the moderate wings of both parties on the subject of the referendum led to coordination in other matters too. Between sessions with congressmen, senators, and committees, the Committee of Nine and the Stearns Republicans came to an informal understanding on future politics. The Republican party soon would schedule a convention for March to make nominations for the state elections, sure to be ordered by Congress. Stearns, Stuart, and their allies agreed that "the leading conservative Republicans should be present at that meeting and endeavor to defeat the nomination of Wells. But if that should be found impracticable, that they should withdraw and nominate some *safe conservative* man, who would honestly and fairly administer the duties of the office. In this connection, the names of Franklin Stearns, William L. Owen, and Gilbert C. Walker were favorably mentioned."[41] If the Stearns Republicans succeeded in ousting Wells and replacing him with an acceptable moderate candidate, the assumption was that centrist Conservatives would join their Republican counterparts, and a Republican party with a new and moderate leadership probably would win the election. If, on the other hand, Wells prevailed and the Stearns men bolted the party, the rebellious moderate Republicans would nominate their own man and would likely be joined by the massive ranks of the Conservatives. Thus, the way was prepared for the coalition that would take control of the state in 1869.[42]

The year had begun with the constitutional convention dominated by a rampant state Republican party. But General Schofield's postponement of the referendum on the constitution, followed by similar delays in Congress, robbed Virginia Republicans of the momentum they had built up in 1867. Governor Wells, an amateur in Virginia politics, had slowed the party's progress further during the summer and fall when he alienated Hunnicutt, numerous freedmen, General Mahone, and General Stoneman.

Just as the radical triumph in the state elections of 1867 had spurred Virginia Conservatives to organize themselves into a new party, the Republican victory in the national campaign of 1868 convinced moderate Conservatives that the time for realism had come, that they should accept Reconstruction and make the best of it. This raised two possibilities—one promising and one ominous—for Virginia Republicans. If they could nominate a new gubernatorial candidate who was less offensive to centrist Conservatives and even some Republicans, adopt universal suffrage and universal amnesty as their own program, and make a grand display of welcoming the old Whigs and Unionists into their party, the Republicans might overcome all their misfortunes and retain control of the state government. The Old Dominion's Republicans had missed a similar chance in 1867 when they had spurned the campaign of Botts, Pierpont, and northern party leaders to incorporate native moderates into their ranks. Now, circumstances were offering them a second opportunity to become a majority party.

On the other hand, if Virginia Republicans lined up behind Wells, rejected universal amnesty, and demanded the retention of the proscriptive clauses of the Underwood constitution, they would probably lose all of the Conservative centrists and most of their own moderates in the next critical election. Decisions made in the spring of 1869 would determine the long-term future of the party.

CHAPTER 8

The End of Reconstruction

THE SIX months following the appearance of the Senex letter and the proposed marriage of Conservative and Republican moderates promised to be among the most exciting and interesting in Virginia's Reconstruction history. Those months would tell whether President-elect Grant would demand a vote on the constitution as a whole or submit the more controversial clauses for a separate vote. If Grant insisted on the whole charter, no one on either side of the political fence could tell what might happen. It was certainly doubtful that the constitution as a whole could be approved in a popular referendum. But if it were rejected by the voters, what then? A new constitutional convention? Continued military government? Even if Grant did allow a separate vote on some clauses, no one knew whether the Republican constitution would be accepted by the white conservative majority of voters.

Whatever President Grant decided, still other questions remained. Which path would the Virginia Republican party take in 1869? If its members rejected Wells and the test oath, nominated a moderate gubernatorial candidate like Stearns or Gilbert C. Walker, and embraced the old Whigs and Unionists—in short, if they moved to the center of the political spectrum—could they retain enough black support to carry the state in 1869? On the other hand, if they persisted with Wells as their leader, clung to the test-oath and disfranchising clauses, and snubbed the Conservative centrists, could strict party discipline alone overcome the massive native white vote? The spring and summer of 1869 would answer a lot of questions.

The True Republicans

While Virginia awaited the results of the New Movement—many believing it had failed—Republicans were preparing for their March 9 nominating convention.[1] The moderates who had recently returned from lobbying in Washington, including Stearns, Rye, Gilbert C. Walker, and the Portsmouth carpetbagger J. H. Clements, were determined to wrest control of the party from Wells. Rye was especially anxious to defeat the governor: "We are going to have a *brilliant fight* in the nominating convention," he told General Mahone. "May I ask that you will give us all the aid in your power." But the dyspeptic former general opposed the moderates' plan. He believed the Wells faction should be given full freedom to control the Republican party and make it as radical as possible. It would be easier to defeat that way. The moderates, however, insisted on resisting the governor within the party.[2] "We are fighting against Wells's nomination, boldly and bravely," Rye told Mahone. "We intend never to surrender, whether he is nominated or not." Clements agreed that Wells had to be destroyed within the Republican organization: "It is nonsense to expect any Candidate of a second or third party can beat the Republican Candidate. Our only safety is in getting a good nominee for the latter party."[3]

On the morning of March 9 Virginia Republicans gathered in the Union Street Colored Methodist Church in Petersburg, the city besieged by General Grant four years earlier, to select their gubernatorial candidate. Many of the Republicans whom Governor Wells had offended in the last year were present, and most of them had a lean and hungry look. J. H. Clements, with popular support in Portsmouth and an unofficial mandate from moderates, was determined to gain control of the convention at the outset. If a friend could win the chairmanship, the battle against Wells would be half won. After the call to order, the Wells and Clements men made their nominations for temporary chairman amid shouting and shoving from both blacks and whites, radicals and moderates. When George Tucker, a Clements man, jumped onto the stage along with several friends, the more numerous Wells supporters swarmed all over them as both factions scuffled, gouged, and punched for control of the convention.[4] The Petersburg city police quickly waded into the scramble, separated the ruffled combatants, and cleared the meeting hall.

That afternoon the Wells men returned in superior numbers, took control of the convention, and adjourned for the day. The next morning the governor's friends, organized and angry, gave him the gubernatorial nomination. The moderates, obviously overpowered, did not bother to resist. The Wells forces then nominated Thomas R. Bowden, a wartime Unionist, for attorney general and Dr. W. C. C. Douglas of Richmond, an ex-Confederate surgeon, for lieutenant governor. Bowden and Douglas, white southerners, would make the Wells ticket much easier to accept for native Virginians. At that moment Lewis Lindsay, the radical black leader from Richmond, nominated J. D. Harris, a native of the West Indies and a prominent black physician, for the office of lieutenant governor. Before the Wells men could make a decent and face-saving detour around Harris to select Douglas, the disgruntled moderates delivered the Wells candidacy a telling blow. In an instant, the quick-witted carpetbagger Edgar Allen seconded the Harris nomination, and the strange combination of black radicals and moderate whites elected Harris over Douglas. In effect, the wily Allen and his allies had crippled the Wells ticket; the overwhelming majority of native whites and many white carpetbaggers would never support any slate of officers with a black man in the second position.[5]

Before adjourning, the delegates resolved (1) that Virginia should be restored to its rightful place in Congress promptly and with its constitution, including the disabling clauses, intact; (2) that no state should deny the vote or officeholding privileges to any citizen (except those disfranchised and disqualified for office by the Underwood constitution); (3) that Virginia would faithfully support U. S. Grant as president; (4) that the Republican party should be the agent of Reconstruction in Virginia (an apparent reference to General Stoneman's refusal to abide by party recommendations for state and local offices); and (5) that the party would remove voting and officeholding restrictions on those "who accept in good faith the results of the war, and cooperate in earnest efforts for a restoration of the State under the Reconstruction laws."[6]

So the Virginia Republican party had made its choice—it would follow Wells, insist on the proscriptive clauses, pass up the possibility of a coalition with centrist Conservatives, and depend on internal party discipline to overcome its minority status on the voting rolls. This was the second time in two years that the state party had turned away from moderate Conservatives who were willing to cooperate with them. This strategy may well have worked in a state with a black voting majority or near majority. In such a state Republicans could win elections and adopt their own programs, undiluted by concessions to native whites. But in the

Old Dominion, with its clear native white majority, the Republican approach was risky, perhaps foolhardy.

The first time Virginia Republicans had turned away native white moderates, in 1867 when Botts and Pierpont had arranged an abortive union of the two groups, the Republicans had not suffered for their action. They went on to sweep most of the seats in the Underwood convention and to write their own new constitution. Conditions were different this time, however. Since 1867, native whites, shaken out of their post-Appomattox apathy, had organized themselves into a new Conservative party composed of antebellum Democrats and Whigs. Moreover, in 1869 the Republican party's own moderates had an understanding with the centrist Conservatives that they would leave the regular Republican organization if it insisted on Wells and proscription. It would be much more difficult for the regular Republicans to win this time.

The moderates had failed to seize control of the party, but they were determined to defeat Wells and the disabling clauses one way or another. At this point two groups of influential moderates held separate meetings and settled on a common course. In Petersburg's Jarratt's Hotel, George Rye, Edgar Allen, C. W. Buttz, Joseph Segar, D. B. White, Mahone (who now allied with the moderates despite his previous disagreement with their tactics), and a few less prominent figures agreed on March 10 to nominate another ticket under the "True Republican" label. For governor they settled on Gilbert C. Walker, a man who possessed all the qualities the moderates needed. He was a northern-born Republican with party and personal connections in Washington; that would satisfy congressional and Virginia Republicans and many freedmen. He was an outspoken critic of the disabling clauses; that would please almost all Virginia whites and some blacks. He was a Norfolk-based stockholder in Mahone's railroads and a strong proponent of consolidation; that would delight Mahone and his business associates.[7]

On the same night, twenty miles to the north in Richmond, other leading Republican moderates held a similar meeting at the home of the wealthy businessman Franklin Stearns.[8] This group, with its own ties to the centrist Conservatives, adopted the same strategy then being discussed in Petersburg and the strategy the Stearns men had earlier discussed with the Committee of Nine. Sometime within the next week participants in the two meetings drew together and agreed on a common plan. Walker would head the True Republican ticket. John F. Lewis and James C. Taylor would run for lieutenant governor and attorney general, respectively. Lewis, the brother of former secretary of state Charles H. Lewis (in the Pierpont wartime government) and descendant of a pre-Revolutionary Rockingham County family, was an unconditional Unionist Whig during the war. Taylor, a lawyer, former state senator, and ex-Confederate soldier whose officeholding disabilities had been removed by Congress, was from Montgomery County in southwestern Virginia.[9]

On March 16 the True Republicans published an address in Richmond newspapers that presented their nominees, asked for public support against "designing and selfish politicians," and denounced the disabling clauses. It was signed by Franklin Stearns, leader of the moderate committee that had cooperated with the Committee of Nine; George Rye, a charter member of the party and now state treasurer; Edgar Allen, chief of the Virginia Union League; G. K. Gilmer, a veteran of the Pierpont Restored government and editor of the *Harrisonburg American Union*; Charles H. Lewis, Pierpont's secretary of state; James W. Hunnicutt, whose enmity for Wells had overcome his radicalism; and about 150 other moderate Republicans.[10]

Years later True Republicans and some Conservatives agreed that the 1869 movement to ally moderate Republicans and centrist Conservatives in the Old Dominion had shown the way for moderates on the national level to form the Liberal Republican party of 1872. Earle Dudley Ross, the Liberal Republican party's first major historian, concurred in 1919: "The Virginia movement was later held, probably with essential correctness, to be a real beginning of Liberal Republicanism."[11] The True Republicans wrought more than they realized in Stearns's living room and in Jarrett's Hotel in March 1869.

Press reaction at the time indicated that moderates in both parties were drawing together against the radicals on both left and right. The *Richmond Whig* believed the True Republican ticket represented "the most benignant policy which, in our present circumstances, can be hoped for." The ultraconservative *Enquirer*, on the other hand, opposed coalition with anyone, especially a carpetbagger Republican, who favored any part of the Underwood constitution. The radical Republican *Richmond State Journal* deplored the moderate maneuver and warned the True Republicans that they were only "catspaws" of the Democrats.[12]

The radical (or regular) Republicans, surrounded now by enemies front and rear, were further embarrassed on March 20 when Edgar Allen and W. H. Samuel, True Republicans, accused Governor Wells, H. G. Bond, and L. E. Dudley of tampering with United States mail. Samuel had written Allen a letter urging opposition to Wells because of the latter's attempts to fill state offices with radicals exclusively. Allen had never received the communication, but it soon turned up in Governor Wells's office. Two days later the governor of Virginia, the chairman of the Republican state executive committee (Dudley), and the Federal register in bankruptcy (Bond), were arrested, despite their protests that the letter had reached them by legitimate means. The United States district attorney released them, however, and dismissed the charges.[13]

Before the case was dropped, General Stoneman, who had been wanting to remove the governor anyway, relieved Wells of his duties. The arrest was apparently the last straw for Stoneman, but he had other reasons as well. The general told one newspaper reporter that he had removed Wells because the governor was too proscriptive toward non-Republicans and too free with the pardoning power as a political tool. Stoneman could have removed Wells for any reason whatever and it would have delighted Conservatives. The *Lexington Gazette* said the general's action had met with "universal satisfaction" and suggested that Wells be sent to prison "to keep company with his betters."[14]

Wells, like Pierpont a year earlier, sought help in Washington. One of the governor's Richmond allies, Dr. Alexander Sharp, was a friend of the President and brother-in-law of Mrs. Grant.[15] Sharp and L. H. Chandler of Norfolk, who had remained in the regular party, asked Grant to countermand Stoneman's order and reinstate Wells. The president apparently was angry with Stoneman for interfering so openly in state politics. Within a few days Stoneman returned Wells to the Governor's Mansion and received orders to proceed to California for a new assignment. General L. S. Webb succeeded Stoneman but served only a few days before being replaced by General E. R. S. Canby, a moderate Republican much like Schofield and Stoneman.[16]

During the missing letter and Stoneman-Wells affairs, moderate Republicans were busy. On March 24 the True Republican state executive committee sent a delegation to Washington to lobby for a separate vote on the disabling and township clauses of the Underwood constitution. Led by G. K. Gilmer, Stearns, and Rye, the group testified before the House Reconstruction Committee on April 3 and visited President Grant, who promised to cooperate. That night they talked to as many members of

Congress as they could locate. They also presented a written memorial to Congress asking for a separate vote on the three provisions and estimating that not over 10,000 Virginia voters still opposed political and legal equality for blacks.[17]

The combined assaults on the constitution by the True Republicans and the Committee of Nine finally succeeded. On April 7 President Grant asked Congress to provide money for an election in Virginia and requested permission to submit certain clauses of the constitution to a separate vote. The next day Benjamin F. Butler, target of so much Conservative ridicule during the Underwood convention, reported the Reconstruction committee's bill to the House. Unanimously approved by the committee, the bill authorized the president to set an election for whatever date he wished and to "submit to a separate vote such provisions of said constitution as he may deem best." The House adopted the measure the same day by a vote of 125 to 25 and sent it to the Senate.

On April 9 Senator Oliver P. Morton of Indiana proposed an amendment requiring the state legislature to ratify the Fifteenth Amendment to the national Constitution (allowing for black male suffrage) before Virginia could be readmitted into Congress. With the support of Charles Sumner and other radicals, the bill passed the Senate by a vote of 44 to 9. The House approved the amended version late that night. The combination of True Republicans, with their Washington connections, and Conservatives, with their superior numbers, was proving a formidable opponent for the regular Republicans in Virginia.[18]

The 1869 Election

While the Old Dominion waited for President Grant to set a date for the election, Conservatives were examining their prospects in the upcoming contest. There were now three parties in the field—Conservatives, True Republicans, and regular Republicans. If the Conservative ticket remained in the race, moderates of both parties would be isolated and suspended in the political center between the radical carpetbagger Wells on one side and the backward-looking Colonel Withers on the other. No one could predict what the results of a three-man race might be. If the Conservative candidates withdrew from the campaign, however, Conservative voters might join the True Republicans to defeat the radical carpet-

bagger Wells. At the same time, the native white party would be supporting another carpetbagger Republican for governor, Gilbert C. Walker.

Although there was disagreement among party leaders about which
course to take, the Conservative rank and file seemed eager to defeat Wells
in any way they could. From all parts of the state came word that the voters
were anxious to withdraw the Withers ticket and unite with the True
Republicans against the radicals. Observers in Abingdon, Wytheville,
Bristol, Nottoway County, Christiansburg, Charlotte Court House, Culpeper, Suffolk, Richmond, and other areas agreed that the voters were
"nearly a unit for the Walker ticket, and they would deplore the folly of a
third ticket."[19]

The Conservatives scheduled a state convention in Richmond on April
28 to settle the matter. Some Conservatives, including the gubernatorial
nominee, Colonel Robert E. Withers, were reluctant to withdraw. They
despised the idea of allying with Republicans of any kind, especially when
the latter were willing to accept most of the Underwood constitution. The
nominee for lieutenant governor, John L. Marye, Jr., of Fredericksburg,
took the opposite view and worked long and hard at the convention to
withdraw the ticket. Withers, realizing that a three-way race could mean
radical victory, finally joined Marye and James A. Walker in resigning as
the Conservative ticket. The convention made no other nominations and
thus effected a silent partnership with the moderate Republicans. A
Conservative address to party followers urged defeat of the disabling
clauses of the Underwood constitution but made no recommendation on
the charter as a whole. It endorsed neither candidate for governor, but that
was unnecessary; everyone knew where the Conservative vote would go.[20]

This decision by the native whites made the True Republican movement much more important than it could have been otherwise. Without
the main body of the Conservatives, the centrists alone probably could not
carry the state. Once the rank-and-file Conservatives joined them, however, the two parties had excellent prospects of winning. Unfortunately for
the True Republicans, their smaller number compared to the masses of
Conservatives meant that the native whites would control the Republicans, not vice versa.

General Mahone played no prominent role in the Conservative withdrawal. He did not convince Withers to resign, for the two men were
personal and political enemies and would remain so for many years.
Withers withdrew because practical politics and most of his colleagues

demanded it. He did not retire to further Mahone's railroad scheme; indeed, Withers vigorously opposed it. It was clear to most Conservatives that the voters wanted to ally with the Walker ticket. In short, the Conservatives probably would have withdrawn their candidates whether Mahone wanted them to or not.[21]

The only item of political interest in early May other than the gubernatorial campaign was President Grant's forthcoming proclamation on the election. Would he order a separate vote on some clauses? Which provisions, if any, would he detach from the body of the constitution? Would he give both parties enough time to campaign? The answers came on May 14 when Grant set the referendum for July 6 and ordered a separate vote on the disfranchising and test-oath clauses. Some Conservatives had wanted to include the township provision among the separate items, but General Canby and the president's cabinet had discouraged it. The public school system was intimately connected with the township arrangement; to destroy one was to destroy the other. The president therefore refused to separate the third clause from the rest of the constitution. Conservatives were disappointed, but they were powerless to counteract the presidential directive.[22]

General Canby went to great lengths to ensure a fair and free election in July. He informed his superiors in Washington that he would need to find "about three thousand" election registrars and poll managers to oversee the electoral machinery. At the request of the mayor of Alexandria, Canby sent a cavalry unit to that city to supplement the regular police force on election day. While the general did not expect trouble, he did ask the army's adjutant general in Washington for permission to place three artillery companies at Fort Monroe in order to forestall any incidents in that part of the state. General Canby also arranged for each political party to have up to three observers present at the counting of ballots at the various polling places around the state on election night. If there was to be any intimidation or fraud in July, Canby wanted to know about it.[23]

The 1869 campaign was one of the hardest fought in Virginia's history. Governor Wells and L. H. Chandler visited every section of the state, exhorting freedmen and radical whites to support their ticket. Charles H. Porter, one of the most active and energetic speakers in the radical camp and now a congressional candidate, addressed audiences in Prince Edward, Buckingham, Bedford, New Kent, and Charles City counties, then con-

tinued to Appomattox Court House, Lynchburg, Richmond, Charlottesville, and Amherst—all in two weeks. The radicals left no corner of the
state untouched.[24]

The thrust of their argument was that the True Republicans were mere
tools of the crafty Conservatives. Walker, they insisted, was no more than a
stalking-horse for the old secessionist Democrats and Whigs. He and his
running mates were "the ticket of the Rebel Conservatives disguised in
Union Blue." Wells and the *State Journal* warned freedmen that Walker was
supported and controlled by men who privately opposed black suffrage,
black officeholding, and black legal equality. The True Republicans were
the party of slaveholders and secessionists; the governor represented freedom and justice. In short, said the *State Journal*, "it is for the colored
people to decide whether they will entrust the administration of the
principle [of equal rights for all] to friendly or unfriendly hands."[25]

Wells attempted to win back some of the moderate vote in May by
surrendering on the disabling clauses. He published a letter expressing his
determination to vote against the two provisions and claiming that he had
urged President Grant in April to provide for a separate vote. Despite his
own view, he concluded, he would abide by the decision of the voters.[26]
This reversal accomplished little or nothing for the governor. He was the
man who had asked Congress not to reopen the registration rolls in 1868,
the man who had opposed the Committee of Nine, the man who had
resisted the movements for a separate vote on the disabling clauses. He was
indelibly marked as a proscriptive radical in the minds of moderates and
Conservatives.

Added to this handicap, of course, was the reputation Wells had
gained—fairly or not—as a mail thief, a shady lawyer, and an opponent of
state interests. While sitting in the Governor's Mansion he had been
arrested for a Federal crime. And though the case had been dropped, he
had never fully explained how he acquired the missing letter. He was
surrounded by radical carpetbaggers like Porter and Platt, was the freedmen's favorite candidate, and had a black running mate—a tremendous
burden in Reconstruction Virginia. While governor he had served as
counsel for the defense in a whiskey-fraud case and as a lawyer for the
plaintiff against a railroad owned partly by the state. Finally, he had
cooperated with agents of an out-of-state corporation, the B&O, in a plan
to sell the state's interest in the Virginia and Tennessee Railroad. This was

an affront not only to those who were personally connected with consolidation but to all those Virginians who saw the B&O, a major cog in the Union war machine, as an alien Yankee institution.

The regular Republicans were no match for the True Republican–Conservative coalition. The latter, realizing that Wells's greatest strength was among the freedmen, mounted a powerful campaign to split the black vote. Hunnicutt, still popular among blacks despite his recent alliance with moderates and Conservatives, appealed to freedmen to support Walker and defeat the disabling clauses. The old editor was running on the True Republican ticket for the same congressional seat sought by the radical carpetbagger Charles H. Porter. The True Republicans backed Daniel M. Norton, the powerful black leader of the Peninsula, for a congressional seat. They promised Thomas Bayne an office after the election. Richmond Conservatives also organized biracial barbecues to attract the city's freedmen into their camp. Other Conservatives cited several examples of Governor Wells's disregard for freedmen: he had not invited J. D. Harris, his black running mate, to the Governor's Mansion; he was refusing to campaign with Harris; he sent his children to all-white schools; some of his followers, J. M. Humphreys and L. H. Chandler in particular, had opposed black suffrage until 1867.[27]

One of the most serious charges against Wells was that his advisers were urging antiblack Republicans of the southwest to scratch J. D. Harris's name from the ballot and to substitute a white man's name. Even slander was not ruled out: Wells's family, the Conservatives whispered, had been engaged in the slave trade earlier in the century.[28]

The Walker forces had other means of influencing the black vote as well. White employers threatened to discharge radical freedmen from their jobs. They managed to send their black employees far from the polls on election day; they promised extra wages to those freedmen who would not take the time to vote. The attempt to split or reduce the black vote was successful in some areas, especially in the southeast where several influential black leaders were campaigning for Walker.[29]

The anti-Wells alliance gathered support by other means, too. They established their own newspaper, the *Richmond Independent Republican*, and placed Hunnicutt in the editor's chair. Gilbert C. Walker hinted strongly to Conservative audiences that he would not enforce the township clause; this would eliminate many black officeholders even before they were elected. When some Conservatives hesitated to join one carpetbagger,

Walker, against another carpetbagger, Wells, the Conservative state executive committee openly endorsed Walker in late May. This seemed to end what little resistance there was, and the remaining Conservatives rolled into the Walker camp.[30]

General Mahone, who had cooperated with and followed the True Republicans earlier in the year, played a more prominent role in the 1869 campaign. He furnished funds for one anti-Wells candidate who favored consolidation (James W. Walker of Culpeper); he provided free passes on his railroads in order that twenty Gilbert C. Walker voters could register; he fed gubernatorial candidate Walker information on the positions of prominent politicians; he conferred with the True Republican candidates on the timing and setting of their speeches. No man, other than the candidate himself, worked harder for Walker's success.[31]

The railroad consolidation question doubtless influenced some voters, but not enough to change the results of the election. After an extended tour through the country traversed by John S. Barbour's Orange and Alexandria line, Walker estimated that he might lose 3,000 votes due to the railroad issue. Some people simply would not vote, while others would support Wells.[32] As it turned out, however, 3,000 votes would comprise only slightly more than 1 percent of the total vote in 1869, certainly not enough to worry Walker or to swing the election against him. Offsetting his losses along the Orange and Alexandria, Walker may even have gained the backing of some otherwise radical blacks who were employed on Mahone's lines; the general was not likely to overlook his influence with his own employees.

How important was the railroad issue for those not directly concerned?[33] The question of consolidation rarely appeared in campaign speeches, either moderate or radical. Wells stressed Walker's capture by the Democrats, and Walker emphasized Wells's history of proscription and radicalism. The railroad issue was seldom mentioned by either party, and then only as one of several secondary points.[34] Mahone himself was responsible for this in at least one case. He asked a friendly newspaper editor to concentrate on the evils of the disabling clauses and the radicalism of Wells and to disregard the consolidation question.[35] The general himself apparently realized that the voters feared Wells mainly as a radical, not as a friend of Baltimore.[36]

Finally, it would have been remarkable indeed if blacks and native whites had voted according to the schemes of railroad men. Freedmen supported the radicals because they had campaigned for black suffrage, black officeholding, political equality, public education, and tax reform. The radicals were the freedmen's proven allies and champions. Wells could have backed Baltimore, Norfolk, New York, Pittsburgh, or Chicago, and it would have mattered little to the freedmen. They had more important things to consider. The same pattern held true for native white Conservatives. For them Wells represented proscription, black equality, and northern-flavored radical Republicanism. They resented his scheming with the B&O, but that was hardly the major issue. The real contest was between conservative southern whites and radical Republicans with their black allies. [37]

All the scheming, planning, speechmaking, and hidden maneuvers finally built to a climax in midsummer. On July 6 "at early dawn almost, the colored element were out and at the polls. For four hours they voted in a solid phalanx. The whites were equally zealous." From Norfolk to the Valley and from Alexandria to the southwestern mountains, long lines of voters waited quietly and patiently to mark their ballots. Statewide, 82 percent of eligible voters participated in the long-awaited election. While white participation increased dramatically over the figure for the 1867 election of delegates to the constitutional convention (from 63 to 84 percent), the proportion of registered blacks who voted declined somewhat (from 88 to 81 percent), indicating that Conservative efforts to get out their own vote and to discourage freedmen from voting may have been at least partially successful. On the other hand, the participation by both races was very high, so the Conservative campaign to minimize the black vote was largely a failure. Of course, whites, with a commanding lead in registered voters (149,781 whites and 120,103 blacks), knew they could win simply by getting out their own vote, something they had failed to do two years earlier.

In the heavily black tidewater counties, 87 percent of all registered Virginians voted. Voter participation was as high or even higher in the larger cities as it was statewide. In Richmond, for example, 84 percent of whites and 83 percent of blacks cast their ballots on July 6; in Norfolk the figures were 96 percent and 92 percent; in Petersburg, 88 and 87 percent. In Rockbridge County in the Valley, where whites comprised 70 percent of registered voters, blacks still turned out in large numbers to vote; 85 percent of whites and 78 percent of blacks participated. Despite this keen interest in the results and the crucial nature of the issues to be decided,

General Canby, military commander in the state, reported to Congress that the day passed quietly with very few complaints of fraud or intimidation. While there was a scattering of complaints from both parties in a few places, in the overwhelming majority of counties, Canby concluded, "the election was impartially and fairly conducted."[38]

As the votes were counted that night, it soon became obvious that the True Republican–Conservative forces had won a smashing victory. Walker defeated Wells by more than 18,000 votes (119,535 to 101,204, a majority of 54 percent). John F. Lewis, the True Republican candidate for lieutenant governor, gathered an even larger total in his race with J. D. Harris, Wells's black running mate (120,068 to 99,400, a majority of 55 percent). James C. Taylor completed the sweep, defeating Thomas R. Bowden for attorney general (119,446 to 101,029, or 54 to 46 percent). The constitution was adopted by the overwhelming vote of 210,577 (96 percent of the vote) to 9,136, while the two disabling clauses were decisively rejected (84,410 for and 124,360 against on the disfranchising section; 83,458 to 124,715 on the test oath).[39]

The antiradical coalition elected 30 of the 43 state senators and 97 of the 140 delegates to the lower house. The great majority of winners were Conservatives, and native whites interpreted the election as a Conservative, not True Republican, victory.[40] (Still, nearly thirty black candidates were elected to the General Assembly—6 radicals to the senate, 21 to the house, and 2 moderate Republicans to the house.) The Conservatives and True Republicans also controlled the congressional delegation. Only three radicals—Richard S. Ayer of Warsaw, a native of Maine and a member of the Underwood convention; James H. Platt of Petersburg; and Charles H. Porter of Richmond—won seats in Washington. Lewis McKenzie of Alexandria, elected as a True Republican, joined four Conservatives to complete the eight-man delegation to the House.[41]

Walker carried sixty-eight counties and cities, including all the predominantly white areas of the southwest, Valley, mountains, and northwest, plus a few counties of southeastern Virginia. Wells won thirty-four cities and counties, including seventeen of the eighteen tidewater counties with black majorities and sixteen other counties in eastern and southern Virginia (see map 5). Alexandria, his home base, the center of prewar and wartime northern immigration, and terminal of the Orange and Alexandria Railroad, also gave Wells a majority. Except for Alexandria, every county along the line of the Orange and Alexandria, all of them white,

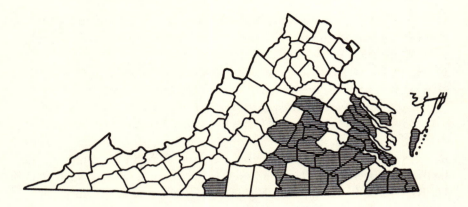

Map 5. Counties voting for Henry H. Wells in 1869. In addition to these counties, the cities of Alexandria, Norfolk, Petersburg, and Portsmouth returned majorities for Wells. From *House Miscellaneous Documents,* 41st Cong., 2d sess., no. 8, pp. 12–14, 23–24.

supported Walker. The railroad issue simply could not overcome the white voters' antipathy for Wells and radicalism. Nearly all the black counties along Mahone's roads voted for Wells; all the white counties favored Walker. In short, Walker won in the white areas of Virginia and Wells in the black.[42]

The day after the election, Governor-elect Gilbert C. Walker traveled from his headquarters in Norfolk to Richmond for a victory celebration. Thousands of Virginia whites gathered at Capitol Square to greet their unlikely hero, a northern carpetbagger. Several excited participants lifted the handsome Walker to their shoulders and carried him to his waiting carriage. A grand procession through the streets of the capital of the Confederacy followed the excitement at Capitol Square.[43]

While a quiet gloom settled over most freedmen and radical whites, the Old Dominion's True Republicans and Conservatives were overjoyed. "Shout the glad tidings, Virginia is free!" exulted the *Lynchburg Virginian.* "The carpetbag and scalawag power has been broken, and Virginians will rule Virginia." A Charlottesville merchant announced a sale on waterproof carpetbags for anyone who might be crossing the Potomac going north. Walker's hometown of Binghamton, New York, fired twenty-four guns to salute his victory. The anti-Wells attitude was succinctly expressed by

John L. Marye: "My friend, ain't it superb?" Northern Republicans, however, were rather suspicious of Walker's white supporters. Horace Greeley of New York regretted that they had "experienced much yet learned little since 1860." He hoped Walker would keep the state out of Conservative control.[44]

The Aftermath

The True Republicans and Conservatives had a brief scare in July and August when General Canby interpreted the Federal Reconstruction Acts to mean that the test oath for officeholders was in effect until after Virginia was readmitted to Congress. Since the General Assembly had to meet before readmission to ratify the Fourteenth and Fifteenth Amendments, it appeared that many of the new legislators would be disqualified and that the readmission process would therefore be halted indefinitely. The matter was settled on August 28 when United States Attorney General E. R. Hoar ruled that the legislators could take office and pass the two amendments but conduct no further business until Virginia was readmitted. One True Republican snickered that "our anticipated embarrassments have been removed by the *virtuous* opinion of a *Hoar*."[45]

After Hoar's action had removed all hope of upsetting the July election, Wells resigned under pressure from many Conservatives and True Republicans. Walker was inaugurated late in September, and the General Assembly passed the two constitutional amendments on October 8, three days after assembling.[46]

Meanwhile, disappointed regular Republicans looked to the future with anxiety. They feared a reversal of all the progress they had enjoyed since the Reconstruction Acts had been passed in the spring of 1867. One northern teacher who had been in Virginia since the war scolded those black voters who had been lured into the True Republican camp by white blandishments: "Some time ago a colored man was put in prison for stealing a hog; and to this day the col'd people say, 'Where are his white friends, who promised to stand by him if he'd vote for Walker? Not one would bail him out. We knew 'twould be just so!' "[47]

Regular Republicans assembled in Richmond on November 24–25 to reorganize the party after the summer electoral disaster. If radical whites were disappointed, Virginia's freedmen must have been even more downcast. Richmond's black community, one of the most active in the state, sent only four delegates of the capital's allotment of twelve to the convention. When the meeting nominated an all-white slate of party officials, black complaints resulted in the addition of only two blacks to the list. Led by carpetbagger and Congressman-elect Charles Porter, Thomas Bayne, Lewis Lindsay, Daniel Norton, and other radicals, the convention made one last attempt to convince Congress that the July election was illegitimate. Complaining that the 1869 campaign had been "a Confederate triumph" marked by threats of violence and white promises to fire politically active freedmen, the convention petitioned Congress to schedule a new election on the constitution as a whole or to remove from office those Virginia legislators who could not take the test oath and replace them with their opponents. The Fifteenth Amendment to the national Constitution, they warned, would not be sufficient protection for the Old Dominion's freedmen because "an educational or property qualification prescribed by the legislature of Virginia would destroy the entire influence of colored suffrage" and Conservatives in the General Assembly would prohibit black officeholding and jury service.[48]

Louder voices than those of the defeated radicals called for the Old Dominion's prompt readmission into Congress, however. Henry H. Wells, resigned to the situation, urged Congress to readmit Virginia; delay would serve no useful purpose. A petition by two-thirds of the General Assembly's members reminded Congress that Virginia had met all requirements made of it and deserved to be seated in Washington. In testimony before a congressional committee, Governor Walker echoed the General Assembly's appeal: "We need capital, we need emigration, and neither of those will come to our State until we have a settled civil government." Asked by Benjamin Butler if there was a Conservative plan to rescind any of the 1868 constitution's sections guaranteeing equality, Walker assured him that "I have never heard of any such intention, and I do not believe there is such an intention."[49]

Weary of the endless wrangling in Virginia, President Grant urged Congress to readmit the Old Dominion promptly.[50] Some radical Republicans, however, feared that Virginia, like Georgia before it, would repudiate certain portions of its constitution once it reentered Congress. Senator Charles Sumner of Massachusetts complained that the General Assembly was "steeped in treason to the lips." To guard against Virginia's repudiation of any Reconstruction reforms, both chambers required Virginia to promise in advance that it would carry out all provisions in its constitution and make no changes in it. John A. Bingham of Ohio, himself a veteran radical, attacked the provisos as "conditions-subsequent"—meaning that such conditions implied a Union of unequal states. They were adopted despite Bingham's protests but had only questionable authority over the Old Dominion. The bill admitting Virginia into Congress passed the Senate on January 21 and the House three days later. President Grant signed it on January 26, bringing Reconstruction to a close in the old Mother of States.[51]

When word reached Virginia that the readmission bill had been signed, True Republicans and Conservatives celebrated their deliverance from Reconstruction. The scene in Petersburg doubtless was duplicated in many other parts of the state: "Conservative citizens rejoiced at the news, crowds gathered in the streets, barrooms were filled with gentlemen toasting the new era, church bells and fireworks added to the joys of the moment."[52]

Although the True Republicans had succeeded in defeating Wells, they were the vehicle by which the Conservative party won control of the state. The True Republicans alone, without the aid of the Conservatives, could not have won the election. The meat and bones of the victorious coalition were the native whites who were supporting Walker as the lesser of two evils. They elected him governor but also installed a solid Conservative majority in the General Assembly.[53] In the next state election a prewar Democrat, James L. Kemper, and a thoroughly Conservative legislature succeeded Walker and his moderate allies.

Given the facts of political life in the Old Dominion—an aroused native white majority, intense interest in the election, and widespread antipathy toward Wells and the disabling clauses—perhaps the state's Republicans should have heeded the earlier advice of Pierpont, Botts, and Stearns. The crucial center, composed of moderate Republicans and antebellum Whigs and Unionists, was necessary for success. It included tens of thousands of voters, long experience in state politics, prominent names, and Washington connections. This middle swing vote was twice pushed away by the Republicans but accepted, however grudgingly, by the Conservatives. The Conservatives' hardheaded realism proved more potent than the radical Republicans' vaunted party discipline, and the result was an end to Reconstruction in Virginia.

A Republican party that included some former Confederates and slaveholders would not have been as reform-minded or as concerned about freedmen's rights as a more radical party would have been. But a diluted Republican party would have had something that a radical party could not have—power. And power with less lofty goals would have been more productive for Virginia Republicans than pure ideals and no power.

CHAPTER 9

Conclusion

THE CRUSHING victory of the Conservative juggernaut in 1869 seemed to spell doom for the divided and defeated Republicans of Virginia. In the next gubernatorial election a former Confederate general and a staunchly Conservative legislature succeeded Walker and his True Republican allies. Taking advantage of their strength, Conservatives amended the Republicans' Underwood constitution in the early and middle 1870s. They altered the system of local government to reduce the power of local black leaders, reduced the number of legislative sessions and the number of legislators, disfranchised those convicted of petty larceny (primarily freedmen) and those who had not paid their poll tax, and removed the limit on interest rates. Meanwhile, one Conservative governor after another took his place in the Governor's Mansion once occupied by Pierpont, Wells, and Walker.[1]

The plight of the Old Dominion's Republicans no doubt seemed hopeless to those observing these events from afar. The Virginia Republican party did not shrivel and die in 1869, however. It remained active, at least in places, throughout the last three decades of the century. General Grant, conqueror of Virginia Confederates in 1865, won the Old Dominion's electoral vote for the Republican party seven years later. The ideas of the Liberal Republican movement in the North coincided with those of Virginia moderates, and the state's Republicans managed to elect five of the state's nine members of the United States House of Representatives in 1872. A total of eighty-seven black Republicans served in the General Assembly from 1869 to 1890. While Conservatives did amend the Underwood constitution to remove some of its more radical features, still the Republican-inspired public school system, black suffrage, and black officeholding remained part of the basic law of Virginia. [2]

In the heavily black counties of tidewater Virginia, local and county Republican organizations continued to elect their members on a regular basis into the 1890s. Elections in the tidewater for the quarter century after 1869 were "quiet, orderly, with extensive voter participation, and with an accurate count of the votes." In some of these counties Republicans won every election from 1867 to 1896. [3]

Republicans enjoyed other post-Reconstruction success when they allied with William Mahone's Readjuster party in the late 1870s and early 1880s. This coalition of black Republicans, mountain whites, and disgruntled politicians won both United States Senate seats, gained control of the state legislature in 1879, elected a governor in 1881, and sent five of the state's ten members to the House of Representatives in Washington in 1882. The Readjuster-Republicans also reversed at least part of the conservative trend since 1869. They "readjusted" the state's debt downward, reformed state finances, increased support for public schools, abolished the whipping post, repealed the poll-tax suffrage requirement, created a black state college, appointed many freedmen to lower state offices, and gave black schools black teachers with pay equal to that of whites. The successes of the Readjuster-Republicans during this period dramatically illustrate what might have happened during the late 1860s if Reconstruction Republicans had managed to tie their future to that of the numerous lower- and middle-class whites in the Valley and in the southwestern mountains of the state. [4]

The Republican resurgence of the late 1870s and early 1880s gradually succumbed, once again, to superior Conservative numbers and organization. After the Readjuster-Republican successes of that period, Republican victories were fewer and fewer and were confined increasingly to the tidewater counties with significant black majorities and to a few mountain counties of the far southwest. The proscriptive Democratic state constitution of 1902 eliminated from the voting rolls "the overwhelming majority of blacks" and "tens of thousands of illiterate, impoverished or apathetic whites." As a result, Virginia's Republican party entered a dormant stage from which it would not emerge until a century after the stirring and emotional events of Reconstruction. [5]

The history of the Virginia Republican party during Reconstruction is in many ways informative about the nature of American and southern politics. Interested readers may well ask why the Virginia party, the only Republican party organized in the antebellum South, failed to achieve more than it did, given its relatively early origins. The birth date of the Old Dominion's party is, of course, somewhat deceiving. Antebellum Republicans were primarily westerners from beyond the Appalachian Mountains, men who joined the party as a protest against the slaveholding hegemony east of the Blue Ridge. When West Virginia split away to become a separate state in 1863, well over 90 percent of the state's Republicans were lost to the party organization. The remaining Unionists huddled in Alexandria and a handful of Union-occupied counties in northern and eastern Virginia during the war, but they were so few and impotent that even their own party and the Republican-dominated United States Congress paid them little heed. These "Restored government" Unionists did manage to write a new antislavery constitution in 1864, but they allowed party machinery to rust while the war raged around them. Thus, when the war ended in 1865, the Restored governor, Francis H. Pierpont, could take only about two dozen Unionist members of the General Assembly with him to Richmond. In short, the party's early birth provided only a thin and shaky foundation for its postbellum work.

Other aspects of the Virginia party's history are equally interesting. It appears that mid-nineteenth-century Republicanism and most white Virginians were not a natural mix. Northerners such as John C. Underwood, George Rye, and others were the true founders of the party in the 1850s, not native Virginians. Men of northern birth continued to provide much of the party's leadership during the Civil War and Reconstruction—men such as Gilbert C. Walker, Henry H. Wells, Franklin Stearns, and Edgar Allen. Those Virginians who did participate intensely in party affairs were men from the periphery of the state's established class—freedmen, westerners with western concerns such as Pierpont, and political mavericks like James Hunnicutt.

Virginia's close proximity to the North doubtless contributed to the flow of northern Republicans into its borders before and after Appomattox. Moreover, the Old Dominion's status as the political center of the Confederacy made it an obvious and convenient target for northern reform efforts. Certainly, northern Republicans, whether they claimed Virginia as their new home or merely wanted to change its ways, played a more prominent role in the Reconstruction of the Old Dominion than in that of most other southern states.

Republicans, whether northern or native, were divided from Conservatives by some fundamental issues during the 1860s. Some earlier historians of Reconstruction in Virginia interpreted the era as an economic conflict between the railroad empire controlled by the Baltimore and Ohio and the lines owned or coveted by General William Mahone. While the consolidation question doubtless did shape the political behavior of some Virginians, notably Mahone himself, railroad wars were not foremost in the minds of most Virginians during this period.

The postwar status of the freedmen and the position of former Confederates were much more important to most voters. Those Virginians who voted for the radical carpetbagger Henry H. Wells in 1869 did so because he promised to protect the rights and privileges of freedmen and white Unionists, because he represented extensive change and reform. Those who supported the moderate carpetbagger Walker did so because he represented the interests of moderates and conservatives and because he was their only realistic hope to stem the tide of change that threatened to move Virginia even further away from its antebellum past. Whether Virginia railroads connected to Norfolk or to Baltimore seemed far less important to most Virginians than whether black and white Republicans would be allowed to control state politics for the next several years.

The party that these blacks and white Unionists created was considered at the time to be quite radical. While northern Republicans of the 1860s may have looked upon the goals of the Virginia party as quite fair, reasonable, and moderate, to most white Virginians and to many northern whites the Old Dominion's Republican party appeared to be a dangerous, disruptive force. It sought to inject into the state's ancient political process people who, until very recently, were beneath political consideration. A few Republicans threatened even the right of private property by calling for land confiscation. Virginia Republicans sought to educate former slaves and raise them to the level of their former masters. Republicans consorted openly with men who had verbally lashed Virginia for many years— Charles Sumner, Thaddeus Stevens, Benjamin Wade, Henry Wilson. To the student of history in the late twentieth century, Virginia Republicans of the 1860s seem quite moderate. But in the new world created by defeat and Reconstruction, most white Virginians considered the party to be a threatening and alien force.

Historians interested in the Civil War and Reconstruction have debated for decades whether the war and its aftermath represented a watershed in the history of the South or merely a slight and temporary divergence from its normal path of development.[6] If the perceptions of the people who lived through those years in Virginia count for anything, we may safely conclude that their world really did change significantly during the 1860s. While neither white Virginians nor even most white northerners suddenly accepted the freedmen as their true equals, still the lives of Virginia blacks were changed in dramatic ways by the war and Reconstruction.

Freedmen were no longer property. Their families could no longer be separated at the whim of white slaveowners. Freedmen now had at least the legal right to move to areas of greater opportunity, and many of them took advantage of that right. They could no longer be legally whipped or punished as they had been as slaves. Black field hands could now seek different kinds of employment. Blacks were now guaranteed, in both state and Federal constitutions, rights they had never enjoyed before—the right to vote and the right to hold public office. Former slaves by the tens of thousands cast their first ballots, and scores of them took their seats in legislative halls and county courthouses where they would have been allowed only as servants a few years previously.

The world of Virginia whites changed too. Their former slaves, people they had regarded as simpleminded and childlike if they knew them personally or ignored as invisible men if they did not know them, were no longer childlike or simple or invisible. White planters and farmers had no choice but to stand by and watch the disruption of their antebellum labor system and the overturning of their old racial structure. Freedmen by the thousands moved off the old farms and plantations for their own reasons, refused to work in gangs under drivers or overseers, bargained for fair wages and working conditions, left the old churches controlled by whites, participated in political meetings, voted, held public office—in other words, asserted their wills and changed life in Virginia forever. White southerners certainly felt the changes sweeping over them. One former planter lamented the passage of the old order: "The houses, indeed, are still there, little changed, it may be, on the outside, but the light, the life, the charm are gone forever. 'The soul is fled.'"[7]

When had powerful white politicians asked black community leaders for their support before? When had former slaveholders invited blacks to political barbecues? When had white men considered it necessary to make speeches to masses of black men or been forced to regard blacks as thinking beings with their own ideas and interests? And while the bargaining and barbecues proceeded on the economic and political fronts, white Virginians paid taxes so that tens of thousands of black (and white) children could learn the alphabet, write their first sentences, and read their first books and newspapers.

Of course, many of the new rights and privileges the freedmen enjoyed in the 1860s eventually were eroded by southern white resistance and northern white indifference. As the decades passed, fewer and fewer black men voted or held office. Fewer black children were given the opportunity to read and write. The hard task of making a living and supporting a family required former slaves, and many poorer whites, to accept working conditions and labor arrangements that promised little progress toward a higher standard of living.

Nevertheless, even under the worst postwar conditions, black men and women were never again slaves. They were citizens now, not chattel. Their marriages and families were never again broken because some slaveholder had lost too much money on a horse race and recouped his losses by selling his human property. Slavery was in the past. Moreover, at least one generation of American blacks enjoyed freedoms and rights—and power—that none of their ancestors in America had ever known. In some parts of Virginia black voters controlled entire counties or towns for twenty-five years before the nation allowed these freedmen to be pushed back into political impotence. But their slide, as long and painful as it was, was never a return all the way back into human bondage. The postwar world for black and white Virginians never did live up to the promise of the Declaration of Independence. But it was different from anything slaveholders and slaves had ever known before.[8]

Historians have frequently speculated on the impact of factionalism in southern Republican parties during Reconstruction. "Was southern Republicanism so radical that it alienated too many whites to succeed? Or was it so moderate and so tainted by internal racism that it failed to mould the kind of strength and organization [among blacks] necessary to success?"[9] In the case of Virginia, blacks enthusiastically supported the party and voted in large numbers for its candidates. More than 80 percent of blacks who were registered to vote usually did vote, and the evidence indicates that the proportion of blacks who registered to vote was at least equal to the proportion of whites who registered.[10] So, the second possibility does not hold.

The first possibility seems more likely as an explanation. Understandably, the freedmen's fear and suspicion of native whites so soon after blacks had been bound in slavery inclined freedmen to trust only each other and radical northern whites. Moreover, northern-born white Republicans in Virginia doubted the good intentions of native whites, usually for solid reasons, and stood to gain politically if these native whites were excluded from positions of power within the state's Republican party. A political party composed of such disparate elements with so many conflicting interests, especially a new party with a limited history of success and internal discipline, was bound to suffer more than most from factionalism.[11]

Among native whites the resentment toward outspoken and critical northern reformers that had built up since the 1830s and southern white embarrassment at their invasion, defeat, and occupation by northern armies predisposed Virginia whites to regard Republicans, black or northern, as meddling aliens. Furthermore, the Republicans' clear intention to move the Old Dominion away from its antebellum past sent a shudder through the conservative white community. This, of course, greatly increased the political, economic, and social risks for those native whites who contemplated an association with the Republican party. One of the unlikeliest of white Republicans, Colonel John Singleton Mosby, the "gray ghost of the Confederacy," bore strong witness to the pressures white men faced when they joined with Republicans. Asked if he believed in Hell, the former partisan leader "answered stonily that of course he did—that any Southerner who did not believe in it had obviously never tried to vote Republican and live in Virginia."[12]

No major second party in the Old Dominion's history ever faced a wider array of obstacles to success than the Republican party of the 1860s. Virginia Republicans, like those in the other Confederate states, suffered from a severe shortage of financial resources. This is not surprising in a party composed primarily of virtually penniless freedmen. Their poverty meant not only that campaign coffers were usually bare. It also meant that poorer Republicans, particularly black laborers, were often pressured by white employers to refrain from political activity, especially voting. Furthermore, their leaders—whether carpetbaggers, scalawags, or blacks—

were often intelligent and usually well intentioned, but they were strangers to the inner workings of Virginia politics. They did not have the network of personal contacts or the history of favors given and received that smoothed the path for politicians more experienced in Virginia affairs. They had to learn about each other and build such networks from the ground up, a formidable task in a society still staggering from the war. Partly as a result, Virginia's Republican leaders did not build a bridge to potential allies among white voters in the southwest mountains and Shenandoah Valley. Fifteen years later another group of political dissidents, white native-born Readjusters, built such a bridge between the two groups and won control of the state's political machinery. [13]

Moreover, Virginia's Republicans inevitably were identified in the minds of most white Virginians with the conquering North. The Republicans' ties to prominent northerners like Charles Sumner, Thaddeus Stevens, Benjamin Butler, Henry Wilson, and the Union Leagues automatically earned them the suspicion and even hatred of tens of thousands of white voters, many of them Confederate veterans. To a proud people tasting the ashes of defeat, the very word "Republican" stirred bitter memories of sons and husbands buried, homes burned, and hopes blasted. When conservative whites finally girded themselves to battle Republicans for control of state politics, they battled with an unusual fervor. Unfortunately for southern Republicans, their northern allies were more powerful and aggressive in war than in peace. Northern Republicans in general eventually tired of Reconstruction politics and the seemingly endless wrangling south of the Potomac. Their unwillingness to maintain martial law indefinitely and to give greater support to their southern associates contributed to the Virginia party's troubles.

Even more damaging to Republicans' prospects than their poverty, their inexperience in state politics, their isolation from potential allies, and their identification with the hated North was the perverse and powerful racism that ran so powerfully through the white community. The great majority of the Old Dominion's white citizens could not take seriously a political party composed primarily of former slaves. [14] This refusal to grant legitimacy to the new Republican party hampered every move Republicans attempted to make. James W. Hunnicutt, the radical white leader, pointed up the difference between the all-white politics of Democrats and Whigs before the war and the situation in the Underwood constitutional convention. Did antebellum Virginia newspapers, he asked, "ever advise the Democrats to turn off, to drive out, to starve and to punish, any one of the party that voted the Whig ticket?" "Was there ever such political intolerance known, read of, heard of, or thought of by men, as the political intolerance that is put in exercise by the opposition."[15]

Until former Confederates could bring themselves to think of the freedmen (and to a lesser extent, the carpetbaggers and scalawags) as thinking, feeling men with real interests to be protected, Republicans faced a long, uphill struggle for legitimacy. Most white conservatives were willing to accept almost any alternative to Republican rule, even continued military occupation. Under these circumstances, only a prolonged and expensive commitment by the North to protect and nurture Reconstruction could have preserved the reforms that southern Republicans had so painfully gained. Unfortunately, the combination of southern white racism and the North's flagging reform spirit spelled political doom for Republicans in Virginia and other states.

With so many heavy burdens to bear, it is remarkable that the Republican party in Virginia managed to accomplish as much as it did. Of course, one of the themes of this book is that Republicans, despite their numerous problems, might have achieved even more—not enough to dominate Virginia politics into the twentieth century, perhaps, but enough to form a stronger, broader-based party that could have protected their interests into the 1870s and 1880s. Given the failure of Reconstruction Republicans in every Confederate state by the 1870s, this may be all that could have been expected from the Virginia Republicans.[16]

Even the most sympathetic observer of the state's Republicans comes finally to the conclusion that they contributed to their own demise as the party in power.[17] Finding the farthest limits of politically feasible reform in the postwar world proved to be a knotty, troublesome task. In the first two years of Reconstruction, Virginia Republicans managed to push those limits beyond the vision of some of their early leaders. Their conservative Unionist chieftans of 1865, mostly native whites led by Governor Francis H. Pierpont, initially led them down a path of very minimal changes. Governor Pierpont, in the first several months after the war, would have been satisfied with the death of slavery, the restoration of the Union, and a few cosmetic reforms, such as legalized slave marriages and a repudiation of the Confederate debt. If Republicans had followed this lead, the more conservative white Unionists of 1865 would have consigned their future black allies to a separate, castelike status—somewhere between slavery and citizenship—marked by vagrancy laws, gang labor reminiscent of slavery, planter combinations to control black workers, lily-white political parties, and demeaning laws to separate blacks from the larger community.[18] Fortunately for black Virginians and their more reform-minded white allies, their own vigorous protests and similar complaints from throughout the former Confederacy led Congress to reject the minimalist Reconstruction policy offered by President Johnson and Governor Pierpont in the latter's first months in Richmond.

The Old Dominion's Republicans avoided this early pitfall but then divided over which direction to take next. Some Republicans, notably Hunnicutt, Underwood, and other radicals, proposed to build the party by removing conservative whites from the political process and by developing Republican strength from within—by getting every potential Republican voter to the polls on election day, by stressing party discipline, and by holding to a strict party platform of reform. Those committed to this approach believed they could win elections with strongly dedicated Republicans alone, without the aid of former slaveholders and Confederates who would be lukewarm about Republican ideals.

A second strategy—championed by Governor Pierpont, John Minor Botts, Franklin Stearns, and northern party leaders—was to unite freedmen and northern immigrants on the one hand with native-born former Whigs and Unionists on the other hand. This approach would require former political enemies to embrace within the same organization—a definite problem—but it could also add tens of thousands of native whites, many of them wealthy and prominent, to the Republican cause.[19]

A third possibility, one that would prove very successful fifteen years later, was to join white farmers and herdsmen from the Valley and southwestern mountains with the black and white Republicans of the tidewater. By dealing with the economic grievances of the Valley and southwest, Republicans might have added enough native white votes to their totals to sweep into office. Such a coalition, if formed early during Reconstruction, might have enabled Republicans to build a powerful and stable party, able to withstand Conservative assaults for decades.

As it turned out, the third possibility was never seriously attempted during Reconstruction. A few southwestern mountain whites did join the party, and they even elected a handful of delegates to the Underwood convention of 1867–68. But the thought of joining with recently freed slaves was just as repugnant in the mountains as it was in the tidewater, and most voters of the southwest remained in the Conservative fold in the 1860s. In addition, black and carpetbagger Republicans of the eastern part of the state had few contacts in the southwest and were generally unfamiliar with conditions in the mountains. Party leaders like Senator Henry Wilson and Horace Greeley on the national level or Wells and Hunnicutt within the state would have had to take the initiative, to offer economic incentives, to tour and campaign in the southwest to overcome the political inertia in those counties. But that rarely happened, and the potential in this strategy was not fully developed until the Readjuster-Republican coalition of the late 1870s and 1880s.

The second possibility—adding native white Whigs and Unionists to the primarily black and carpetbagger Republican organization—was pursued vigorously by Republican "cooperators" like Governor Pierpont and John Minor Botts and by northern Republicans like Wilson, Greeley, and John Jay. In the summer of 1867 and again in the winter and spring of 1869 moderates attempted to join the two groups and create a political majority in the Old Dominion. Whether a successful alliance with more moderate native whites would have resulted in better times for black and white Republicans in the 1870s and 1880s is something we will never know. Some historians believe that native whites—no matter how moderate or Whiggish they seemed—would not have been as determined to reform the Old Dominion as Republicans were.[20] Perhaps—even probably—these scholars are correct in their skepticism. On the other hand, they sometimes assume that moderate native whites—the old antebellum Whigs and conditional Unionists—would have quickly and easily dominated the party and turned it away from its reform path. This implies that more radical black and white Republicans could be easily deceived and manipulated. In Virginia the proposed union of Republicans with centrist whites would have placed the latter group in a clear minority position. Well over half of all Republican votes would have come from black freedmen, and their desire for change would have been seconded by radical white leaders. In other words, the old Whig element would have found it very difficult to dominate a Republican party in which they were a minority and to turn the organization to their own uses at the expense of the rank-and-file voters, especially when those voters regarded them with some suspicion, were keenly aware of their own interests, and were already organized. In any event, Virginia's Republicans doubtless would have benefited more if they had been uncomfortable allies of moderate whites who owed their election to office to radical black and white voters than if—as happened—Republicans were shut out almost entirely from the circle of political power by other, more conservative white politicians who owed them nothing.

The freedmen's and white radicals' suspicion of former Confederates claiming to be the black man's friend had an air of inevitability about it, of course. Politics may make strange bedfellows, but this proposed union of freedmen and their former masters seemed remarkably perverted to many Republicans, especially those who had suffered the pains and indignities of bondage. The marriage was never consummated, and the result was electoral defeat in 1869, leaving Virginia as one of only two states of the Reconstruction South that failed to elect a Republican governor and state legislature after readmission to Congress (Tennessee being the other).

The exclusionary strategy was successful in 1867 when native whites were still reeling from the devastation of war and had not yet organized themselves into a political party. Conservative apathy and drift were only temporary, however. The Republican victory in the 1867 election of delegates to the constitutional convention shocked native whites and spurred them into action. By early 1868 former Democrats and Whigs had joined in a new Conservative party, and the possibility of another Republican victory based on party discipline and Conservative inertia vanished.

Radicals like Hunnicutt, Wells, and many freedmen and carpetbaggers failed to sense the changed conditions of the contest, however. They continued to spurn advances by centrist native whites and clung to the strategy of exclusion, depending on disfranchisement of former Confederates and internal unity to carry the day. Radical hopes and dreams of political power crashed around their heads in 1869 when the former Whigs and Unionists they had twice rejected drifted rightward at the invitation of Conservatives and melded into the new Conservative–True Republican alliance. Governor Wells and his radical allies were soundly defeated, and their proscriptive constitution was amended to remove the disabling clauses.

Thus, Virginia's Conservatives managed to do something the state's regular Republicans would not do—bend a little in order to gain a lot, ally with people with whom they preferred not to associate in normal times, give up some of their goals in order to attain others. The Old Dominion's Conservatives operated at a level of political experience and maturity that the young Republican party had not yet achieved. Only a century later would Virginia Republicans match their opponents in organization, experience, and the long view of politics.

In another southern state with a black majority or a Republican majority of blacks and mountain whites, the policy followed by men like Hunnicutt and Wells might have succeeded. Under those conditions Republicans might have built a successful political party without diluting their membership with former Confederates and slaveholders. But in the Old Dominion, with its politically active native white majority and conservative tradition, dependence on party discipline by a minority was sure to fail. The 1869 campaign brought Republican control of Virginia, brief as it was, to a close and branded the state's Republicans as merely a radical minority.[21]

Nevertheless, Republicans had accomplished some of their goals before they were overwhelmed in 1869. With the help of the Republican majority in Congress, they had brought black Virginians into state political life and even elected some former slaves to the General Assembly. They had also written a new constitution, a document that made numerous needed reforms, provided a system of free public schools, democratized the government of Virginia in several respects, and served the state well for over thirty years. And despite their political burdens and failures, they had established the nucleus of a party that would champion the forgotten black man for several decades and, a century hence, would become once again a powerful factor in state politics. The Republican party of Reconstruction, then, helped to move Virginia away from its Old South past and into the modern age. It was a constructive force in the history of the Old Dominion.

Appendix
Notes
Bibliography
Index

Members of the Underwood Convention of 1867–68

Blacks	Carpetbaggers	Scalawags	Conservatives
Andrews, W. H.	Allen, E.	Babcock, L. E.	Berkeley, N.
Barrett, J. D.	Ayer, R. S.	Bowden, H. M.	Broadus, J. W.
Bayne, T.	Clements, J. H.	Carr, D. C.	Campbell, J. T.
Bland, J. W. D.	Curtiss, G. G.	Dickey, W. R.	Cowan, G. R.
Breedlove, W.	Dixon, J. W.	Eastham, J. B.	Duncan, C.
Brown, J.	Dodge, S. M.	Flanagan, A. H.	French, J. M.
Canada, D.	Hine, O. E.	Fuqua, S.	Gibbony, J.
Carter, J. B.	James, W.	Hawxhurst, J.	Gibson, E.
Cox, J.	Leahy, W.	Hunnicutt, J. W.	Gibson, J. C.
Hodges, W. A.	Lee, L., Jr.	Lydick, W. H.	Gravatt, J. J.
Holmes, J. R.	Maddox, S. F.	Massey, E. W.	Harris, A. W.
Jones, P. K.	Morrissey, J.	Milbourn, A.	Harrison, P.
Kelso, S. F.	Nash, E.	Parr, W. J.	Hunter, F. S. C.
Lindsay, L.	Nickerson, L. M.	Reed, W. R.	Kennerly, J. M.
Morgan, P. G.	Platt, J. H., Jr.	Snead, E. K.	Lee, H. H.
Moseley, W. Q.	Poor, F. W.	Staley, D.	Lewis, B. F.
Moss, F.	Porter, C. H.	Thomas, C. Y.	Liggitt, J. N.
Nelson, E.	Swan, G. W.	Thompson, C. L.	Linkenhoker, L.
Norton, D. M.	Thayer, L. C.	Wicker, H. A.	McLaughlin, W.
Robinson, J.	Toy, J. C.	Williamson, S. D.	Marye, J. L., Jr.
Taylor, J. T. S.	Underwood, J. C.	Winston, F. A.	Mauzy, F.
Teamoh, G.	White, D. B.		Mayse, J.
Toler, B.	Williams, J. H.*		Owen, W. L.

Blacks	Carpetbaggers	Scalawags	Conservatives
Watson, J.			Plaster, G. E.
			Robertson, M. F.
			Robertson, W. H.
			Rust, G. W.
			Scott, R. T.
			Seay, S. R.
			Southall, J. C.
			Taylor, W. F. B.
			Thompson, J. H.
			Waddell, J. A.
			Watson, M.
			Wilson, N.
			Woodson, J. C.
24	23	21	36

Note: R. S. Beazley did not take his seat and was not replaced in the convention.

*J. H. Williams was a carpetbagger but consistently voted with the Conservatives and was regarded by Republicans as a Conservative.

Notes

Introduction

1. A more detailed summary of the traditional interpretation of Reconstruction may be found in Eric Foner, *Reconstruction*, xix–xxi.

2. WPA, *Negro in Virginia*, 231

3. See Eric Foner, *Reconstruction*, xxi–xxii.

4. See Engs, *Freedom's First Generation*; McDonough, *Schofield*; Hodges, *Free Man of Color*, and the three essays by Lowe, Hickin, and Shifflett in Younger, *Governors of Virginia*.

5. The best historiographical treatment of postrevisionism is Eric Foner, "Reconstruction Revisited." A concise statement of the postrevisionist viewpoint is in Benedict, "Preserving the Constitution."

Chapter 1

1. Like many northerners, western Virginians feared the "slave power" more than they did slavery (Gara, "Slavery and the Slave Power").

2. Ambler, *Sectionalism in Virginia*. For refinements of Ambler's work, see Richard O. Curry, *House Divided*.

3. *Wheeling Intelligencer*, Oct. 1, Dec. 12, 1856. See also Lowe, "Republican Party in Antebellum Virginia."

4. Abbott, "Yankee Farmers in Northern Virginia"; George Winston Smith, "Ante-Bellum Attempts of Northern Business Interests to 'Redeem' the Upper South"; Rice, "Eli Thayer and the Friendly Invasion of Virginia"; Lowe, "Republican Newspapers in Antebellum Virginia"; *Wheeling Intelligencer*, May 3, June 4, Dec. 24, 1859; *Brooklyn (N.Y.) Transcript*, reprinted in *Wheeling Intelligencer*, July 21, 1859; Lowe, "Republican Party in Antebellum Virginia," 273–75.

5. *Proceedings of the First Three Republican National Conventions*, 111–24 and passim; Halstead, *Three against Lincoln*, 150–66; *Richmond Examiner*, Aug. 15, Oct. 24, 1860; *Richmond Daily Dispatch*, July 28, 1860; *Alexandria (Va.) Gazette*, July 28, 1860;

Wheeling Intelligencer, Oct. 12, 13, 30, 1860; *The Tribune Almana and Political Register, 1861*, 50–51; Burnham, *Presidential Ballots*, 816–42, 852–64.

6. See Lowe, "Republican Newspapers in Antebellum Virginia," 282–84; Lowe, "Republican Party in Antebellum Virginia," 279n and passim; and Lowe, "Republicans, Rebellion, and Reconstruction," chaps. 1–4.

7. Shanks, *Secession Movement in Virginia*, 190, 204.

8. *Wheeling Intelligencer*, Apr. 15, May 6, 1861; *Wellsburg Herald*, Apr. 26, May 10, 1861, and various other issues. Most unconditional Unionists, no matter what their previous political affiliation, sooner or later drifted into the Republican party. See Harris, "The Southern Unionist Critique of the Civil War," for the views of such white southerners.

9. Hall, *Rending of Virginia*, 126–27; *New York Times* and *New York World*, reprinted in *Wheeling Intelligencer*, Apr. 13, 1861.

10. Lewis, *How West Virginia Was Made*, 14–23; Ambler, *Francis H. Pierpont*, 80.

11. "Proceedings of the First Convention of the People of Northwestern Virginia at Wheeling, Virginia," in Lewis, *How West Virginia Was Made*, 35–71. The best secondary account of the Union and statehood movements is Richard O. Curry, *House Divided*.

12. The official vote on secession was never ascertained. Governor John Letcher, using official returns and estimates for some counties not reporting, announced the total Virginia vote as 128,884 to 32,134. The authority on the statehood movement, however, has estimated the northwestern Unionist vote as 34,677. In any case, secession was easily approved by a ratio of about three or four to one (*Richmond Enquirer*, June 18, 1861; Richard O. Curry, *House Divided*, 141–47).

13. The only full-length biography is Ambler, *Francis H. Pierpont*; see also Lowe, "Francis Harrison Pierpont." Late in life Pierpont changed the spelling of his name from Peirpoint to Pierpont; to avoid confusion I have adopted the form used by his biographer.

14. Autobiographical sketch in Francis H. Pierpont Papers, Brock Collection, Henry E. Huntington Library, San Marino, Calif.

15. Randall, "The Partition of Virginia," in Randall, *Constitutional Problems under Lincoln*, 433–76.

16. "Journal of the Second Convention," in Lewis, *How West Virginia Was Made*, 78–157; *Richmond Enquirer*, June 25, 1861.

17. The Cameron and Smith letters are reprinted in Ambler, *Francis H. Pierpont*, appendix. Lincoln's address is in Basler, *Collected Works of Lincoln* 4:427–28.

18. Basler, *Collected Works of Lincoln* 6:26–28; Isaiah Woodward, "Opinions of President Lincoln and His Cabinet on Statehood for Western Virginia." Thaddeus Stevens, the outspoken Pennsylvania radical Republican of postwar Reconstruction, did not accept Lincoln's reasoning: "If ten men fit to save Sodom can elect a Governor and other State officers for and against the eleven hundred thousand Sodomites in Virginia, then the democratic doctrine that the majority shall rule is discarded and dangerously ignored" (*Congressional Globe*, 38th Cong., 1st sess., 317–18).

19. Lewis, *How West Virginia Was Made*, 142n–143n; *Congressional Globe*, 37th Cong., 1st sess., 5–6, 103–9.

20. The best treatment of wartime thinking on Reconstruction is Belz, *Reconstruct-*

ing the Union; see esp. pp. 9, 14–15. The Virginia experiment was specifically mentioned when the Unionist government of Tennessee was established in 1862 (Maslowski, *Treason Must Be Made Odious*, 28).

21. Bates to A. F. Ritchie, Aug. 12, 1861, in Lewis, *How West Virginia Was Made*, 219–20. The similarities between this and Lincoln's "Ten Percent Plan" are obvious. See also Bates to John J. Jackson, Jr., May 7, 1862, in Attorney General's Letter Books, National Archives, Washington, D.C.

22. *New York Times*, June 27, 1861; *Congressional Globe*, 37th Cong., 3d sess., pt. 1, 37–38 (see ibid., 1st sess., 263, 142–44, for similar remarks of Congressman James Doolittle of Wisconsin and Senator Henry Lane of Indiana); Samuel Colver to Pierpont, June 25, 1861, Francis H. Pierpont Executive Papers, Virginia State Library and Archives; *Wheeling Intelligencer*, Mar. 5, 1862; "Journal of the Second Convention," in Lewis, *How West Virginia Was Made*, 103–4, 166. Belz, *Reconstructing the Union*, 30, found that "many Congressmen" regarded the Restored regime in Virginia as a model for Reconstruction in other states.

23. The phrase "rehearsal for Reconstruction" was first used by Willie Lee Rose in her account of that name dealing with wartime Reconstruction in the Sea Islands of South Carolina.

24. See Richard O. Curry, *House Divided*; Ambler, *Francis H. Pierpont*; Randall, "The Partition of Virginia," 433–76.

25. Francis West to Pierpont, July 13, 1863, Gillet F. Watson to Pierpont, Nov. 12, 1863, Pierpont Executive Papers; *Alexandria Gazette*, May 20, Oct 12, Nov. 12, 16, 1863, Jan. 7, June 25, 1864; James, "Establishment of Freedman's Village in Arlington"; Chambers, "Notes on Life in Occupied Norfolk."

26. Ambler, *Francis H. Pierpont*, chaps. 18–20; Lowe, "Republicans, Rebellion, and Reconstruction," chap. 4.

27. Butler, *Private and Official Correspondence*, vols. 3–5, passim; Ambler, *Francis H. Pierpont*, chap. 19; Pierpont Executive Papers, 1863–64, VSL.

28. Butler, *Correspondence* 4:567–74; Ambler, *Francis H. Pierpont*, chap. 19; Johnson, "Contraband Trade during the Last Year of the Civil War," 641; Gordon, *War Diary*, 379–80. Even a sympathetic biographer has criticized Butler's Norfolk activities; see Trefousse, *Ben Butler*, 166.

29. Pierpont to Butler, Jan. 11, 1864, Secretary of War Edwin Stanton, Jan. 20, 1864, in Butler, *Correspondence* 3:282–84; Pierpont to Lincoln, Jan. 16, 1864, Pierpont Executive Papers, VSL; Pierpont, *Letter of Governor Peirpoint*; Beale, *Diary of Edward Bates*, 386–87, 393–94.

30. Lincoln to Butler, Aug. 9, 1864, in Basler, *Collected Works of Lincoln* 7:487–88; Trefousse, *Ben Butler*, 166–73; Mallam, "Grant-Butler Relationship," 266. Butler's successor, General George H. Gordon, worked smoothly with Governor Pierpont and reversed many of Butler's actions (*Alexandria Gazette*, Jan. 11, Feb. 16, 24, 1865; Charles H. Porter to Pierpont, Feb. 28, 1865, Pierpont Papers, Brock Collection, Henry E. Huntington Library). Unionist Governor Andrew Johnson of occupied Tennessee experienced similar problems of overlapping military and civil authority (Maslowski, *Treason Must Be Made Odious*, 20).

31. Herman Belz found that Congress also objected to the military government in

some parts of Restored Virginia (Belz, *Reconstructing the Union*, 115–16; see also pp. 40–42).

32. *Congressional Globe*, 38th Cong., 1st sess., 6, 12, 332, 526, 847–50, 1675–78, 2311–23, 2424–25. Even Virginia's senators were later denied their seats in the second session of the 38th Congress (action of Feb. 17, 1865, ibid., 2d sess., 845–49, 1433–35). The Virginians received belated and useless support from the 43d Congress, which ruled that all persons residing behind Confederate lines were rebels in the eyes of the law. Thus, only those persons within Union lines were entitled to vote (Randall, *Constitutional Problems under Lincoln*, ix).

33. *Alexandria Gazette*, May 28, 1864; Mayer, *Republican Party*, 115–17; *Proceedings of the First Three Republican National Conventions*, 175–93, 203–25.

34. Pierpont's account of this period is in *Richmond Southern Intelligencer*, June 21, 1879. In December 1863 Secretary of the Treasury Chase and his supporters, impatient with Lincoln's moderate policies, briefly considered Pierpont as a potential candidate to oppose Lincoln for the Republican nomination in 1864 (Randall, *Lincoln the President* 4:96). This may explain Chase's close cooperation with the Restored governor.

35. *Journal of the House of Delegates, of the State of Virginia, for the Session of 1863–4*, 3–4, 28, 32; *Journal of the Senate of the State of Virginia, for the Sessions of 1863, 4 & 5*, 3–4, 36–38 (hereafter cited as *House Journal* and *Senate Journal*).

36. *Acts of the General Assembly*, 1863–64, 4–8; *New York Times*, supplement, Dec. 19, 1863 (misdated Dec. 12).

37. *Journal of the Constitutional Convention Which Convened at Alexandria . . .* , 3–4 (hereafter cited as *Convention Journal*).

38. Two clauses limited voting and officeholding (Thorpe, *Federal and State Constitutions* 7:3854–55). One required an oath of allegiance to the United States and Restored governments and a declaration that the swearer had not aided the rebellion since Jan. 1, 1864. This provision would eliminate most Virginians from politics, but the General Assembly could drop the voting restriction whenever it was thought safe to do so. The second clause barred from voting and officeholding all officers, military or civil (except for county officials), who had served the Confederate national or state governments. Only a constitutional amendment could remove this disability from officers.

39. By omitting any reference to race, the convention implied segregated schools. Not until 1870, however, would the state finally provide funds for public education (see Fraser, "William Henry Ruffner and the Establishment of Virginia's Public School System").

40. The democratization was for whites only, however. The delegates, like most white Americans in the North and South, were not ready to consider black suffrage in 1864. The 1851 and 1864 constitutions are in Thorpe, *Federal and State Constitutions* 7:3829–71.

41. *Convention Journal*, 41–49; Pierpont, "History of the Reorganization of the Restored Government of Virginia," 356–57. W. J. Cowing, editor of the *Alexandria Virginia State Journal* and a participant in Restored government affairs, indicated that Pierpont himself lobbied for several days against submission of the charter to the voters (*Alexandria Virginia State Journal*, Aug. 17, 1865).

42. Thomas, *Confederate State of Richmond*, chaps. 11–12.

43. Campbell, "Papers," 69–74; Basler, *Collected Works of Lincoln* 8:386–89, 399n, 405–8; Campbell, *Reminiscences and Documents*; Nicolay and Hay, *Abraham Lincoln* 10:220–28; *American Annual Cyclopaedia and Register of Important Events, 1865,* 798; Ambler, *Francis H. Pierpont,* 253–60; Randall, *Lincoln the President* 4:353–59; Beale, *Diary of Gideon Welles* 2:279–80; Welles, *Civil War and Reconstruction* 1:186–93, 196–99.

44. *Alexandria Gazette,* Apr. 10, 11, 1865; Leech, *Reveille in Washington,* 381–82.

Chapter 2

1. Many Virginians who called themselves Unionists in the winter and spring of 1861 finally did join the Confederacy (i.e., the so-called conditional Unionists). The word "Unionist" is used here to refer to those who remained loyal to the United States throughout the conflict and joined the Republican party either during or after the war. Thus, "Unionist" is used interchangeably with "Republican" for the postwar years unless otherwise specified.

2. Beale, *Diary of Gideon Welles* 2:281–82, 291.

3. Richardson, *Messages and Papers of the Presidents* 6:213–15. Pierpont, like Governor Andrew Jackson Hamilton of Texas and unlike most of the other southern governors who served under President Johnson in 1865, had been an unconditional and consistent Unionist throughout the war. See Carter, *When the War Was Over,* 25–27, for a description of these governors.

4. The journey is described by Pierpont's daughter Anna Pierpont Siviter in her *Recollections of War and Peace,* 154–63.

5. Pierpont's own account of early Reconstruction is in the *Richmond Southern Intelligencer,* June 21, 1879; also see Siviter, *Recollections,* 196. President Johnson's May 29 amnesty proclamation and general plan of Reconstruction is printed in Edward McPherson, *Political History of the United States,* 9–10. Except for this one interview, the governor and the president never discussed Reconstruction, and Pierpont later complained that he had received no instructions or advice of any kind from the White House during Johnson's tenure. In fact, the two men met only once afterward, and then not on business, according to Pierpont's 1879 account. Governor Benjamin Perry of South Carolina also had little contact with the president (Carter, *When the War Was Over,* 30–31). Pierpont's complaint supports the criticism of Johnson in Eric McKitrick's *Andrew Johnson and Reconstruction,* 199–200.

6. Reid, *After the War,* 19–20; Dennett, *South As It Is,* 4–5, 46. See also Squires, *Unleashed at Long Last,* chap. 4.

7. Trowbridge, *South,* 82, 100–101.

8. *Report of the Joint Committee on Reconstruction* 64.

9. Trowbridge, *South,* 209–10, 233.

10. Chesson, *Richmond,* 58–60; Dennett, *South As It Is,* 8; Flournoy, *Calendar of Virginia State Papers* 11:436–38.

11. WPA, *Negro in Virginia,* 216; comments of a former Virginia slave in Duke and Jordan, *Richmond Reader,* 136.

12. The standard work on the bureau is Bentley, *History of the Freedmen's Bureau.*

More recently, postrevisionist historians have indicted the bureau for its alleged favoritism toward local whites and its conservative attitudes. While the racial views of bureau officers certainly did vary, the postrevisionist criticism seems unduly harsh, for the bureau struggled mightily to ease the freedmen's transition from slavery to freedom. For the postrevisionist view, see McFeely, *Yankee Stepfather*; Gerteis, *From Contraband to Freedman*; Litwack, *Been in the Storm So Long*, esp. p. 386.

13. Lucy Chase to "Dear home folks," Feb. 7, 1863, in Swint, *Dear Ones at Home*, 43. The Virginia branch of the bureau is examined in three able works by William T. Alderson: "The Freedmen's Bureau and Negro Education in Virginia," "The Freedmen's Bureau in Virginia," and "The Influence of Military Rule and the Freedmen's Bureau on Reconstruction in Virginia." For the everyday activities of a Virginia bureau agent, see Mugleston, "Freedmen's Bureau and Reconstruction in Virginia." For the bureau's mixed record of success in other states, see Abbott, *Republican Party and the South*, 62–63.

14. Carter, *When the War Was Over*, 214; Reid, *After the War*, 298; *Debates and Proceeding, 1867*, 155, 168, 163; Perman, *Emancipation and Reconstruction*, 22. Eric Foner, *Reconstruction*, 150, 168, agrees that most blacks supported the bureau and that most native whites resented it.

15. Dennett, *South As It Is*, 366–67; *Debates and Proceeding, 1867*, 168.

16. Franklin Stearns, a Vermont native who had prospered in Richmond since the 1830s, was a banker, landowner, and proprietor of a large distillery. Briefly jailed for his Unionism in 1861, he had remained in Richmond during the war and would become a powerful Republican during Reconstruction. Normally, Stearns worked behind the scenes politically, leaving public office to others (Siviter, *Recollections*, 234, 384; Leslie Winston Smith, "Richmond during Presidential Reconstruction," 122; Chesson, *Richmond*, 109).

17. *Richmond Whig*, May 27, 1865; Ambler, *Francis H. Pierpont*, 263–66; Leslie Winston Smith, "Richmond during Presidential Reconstruction," 115–16.

18. Pierpont's belief in the summer of 1865 that most of the work of Reconstruction had been accomplished by Confederate surrender was similar to President Johnson's ideas (Carter, *When the War Was Over*, 30).

19. Pierpont's attempt to build a political following by appealing to moderate whites was similar to the approaches of his counterparts in North Carolina (William W. Holden), Louisiana (James Madison Wells), and other southern states (Abbott, *Republican Party and the South*, 60, 64; Eric Foner, *Reconstruction*, 182, 189; Carter, *When the War Was Over*, 27–28). While Pierpont's Unionism and Republican party affiliation were unquestioned, his racial attitude was far removed from that of more radical Republicans. Like many white Republicans in the North and South, Pierpont was somewhat insensitive to the freedmen's condition. For example, see Pierpont to Secretary of War Edwin Stanton, Jan. 27, 1864, in Flournoy, *Calendar of Virginia State Papers* 11:424–25.

20. Chesson, *Richmond*, 61–63, 146; County Court and Grand Jury of Henrico County to Pierpont, Nov. 5, 1865, in Flournoy, *Calendar of Virginia State Papers* 11:459.

21. The 1864 constitution disfranchised all who had voluntarily aided the Confederacy since Jan. 1, 1864. The General Assembly could alter this provision, however,

whenever it thought safe to do so. In addition, this same class was disqualified for office, and all who had held office under the Confederate national or state governments
(except county officials) were disfranchised and disqualified by another clause of the constitution. The second class of penalties could be removed only by a referendum or constitutional amendment. Thus, in May and early June 1865 only those white men who
had not aided the rebellion since January 1864 and who had not held a Confederate
office—a tiny group at best—were eligible to vote and hold office. The constitution is
in Thorpe, *Federal and State Constitutions* 7:3852–71.

    22. *Fredericksburg Ledger*, June 3, 1865; *Richmond Whig*, June 12, 1865; Siviter,
Recollections, 185; Pierpont's autobiographical sketch in the Pierpont Papers, Brock Collection, Henry E. Huntington Library; Carter, *When the War Was Over*, 31–32.

    23. *Richmond Whig*, June 21, 1865; *Richmond Southern Intelligencer*, June 21, 1879.
Even some prominent northern Republicans agreed with Pierpont that Virginia Union-
ists could not and perhaps should not attempt to govern as a small minority. See Reid,
After the War, 20; Henry Winter Davis to Edward McPherson, May 27, 1865, Edward
McPherson Papers, Library of Congress.

    24. *House Journal, for the Extra Session of 1865*, 3, 6, 11–12. According to the
1864 constitution, neither the 1864–65 regular session in Alexandria nor this June session of 1865 was legitimate, for neither was large enough to comply with article 4, section 2, which required that the Assembly be composed of at least eighty delegates and
twenty senators. The failure to meet this standard would provide ammunition for Republican critics of Pierpont and the special session.

    25. *Acts of the General Assembly*, 1865, 3, 5–6. Most histories of the period confuse
the two disfranchising clauses and are not clear on who was enfranchised at what times.
For example, see Eckenrode, *Political History of Virginia during the Reconstruction*, 30.

    26. *Acts of the General Assembly*, 1865; *House Journal, for the Extra Session of 1865*,
17. The *Richmond Whig*, July 11, 1865, called Pierpont's policy "just, patriotic and liberal." See also ibid., June 21, 1865. Virginia joined several other southern states in
passing a stay law (Carter, *When the War Was Over*, 138–43). Indeed, such statutes were
not unprecedented in the South, for some antebellum legislatures had adopted similar
laws before the war.

    27. *Alexandria Gazette*, July 31, 1865; Siviter, *Recollections*, 178; Chesson, *Rich-
mond*, 93.

    28. Pierpont autobiographical sketch, Pierpont Papers, Brock Collection, Henry
E. Huntington Library; Dorris, *Pardon and Amnesty under Lincoln and Johnson*, 225; John
B. Baldwin to Pierpont, Nov. 18, 1865, Pierpont Executive Papers, VSL; Sefton, *The
United States Army and Reconstruction*, 55–56.

    29. Hickin, "John C. Underwood and the Antislavery Crusade"; Lowe, "Republi-
can Party in Antebellum Virginia," 259–79; Lowe, "Republican Newspapers in Antebellum Virginia," 282–84; *DAB*, s.v. "Underwood, John Curtiss [*sic*]"; John C.
Underwood Papers and Scrapbook, LC.

    30. Randall, *Constitutional Problems under Lincoln*, 289–91; *Alexandria Gazette*,
Feb. 27, Mar. 1, 2, May 27, July 20, 1864; Reid, *After the War*, 323–24; *American
Annual Cyclopaedia and Register of Important Events*, *1863*, 221. The United States Su-
preme Court, to the dismay of Underwood and the Unionist purchasers of confiscated

property, ruled in 1869 that such land and buildings would have to be returned to the original owner's heirs upon the death of the original owner (*Bigelow* vs. *Forrest*, *United States Reports* [9 Wallace 339]).

31. Pierpont autobiographical sketch, Brock Collection, Henry E. Huntington Library. For two public meetings, see minutes of Rockingham County meeting in *Fredericksburg Ledger*, Sept. 29, 1865, and Richmond Citizens to President Andrew Johnson, Aug. 29, 1865, in Andrew Johnson Papers, LC.

32. *Alexandria Virginia State Journal*, reprinted in *Richmond Whig*, May 31, 1865; C. Y. Thomas to Pierpont, June 28, 1865, Pierpont Executive Papers, VSL.

33. Philip A. Tracy to Pierpont, June 21, 1865, Pierpont Executive Papers, VSL; see also George Senseney to Pierpont, Aug. 7, 1865, ibid.

34. *Report of the Joint Committee on Reconstruction*, 11, 24; *Alexandria Virginia State Journal*, Aug. 17, Sept. 4, 12, 1865.

35. *Alexandria Gazette*, May 13, 1863; *Convention Journal*, 10–11; Whitelaw, *Virginia's Eastern Shore* 2:1174; *Report of the Joint Committee on Reconstruction*, 20

36. *Alexandria Gazette*, June 13, 1865. Only a few Virginia Republicans, mostly from the North, favored black suffrage for humanitarian reasons. On the other hand, many northern-born and some native Republicans were willing to accept black suffrage for political reasons. This would later be the case in other southern states (Olsen, "Reconsidering the Scalawags"). For the early positions of Virginia and Louisiana Republicans, see Abbott, *Republican Party and the South*, 63–65. Governor William G. ("Parson") Brownlow in Tennessee also called for black suffrage as early as the summer of 1865 (Carter, *When the War Was Over*, 58).

37. *Alexandria Gazette*, June 23, July 8, 1865; *Richmond Whig*, July 11, 1865. Like Alexandria, Norfolk was home to many northern immigrants before and during the war, and northern influence was probably the driving force behind the white Norfolk Republican organization. For one reference to heavy northern immigration into Norfolk, see *Report of the Joint Committee on Reconstruction*, 125.

38. *Richmond Whig*, July 6, 1865; Dennett, *South As It Is*, 5. At least two of the three signers of the Alexandria address, and possibly all three, were northern natives who had immigrated to Virginia before or during the war. W. J. Cowing, editor of the wartime Unionist *Alexandria Virginia State Journal*, had participated in the Restored government during its Alexandria tenure and may have been a New Yorker. S. Ferguson Beach was a New York native who had practiced law in Alexandria during the war and served in the Restored constitutional convention of 1864. Lysander Hill had been born and educated in Maine, served two years in the Federal infantry, and opened a law office in Alexandria in 1864 (*National Cyclopaedia of American Biography* 16:136).

39. Dennett, *South As It Is*, 41, 369; Abbott, *Republican Party and the South*, 61.

40. Trowbridge, *South*, 589; Dennett, *South As It Is*, 360; Reid, *After the War*, xv.

41. *Report of the Joint Committee on Reconstruction*, 14–15, 88 (see also pp. 9, 11, 27, 81, 96); Carter, *When the War Was Over*, 54.

42. Philip S. Foner and Walker, *Proceedings of the Black National and State Conventions* 1:80–81, 89, 102–3.

43. *Alexandria Gazette*, June 12, 1865; O'Brien, "Reconstruction in Richmond," 274–78; *Richmond Republic*, Aug. 5, 10, 1865; *Richmond Whig*, Aug. 8, 1865; Philip

S. Foner and Walker, *Proceedings of the Black State Conventions* 2:258–74; *Norfolk Post*, Aug. 12, 1865; see also Abbott, *Republican Party and the South*, 61.

44. J. R. S. Van Fleet to B. F. Butler, Aug. 1, 1865, Loyal League to Butler, Nov. 24, 1865, Benjamin F. Butler Papers, LC; O'Brien, "From Bondage to Citizenship," 328–34; Engs, *Freedom's First Generation*, 90–91; Underwood to Dr. Thomas Bayne, Sept. 27, 1865, in *Alexandria Virginia State Journal*, Oct. 5 (misdated Oct. 4), 1865.

45. Dennett, *South As It Is*, 9–10.

46. Alfred H. Terry to John C. Underwood, Sept. 30, 1865, Frederick Douglass to Underwood, Nov. 14, 1866, John C. Underwood Papers and Scrapbook.

47. O'Brien, "From Bondage to Citizenship," 286–96; Henderson, *Unredeemed City*, 82–83; Engs, *Freedom's First Generation*, 91–94. Numerous Virginia Republicans are also identified in James Douglas Smith, "Virginia during Reconstruction."

48. The interior piedmont county of Albemarle, with no large cities, few scalawags, and no carpetbaggers, was completely unaffected by the various Unionist meetings and manifestos of the summer of 1865 (Vance, "Negro in the Reconstruction of Albemarle County," 14).

49. An excellent treatment of this election is Bromberg, "Virginia Congressional Elections of 1865."

50. *Richmond New Nation*, May 9, 1867; Montague, "Letters Home to Maine from Virginia"; *Who Was Who in America: Historical Volume, 1607–1896*, s.v. "McKenzie, Lewis"; *Alexandria Virginia State Journal*, Oct. 12, 1865; Gaines, *Biographical Register of Members, Virginia State Convention of 1861, First Session*, 52–53; *Norfolk Post*, Oct. 7, 12, 1865.

51. *Norfolk Post*, Sept. 18, 20, 1865; Reid, *After the War*, 20; *Alexandria Virginia State Journal*, Sept. 22, 1865; Underwood to Andrew Johnson, July 10, 1865, Andrew Johnson Papers; *Richmond Republic*, Sept. 20, 1865.

52. Reprinted in *Richmond Republic*, Aug. 12, 1865.

53. Reid, *After the War*, 319; *Alexandria Gazette*, Oct. 21, 1865; *Richmond Republic*, Oct. 17, 1865; *Leesburg Mirror*, Oct. 5, 1865. For vote totals, see Bromberg, "Virginia Congressional Elections of 1865," 95; Maddex, "Virginia: The Persistence of Centrist Hegemony," 116. In eight southern states the 1865 vote of 247,000 was less than half of the 1860 vote of 535,000 (Carter, *When the War Was Over*, 271).

54. *Richmond Republic*, Sept. 15, Oct. 21, 1865; *Alexandria Gazette*, Nov. 17, 1865; Pierpont to J. W. Lewellen, Sept. 7, 1865, in *Fredericksburg Ledger*, Sept. 11, 1865; ibid., Sept. 22, 1865; *Richmond Whig*, Oct. 10, 1865; Bromberg, "Virginia Congressional Elections of 1865," 96–97; *Norfolk Post*, Oct. 19, 1865.

55. *Richmond Whig*, Oct. 20, 1865; *Fredericksburg News*, Dec. 7, 1865; Carter, *When the War Was Over*, 65–67.

56. Wertenbaker, *Norfolk*, 263; *Norfolk Day Book* clipping, n.d., in John C. Underwood Papers and Scrapbook.

57. Gillet F. Watson and J. M. Humphreys to Thaddeus Stevens, Dec. 5, 1865, Thaddeus Stevens Papers, LC; *Hampton True Southerner*, Nov. 30, 1865.

58. Reid, *After the War*, 429–38.

59. Maddex, "Virginia: The Persistence of Centrist Hegemony," 115–16.

60. Many freedmen, unwilling to obligate themselves for long periods of time and believing they would soon be given land by the Federal government, broke their labor contracts in the fall of 1865. Pierpont probably feared the effect that coercive wage and contract laws would have on northern opinion. The black codes of some other southern states were arousing widespread concern in the North. See Alderson, "Influence of Military Rule and the Freedmen's Bureau on Reconstruction in Virginia," 169–70; Reid, *After the War*, 335–36; Wilson, *Black Codes of the South*.

61. *Senate Journal*, 1865–66, 11–36. For other comments by Pierpont on railroad consolidation, see Trowbridge, *South*, 234n. The voters had evidently balloted on the assumption that disqualified candidates could be elected if the General Assembly would amend the constitution before proceeding to other business—a virtual certainty. But being disqualified, these legislators could not lawfully amend the constitution. Only the Republicans complained of this maneuver.

62. One Virginia Unionist, Jacquelin M. Wood, told the Joint Committee on Reconstruction a few weeks later that Governor Pierpont had been popular among white conservatives "when they intended to use him; but when the time came that it suited their interests they abused him. I think they will do the same with President Johnson—use him first, and abuse him afterwards." Louisiana governor James Madison Wells suffered the same embarrassment in his state (*Report of the Joint Committee on Reconstruction*, 88; Eric Foner, *Reconstruction*, 182, 188–89, 269).

63. *Acts of the General Assembly*, 1865–66, 197; *Senate Journal*, 1865–66, 98–101, 252, 295, 300; *Report of the Joint Committee on Reconstruction*, 144–45; *House Journal*, 1865–66, 307, 416.

64. *Acts of the General Assembly*, 1865–66, 91–93. Virginia, like some other southern states, was filled with stories of a Christmas uprising by the freedmen. The Freedmen's Bureau even hired special agents to investigate the rumors. Several meetings of blacks denied the accusations, and in fact, a second Nat Turner never emerged. Many cases of Negro burglary, poaching, and property destruction were reported in late 1865, however, perhaps prompted by the freedmen's frustration at not receiving land from the government, land that some bureau agents had promised. These incidents doubtless contributed to the General Assembly's fears (Carter, "Anatomy of Fear"; *Richmond Republic*, Dec. 23, 1865; Alderson, "Influence of Military Rule and the Freedmen's Bureau on Reconstruction in Virginia," 50–52).

65. Berlin, *Freedom*, ser. 2, *Black Military Experience*, 721–23; Alderson, "Influence of Military Rule and the Freedmen's Bureau on Reconstruction in Virginia," 9, 58; Engs, *Freedom's First Generation*, 30; Henderson, *Unredeemed City*, 44, 46; Chesson, *Richmond*, 90.

66. Edward McPherson, *Political History of the United States*, 41–42; *Fredericksburg Ledger*, June 10, 1865; *Richmond Enquirer*, Jan. 26, 1866; *Hampton True Southerner*, Feb. 1, Mar. 22, 1866. On numerous occasions General Terry intervened in Virginia affairs to assure fair treatment for the freedmen. See O'Brien, "Reconstruction in Richmond," 280; Leslie Winston Smith, "Richmond during Presidential Reconstruction," 61–62. Terry's distinguished military career is outlined in Sifakis, *Who Was Who in the Civil War*, s.v. "Terry, Alfred Howe."

67. Virginia, like other upper South states, wrote its black code on an ad hoc

basis. In several lower South states, by contrast, the generally harsher black codes were the result of special committees that systematically rewrote state law (Carter, *When the War Was Over*, 217).

68. *Acts of the General Assembly, 1865–66*, 83; Alderson, "Freedmen's Bureau in Virginia," 176–77.

69. Wilson, *Black Codes of the South*, 100–102; Alderson, "Influence of Military Rule and the Freedmen's Bureau on Reconstruction in Virginia," 67–71; Wicker, "Virginia's Legitimization Act of 1866."

70. Carter, *When the War Was Over*, 177, 187, makes a similar point.

71. *Acts of the General Assembly, 1865–66*. The reactionary behavior of the first postwar General Assembly in Virginia was not unusual in the old Confederacy. For example, the first such legislature in Texas also adopted measures that stunned and disappointed Unionists in the Lone Star State. See Moneyhon, *Republicanism in Reconstruction Texas*, 49–52.

72. Underwood to Theodore Tilton, Mar. 22, 1866, John C. Underwood Papers and Scrapbook, 111; T. J. Pretlow to Thaddeus Stevens, Dec. 27, 1865, Thaddeus Stevens Papers; *Richmond Republic*, Mar. 2, 1866.

73. Carter, *When the War Was Over*, 56, describes similar disappointment among southern Unionists in other states.

Chapter 3

1. Jackson, *Negro Office-Holders in Virginia*, 30; Engs, *Freedom's First Generation*, 89, 91, 94–96, 104–5, 131; *Report of the Joint Committee on Reconstruction*, 49–51, 60–63, 54–55; *Hampton True Southerner*, Feb. 8, 15, 1866.

2. *Alexandria Gazette*, Feb. 6, 1866; *Congressional Globe*, 39th Cong., 1st sess., 873.

3. See the testimonies of John C. Underwood and Union general John W. Turner, *Report of the Joint Committee on Reconstruction*, 3, 9. McKitrick, *Andrew Johnson and Reconstruction*, emphasizes this apparently lost opportunity.

4. *Report of the Joint Committee on Reconstruction*, 150, 7.

5. Ibid., 8, 23, 14. Even with military protection the situation could be dangerous. The assistant commissioner of the Freedmen's Bureau in Virginia, a wise and sensible officer by all accounts, reported late in 1866 that eighteen blacks had been killed by Virginia whites for the year ending in September 1866. Moreover, some assaults went unreported for fear of white reprisal (Alderson, "Freedmen's Bureau in Virginia," 18).

6. *Report of the Joint Committee on Reconstruction*, 1, 8, 12, 21, 27. Some southerners would have concurred. "Never have I failed to negative all ideas of repenting ought of my past," wrote former Confederate general and future governor James L. Kemper in 1873 (Kemper to Henry A. Wise, Aug. 30, 1873, James Lawson Kemper Papers, University of Virginia Library).

7. *Report of the Joint Committee on Reconstruction*, 22, 10, 83–84, 43. As mentioned in chapter 2, the charge that the 1865 legislature had been too small to be legitimate was true. But the 1864–65 regular session in Alexandria had also been too small, and

no Unionists had complained then. Indeed, that session had elected Underwood to the United States Senate (although he had never been allowed to take his seat).

8. Ibid., 6, 18, 24, 121.

9. Ibid., 6–10, 14–17, 1–6, 10–14, 18–20, 22–25, 80–84, 114–23.

10. Ibid., 162–63, 159.

11. Ibid., 54–55, 56. There is little reason to doubt Newby's story about thumb-tying since both armies had used the same punishment for white soldiers during the recent war (Robertson, *Soldiers Blue and Gray*, 133).

12. *Report of the Joint Committee on Reconstruction*, 51, 52.

13. Ibid., 52, 58, 59.

14. Ibid., 56, 58.

15. *Richmond New Nation*, Apr. 12, 1866; *Norfolk True Southerner*, Mar. 29, 1866.

16. Underwood's attempt in September 1865 to establish a newspaper called *The Nation* was doubtless connected to the *New Nation* of 1866. See chap. 2 above.

17. *Richmond New Nation*, Mar. 22, 1866; Hunnicutt, *Conspiracy Unveiled*; *Richmond Register*, Jan. 10, 1868; *Washington (D.C.) Chronicle*, Dec. 20, 1863, Jan. 4, Feb. 13, 1864. For an analysis of Hunnicutt, John Minor Botts, and other southern Unionists, see Harris, "Southern Unionist Critique of the Civil War," 39–56.

18. *Richmond New Nation*, Mar. 22, May 24, July 19, Aug. 16, 1866, Jan. 10, 1867, Dec. 18, 1868; Abbott, *Republican Party and the South*, 64; *Alexandria Virginia State Journal*, Dec. 27, 1865; John C. Underwood to Gerrit Smith, Feb. 1, 1868, Gerrit Smith Papers, Syracuse University Library.

19. The black Rising Christian Association of Richmond donated twenty-five dollars to the *New Nation* in June, and individual subscribers from Providence, Rhode Island, and New Bedford, Massachusetts, contributed fifteen dollars more. Advertisers in the *New Nation* included Horace Greeley's *New York Tribune*, a wholesale merchant in Portland, Maine, a petroleum company in Boston, a bookseller in Philadelphia, and the Alexandria law firm of fellow Virginia Republicans Lysander Hill and George Tucker (*Richmond New Nation*, June 21, 1866).

20. Ibid., Mar. 22, 1866; Hunnicutt, *Conspiracy Unveiled*, 34–35, 131; *Alexandria Gazette*, Jan. 6, 1864.

21. *Fredericksburg Herald*, Apr. 16, 1867; *Richmond New Nation*, Mar. 22, Apr. 12, July 26, Nov. 29, 1866.

22. Cappon, *Virginia Newspapers*, 25–27.

23. Thus, the 1866 convention was not the birth of the Virginia Republican party. Eckenrode, *Political History of Virginia during the Reconstruction*, 47, and several other works make this error.

24. The Loyal Association of Alexandria had called for a state convention as early as November, and Hunnicutt and several others had echoed the suggestion in March (*Hampton True Southerner*, Nov. 24, 1865; *Richmond New Nation*, Mar. 22, 1866).

25. *Alexandria Virginia State Journal*, May 18, 1866; *Alexandria Gazette*, May 19, 1866. Underwood later claimed that he had attended no political meetings since his appointment to the district judgeship (unidentified clipping, John C. Underwood Papers and Scrapbook, 187).

26. Some Unionists, such as Virginia native John Minor Botts, had given up slav-

ery only reluctantly. Others, like the New York–born John Hawxhurst, advocated black rights on ideological grounds (Botts, *Great Rebellion*, 312–14; *Alexandria Gazette*, May 19, 1866).

27. Botts, *Great Rebellion*; Thomas, *Confederate State of Richmond*, 7–8, 82; Nevins, *Emergence of Lincoln* 2:62.

28. *Richmond Whig*, May 19, 1866; *Alexandria Gazette*, May 18, 1866; Botts, *Great Rebellion*, 339–44.

29. *Richmond Whig*, May 21, 1866; *Staunton Valley Virginian*, May 23, 1866; *Fredericksburg Ledger*, May 18, 1866; *Richmond New Nation*, May 24, 1866; *Nation* 2 (May 24, 1866): 657–58. Conservatives often labeled Unionists "ferrets" because some Republicans revealed the Confederate past of white Virginians recommended for public office (Leslie Winston Smith, "Richmond during Presidential Reconstruction," 119–20).

30. Leslie Winston Smith, "Richmond during Presidential Reconstruction," 257–58; O'Brien, "From Bondage to Citizenship," 352–53; John Hammond Moore, "Norfolk Riot," 164.

31. Leslie Winston Smith, "Richmond during Presidential Reconstruction," 259–62; O'Brien, "From Bondage to Citizenship," 334–42; John Hammond Moore, "Norfolk Riot," 155–64.

32. Engs, *Freedom's First Generation*, 89; O'Brien, "From Bondage to Citizenship," 346–49.

33. *New York Times*, May 12, 1866; *Richmond Whig*, May 10, 1866; Nichols, "United States vs. Jefferson Davis."

34. *Petersburg Index*, quoted in *Richmond Whig*, May 12, 1866; ibid., May 11, June 6, 1866; *Norfolk Virginian*, May 10, 1866; *Abingdon Virginian*, June 29, 1866; *New York Times*, June 8, 1866; *Nation* 2 (June 8, 1866): 722; Nichols, "United States vs. Jefferson Davis."

35. *Richmond New Nation*, July 5, 1866; Chesson, *Richmond*, 110; Butler, *Private and Official Correspondence* 5:623–24, 633.

36. *Richmond Enquirer*, July 6, 25, 30, 1866; *Richmond Whig*, July 6, Aug. 1, 1866; *Richmond New Nation*, July 5, 1866.

37. Ashby, *Shenandoah County, Virginia, Marriage Bonds*, 264; Wayland, *History of Shenandoah County*, 291; Lowe, "Republican Party in Antebellum Virginia," 260–62 and passim.

38. *Harrisonburg Rockingham Register*, Aug. 9, 16, 1866; *Staunton Valley Virginian*, Sept. 5, 1866; Alderson, "Influence of Military Rule and the Freedmen's Bureau on Reconstruction in Virginia," 136–38.

39. *Richmond Whig*, July 23, 1866; Underwood to Greeley, Aug. 8, 1866, Horace Greeley Papers, New York Public Library.

40. *Senate Executive Documents*, 39th Cong., 2d sess., no. 29, 17–37. In *ex parte Milligan* (4 Wallace 2) the Supreme Court had held that military commissions could not try civilians in areas remote from the theater of war. For the events surrounding the 1866 elections, see Randall and Donald, *Civil War and Reconstruction*, 587–91.

41. Maddex, *Virginia Conservatives*, 40–41; Randall and Donald, *Civil War and Reconstruction*, 589–90. Hunnicutt called the convention "a conclave of traitors and treason" (*Richmond New Nation*, Aug. 16, 1866).

42. *Southern Loyalists' Convention*, 1–2; *Richmond New Nation*, July 19, Aug 16, 1866; *Alexandria Gazette*, Aug. 24, 30, 1866.

43. Included in the delegation were John Hawxhurst, John Minor Botts, Lysander Hill, George Rye, Burnham Wardwell, Hunnicutt, and Lewis McKenzie. See *Richmond Whig*, Sept. 5, 1866, for a partial list of Virginia members. No Virginia blacks and only a handful from the rest of the country attended the convention.

44. Botts labeled the Democrats "the most wicked party, as I religiously believe, that the Almighty, in his infinite wisdom, ever permitted to exist on earth." He longed for a Republican party led by antebellum pro-Union Whigs (*Great Rebellion*, 369 and passim).

45. Meier, "Afterword" 399, stresses the problem of factionalism within the southern Republican state parties during Reconstruction.

46. *Richmond Whig*, Sept. 5–10, 1866; *New York Times*, Sept. 4–6, 1866; *Southern Loyalists' Convention*.

47. *Richmond New Nation*, July 19, Sept. 6, 20, Oct. 4, Nov. 8, 1866; Hyman, *Radical Republicans and Reconstruction*, 342–48.

48. The *Richmond Examiner*, Apr. 17, 1866, called Charles H. Lewis, the erstwhile secretary of the commonwealth and then a newly appointed aide to Pierpont, a "Despicable White" and attacked the governor for retaining him.

49. Ambler, *Francis H. Pierpont*, 285–86, 434–35; Pierpont to Waitman T. Willey, Feb. 8, 1866, Waitman T. Willey Papers, West Virginia University Library; Pierpont to William Seward, July 17, 1866, Pierpont Executive Papers, VSL.

50. Ambler, *Francis H. Pierpont*, 285–86, 434–35; *Alexandria Gazette*, Aug. 27, 1866; O'Brien, "From Bondage to Citizenship," 379; *Richmond New Nation*, Nov. 8, 1866.

51. The amendment defined citizenship to include blacks, reduced the congressional representation of those states prohibiting black suffrage, disqualified for office certain classes of Confederates, repudiated the Confederate debt, and guaranteed the Federal debt.

52. *Senate Journal*, 1866–67, 4–34. For the hostile reaction of conservative newspapers, see *Richmond Enquirer*, Dec. 7, 1866; *Leesburg Mirror*, Dec. 12, 1866.

53. Schofield, *Forty-Six Years in the Army*, 394–95; report of Richmond correspondent in *New York Times*, Dec. 31, 1866.

54. Alexander Sharp to Elihu Washburne, Dec. 19, 1866, Elihu Washburne Papers, LC; Schofield, *Forty-Six Years in the Army*, 394–95; *New York Times*, Dec. 31, 1866.

55. *Senate Journal*, 1866–67, 102–3; *House Journal*, 1866–67, 108; *Richmond Dispatch*, Jan. 10, 1867; *New York Times*, Dec. 31, 1866; Schofield, *Forty-Six Years in the Army*, 394–95.

Chapter 4

1. William B. Downey to Thaddeus Stevens, Jan. 7, 1867, Thaddeus Stevens Papers; *Richmond New Nation*, Jan. 31, Feb. 21, 1867; O'Brien, "From Bondage to Citizenship," 415–17.

2. *Richmond New Nation*, Jan. 31, Feb. 7, 1867; Shanks, "Disloyalty to the Confederacy in Southwestern Virginia"; Withers, *Autobiography of an Octogenarian*, 235, 240–42. For an excellent study of mountain Republicans throughout the South, see McKinney, *Southern Mountain Republicans*, esp. pp. 56–60.

3. The text of the Reconstruction Act is in Edward McPherson, *Political History of the United States*, 191–92.

4. Perman, *Emancipation and Reconstruction*, 55; see also Eric Foner, *Reconstruction*, 308.

5. *Charlottesville Chronicle*, Mar. 14, 1867; *Lynchburg Virginian*, Mar. 4, 1867; Wardwell to Butler, Mar. 6, 1867, Benjamin F. Butler Papers; Samuel Campline to Thaddeus Stevens, Mar. 5, 1867, Thaddeus Stevens Papers; *New York Times*, Mar. 11, 1867.

6. Ambler, *Francis H. Pierpont*, 295–96; Edward McPherson, *Political History of the United States*, 192–94 (text of second Reconstruction Act); Pierpont to Waitman T. Willey, Mar. 13, 1867, Waitman T. Willey Papers.

7. Schofield, *Forty-Six Years in the Army*, 373–76 and passim; McDonough, *Schofield*, 237–39; General Assembly to President Andrew Johnson, Mar. 8, 1867, Andrew Johnson Papers.

8. "Correspondence Relative to Reconstruction," in *Senate Executive Documents*, 40th Cong., 1st sess., no. 14, pp. 33, 42–43. See also McDonough, *Schofield*, 173; Alderson, "Influence of Military Rule and the Freedmen's Bureau on Reconstruction in Virginia," 159–60; Alderson, "Freedmen's Bureau in Virginia," 40–42.

9. Abbott, *Republican Party and the South*, 100–102; Mugleston, "Freedmen's Bureau and Reconstruction in Virginia," 51.

10. *Richmond New Nation*, Apr. 11, 1867. For similar movements in other Confederate states, see Abbott, *Republican Party and the South*, 112–13.

11. *Richmond New Nation*, Apr. 11, 18, 1867; Henderson, *Unredeemed City*, 164; Chesson, *Richmond*, 105.

12. For Whittlesey, see *New York Times*, Nov. 3, 1868; for Bowden, see *Richmond New Nation*, Oct. 3, 1867.

13. Jackson, *Negro Office-Holders in Virginia*, 2–4, 21, 25; see also Leslie Winston Smith, "Richmond during Presidential Reconstruction," 141–42. Bland was regarded by some of his fellow black Republicans with great respect, but they doubted his total commitment to radical Republicanism (see George Teamoh Journal, Carter Woodson Papers, LC).

14. Hodges, *Free Man of Color*, xv–lxxiii.

15. For Beckley, see *Richmond Enquirer*, Apr. 19, 1867.

16. *Richmond New Nation*, Apr. 18, 25, 1867; *Richmond Enquirer*, Apr. 18, 19, 1867. For Cook, see Leslie Winston Smith, "Richmond during Presidential Reconstruction," 139; O'Brien, "Reconstruction in Richmond," 274; Rachleff, *Black Labor in the South*, 31.

17. In Petersburg those blacks who had been born free or were freed before the war wielded more power and influence in local affairs than slaves emancipated in 1865. In Richmond there were several subgroups within the black community: antebellum free blacks, urban slaves, rural slaves, young and old, radical and moderate, and followers of

one leader or another. Throughout the southern states those who had been free before
the war or owned property or were educated tended more toward moderation than
slaves emancipated during the war (Henderson, *Unredeemed City*, 85; Chesson, *Richmond*, 97; Hume, "Negro Delegates to the State Constitutional Conventions of 1867–
1868," 143). For an extreme case of black class conflict, certainly not typical of affairs
in Virginia, see Holt, *Black over White*

18. *American Annual Cyclopaedia and Register of Important Events, 1867*, 758–59;
also Edward McPherson, *Political History of the United States*, 253–54.

19. *Richmond New Nation*, Apr. 25, 1867; *Richmond Enquirer*, Apr. 19, 1867. For
Hine, see James Douglas Smith, "Virginia Constitutional Convention of 1867–1868,"
54.

20. *New York Tribune*, Apr. 18, 19, 1867; *New York Times*, Apr. 19, May 18,
1867.

21. *American Annual Cyclopaedia and Register of Important Events, 1867*, 759; *Richmond New Nation*, May 9, 14, 1867; *New York Tribune*, May 10, 1867; Chesson, *Richmond*, 102–4.

22. Henderson, *Unredeemed City*, 166–68; Maddex, *Virginia Conservatives*, 52–53;
Richmond Whig, May 1, 1867.

23. Carter, *When the War Was Over*, 275, and Eric Foner, *Reconstruction*, 560, both
express some skepticism of native white moderation. On the other hand, Jack P. Maddex, Jr., stresses the importance of Virginia moderates in "Virginia: The Persistence of
Centrist Hegemony."

24. *Richmond Whig*, Apr. 22, 1867; *Richmond Enquirer*, Apr. 23, 1867. Apprecia-
tive of the *Whig*'s efforts, General Orlando Brown, head of the state's Freedmen's Bureau, and Senator Henry Wilson of Massachusetts cooperated to direct Federal
patronage to the Richmond newspaper (Abbott, *Republican Party and the South*, 133; C.
H. Lewis to Henry Wilson, Nov. 19, 1867, Henry Wilson Papers, LC; Orlando Brown
to O. O. Howard, June 13, 1867, Oliver O. Howard Papers, Bowdoin College Library).

25. Abbott, *Republican Party and the South*, 113–15, indicates that Governor John
Andrew, Senator Henry Wilson, and John Murray Forbes—all prominent Massachusetts Republicans—were cooperating closely with Pierpont and John Minor Botts
in Virginia in the spring of 1867.

26. Abbott, *Republican Party and the South*, 113–17; *New York Tribune*, Apr. 22–23,
25–26, 1867; *Richmond Enquirer*, Apr. 23, 1867. Wilson later revealed that Governor
Pierpont, who was "exceedingly anxious" to build a biracial Republican party, and about
thirty members of the General Assembly had invited him to speak in Richmond (*New
York Independent*, July 24, 1869, reprinted in Squires, *Unleashed at Long Last*, 253–55).

27. *Richmond New Nation*, Apr. 23, 1867; *Richmond Enquirer*, Apr. 20, 1867.

28. *New York Tribune*, May 15, 17, 22, 1867.

29. *New York Tribune*, Apr. 12, 1867; *Richmond New Nation*, Apr. 18, 1867; *Richmond State Journal*, June 15, 1869.

30. Schofield to Botts, Mar. 21, Apr. 6, 1867, John M. Schofield Papers, LC;
Richmond New Nation, May 9, 1867; *New York Times*, May 18, 1867; Abbott, *Republican Party and the South*, 122–23.

31. *Alexandria Virginia State Journal*, reprinted in *Richmond New Nation*, May 9, 1867; *New York Times*, May 18, 1867; *New York Tribune*, May 11, 1867; *Richmond New Nation*, May 2, 14, 1867, Dec. 18, 1868. During the war Botts, like Hunnicutt, had suffered for his Unionism at the hands of Confederates. Partly as a result, Hunnicutt had more sympathy for Botts than for many of Botts's allies. In fact, despite their differences, the two men seemed to respect and even like each other (ibid., Apr. 11, 1867).

32. Scroggs, "Southern Reconstruction"; Abbott, *Republican Party and the South*, 123; Perman, *Emancipation and Reconstruction*, 125–26. For the more typical situation of northern party nonintervention, see Klingman, *Neither Dies nor Surrenders*, 14.

33. Jay, an antebellum abolitionist and founder of the New York Union League Club, would serve as president of the American Historical Association in 1890 (*DAB*, s.v. "Jay, John").

34. See *Report of the Proceedings of the Conference at Richmond* for details of the meeting. See also remarks by Henry Wilson in *New York Tribune*, July 22, 1869.

35. See Perman, *Road to Redemption*, 23 and passim.

36. Alexander Rives to B. J. Barbour, July 10, 1867, James Barbour Papers, UVA Lib.

37. *Richmond Enquirer*, June 13, 14, 1867; *New York Tribune*, June 15, 1867; *Nation* 3 (July 18, 1867): 42.

38. *Richmond Whig*, July 2, 1867; *Richmond Enquirer*, July 3, 1867.

39. Eckenrode, *Political History of Virginia during the Reconstruction*, 75; *Richmond Enquirer*, July 6, 1867; *Richmond Whig*, July 9, 23, 25, Aug. 1, 1867; *New York Times*, July 21, 1867.

40. Rachleff, *Black Labor in the South*, 45; *Richmond Dispatch*, Aug. 1, 1867; *New York Times*, Aug. 1, 1867.

41. *Richmond New Nation*, Aug. 22, 1867. The exact numbers of both factions at the meeting are impossible to determine, but radicals, especially blacks, were apparently a large majority of all those present. Botts later estimated that 200 to 300 "white Republicans" were in Richmond for the convention (Botts to Joseph Cox, Lewis Lindsay, Fields Cook, John Oliver, et al., Dec. 24, 1867, in *Richmond Register*, Jan. 15, 1868).

42. Eyewitness account, *New York Times*, Aug. 6, 1867. Speeches such as this one by Hunnicutt led at least one northern Republican journalist to refer to him as "Hunnicutt or Honeypot, or whatever that crazy Virginia devil's name may be" (*Cincinnati Commercial*, quoted in Abbott, *Republican Party and the South*, 129).

43. Born in St. John's, Canada, in 1837, James H. Platt had received a medical education at the University of Vermont. He had settled in Petersburg in April 1865 and was a successful local businessman. He would represent Virginia in Congress from 1870 to 1875 then move to New York in 1876 (*Biographical Directory of the American Congress*, 1463; Henderson, *Unredeemed City*, 106–7, 111).

44. Alrutheus Taylor, a leading historian of black Virginians, described Bayne as "one of the shrewdest politicians of his time" (Taylor, *Negro in the Reconstruction of Virginia*, 220).

45. The Botts address is in *American Annual Cyclopaedia and Register of Important Events, 1867*, 761. At least three, and probably more, moderate blacks—Fields Cook,

Cornelius Harris, and John Oliver—expressed support for Botts's ideas (Taylor, *Negro in the Reconstruction of Virginia*, 220).

46. *Richmond New Nation*, Aug. 8, 1867. All eyewitnesses mentioned the disorderly tone of the meeting. Even Hunnicutt regretted the "great confusion and cries of disorder" and criticized the "many zealous orators who frequently forced themselves upon the assembly," doubtless a reference to Bayne (ibid.).

47. *Richmond Enquirer*, Aug. 2, 3, 8, 15, 22, 1867; *New York Tribune*, Aug. 2, 3, 1867; *New York Times*, Aug. 2, 3, 1867.

48. *New York Tribune*, Aug. 5, 1867; *Richmond New Nation*, Aug. 8, 1867; *New York Times*, Aug. 6, 1867. Sixteen months later even Hunnicutt admitted that the August convention had accomplished "little or no good." Of course, this was after he had lost in his bid for the governorship and while he was in the process of losing his newspaper (*Richmond New Nation*, Dec. 18, 1868).

49. *Charlottesville Chronicle*, Aug. 6, 1867; *Richmond Enquirer*, Aug. 3, 1867.

50. Botts to Joseph Cox et al., Dec. 24, 1867, in *Richmond Register*, Jan. 15, 1868; Lewellen to G. C. Walker, Feb. 20, 1870, Gilbert C. Walker Executive Papers, VSL.

51. *Congressional Globe*, 41st Cong., 2d sess., 335; *New York Tribune*, July 22, 1869.

52. See William E. Parrish, "Reconstruction Politics in Missouri, 1865–1870" (pp. 1–2), Thomas B. Alexander, "Political Reconstruction in Tennessee, 1865–1870" (p. 50), Richard O. Curry, "Crisis Politics in West Virginia, 1861–1870" (pp. 98–100), Jacqueline Balk and Ari Hoogenboom, "The Origins of Border State Liberal Republicanism" (pp. 226–27), all in Richard O. Curry, *Radicalism, Racism, and Party Realignment*; Warren A. Ellem, "Who Were the Mississippi Scalawags?" 240; Klingman, *Neither Dies Nor Surrenders*, pt. 1 (Florida); Moneyhon, *Republicanism in Reconstruction Texas*, 61.

53. The southern Republican party's need for experienced and prominent white supporters, not only for their numbers but also for the legitimacy they would confer on the party, is also emphasized in Summers, *Railroads, Reconstruction, and the Gospel of Prosperity*, 29.

54. The Virginia party's failure to incorporate large numbers of western white voters is seen as particularly significant in Maddex, "Virginia: The Persistence of Centrist Hegemony," 130–32. Abbott, *Republican Party and the South*, 239, adds that the national party leadership offered few economic inducements to attract the votes of most southern whites. The success of the Readjuster-Republican party in the late 1870s and early 1880s, a success based on the melding of western whites and eastern blacks, demonstrated what might have happened during Reconstruction had conditions been different.

55. Carter, *When the War Was Over*, 231, 275, doubts that the Unionist Whig element would have benefited the southern Republican parties.

Chapter 5

1. U.S. Bureau of the Census, *Statistics of the Population, Ninth Census*, 68–70. The Ninth Census summarizes the 1860 population statistics according to the post-1863

boundaries of the state. The 1870 census counted 712,089 whites (58.1 percent of the total population) and 512,841 blacks (41.9 percent) in the Old Dominion five years after the war.

2. Ibid.; U.S. Bureau of the Census, *Population of the United States in 1860, Eighth Census*, 518–20. These numbers exclude the slaves and free blacks living in cities and towns that would separate to form West Virginia in 1863.

3. WPA, *Negro in Virginia*, 189–91, 199–200.

4. Reidy, "Coming from the Shadow of the Past," 404, 410. Magdol, *Right to the Land*, 93–96.

5. Reidy, "Coming from the Shadow of the Past," 404, 414; O'Brien, "Reconstruction in Richmond," 260.

6. Dennett, *South As It Is*, 14, 364; Litwack, *Been in the Storm So Long*, 310–13; Eric Foner, *Reconstruction*, 81.

7. Dennett, *South As It Is*, 365, 48; Trowbridge, *South*, 150.

8. Dennett, *South As It Is*, 44, 51; Magdol, *Right to the Land*, 151; *Report of the Joint Committee on Reconstruction*, 124; L. Chase to "My Dear Friends," July 1, 1864, in Swint, *Dear Ones at Home*, 128. Farm wages tended to be higher in the Deep South than in Virginia (Litwack, *Been in the Storm So Long*, 411).

9. Dennett, *South As It Is*, 15.

10. Reid, *After the War*, 334; Trowbridge, *South*, 151, 230.

11. Gutman, *Black Family in Slavery and Freedom*, 39–41, found that about 80 percent of adult male freedmen in sample Virginia counties were farmers or farm laborers in 1865–66. Moreover, most ex-slave families in the state included both parents (ibid., 9–10).

12. See chapters 6 and 8 below for black voting patterns. In the 1870s rural and black belt freedmen would assume more prominent roles as political leaders. But during Virginia's abbreviated Reconstruction in the late 1860s, most black leaders were ministers, artisans, free before the war, and urban. See Eric Foner, *Reconstruction*, 112–13; Magdol, *Right to the Land*, 75–76, 136; Rachleff, *Black Labor in the South*, 34.

13. Litwack, *Been in the Storm So Long*, xiii; Charlotte Ann Jackson to ?, n.d., in Swint, *Dear Ones at Home*, 252.

14. Litwack, *Been in the Storm So Long*, 171, 172.

15. Ibid., 170. Richmond freedmen continued to celebrate Emancipation Day (April 3) and Independence Day (July 4) in following years, sometimes massing as many as 2,000 marchers in their parades (Rachleff, *Black Labor in the South*, 39–40).

16. Dennett, *South As It Is*, 15, 6.

17. Reid, *After the War*, 343; Dennett, *South As It Is*, 42–43.

18. Hopkins to Major James Johnson, Jan. 15, 1866, in Berlin, *Freedom*, ser. 2, *Black Military Experience*, 800–801. For a similar incident in Montgomery County, see the report by Freedmen's Bureau officer C. S. Schaeffer to his superior, J. H. Remington, Feb. 14, 1867, ibid., 808–10.

19. Reid, *After the War*, 18, 580; Dennett, *South As It Is*, 25.

20. O'Brien, "Reconstruction in Richmond," 271–72, 280, 278.

21. Gutman, *Black Family in Slavery and Freedom*, 397–98.

22. Trowbridge, *South*, 176.

23. Gutman, *Black Family in Slavery and Freedom*, 412–13; Litwack, *Been in the Storm So Long*, 244.

24. O'Brien, "Reconstruction in Richmond," 261–63; Litwack, *Been in the Storm So Long*, 465.

25. S. E. C. to ?, Apr. 18, 1865, Lucy Chase to Miss Lowell, Apr. 20, 1865, in Swint, *Dear Ones at Home*, 156–57; Dennett, *South As It Is*, 370.

26. Dennett, *South As It Is*, 56; Reid, *After the War*, 14–18; Litwack, *Been in the Storm So Long*, 172; report on schools by J. W. Alvord of Freedmen's Bureau, Jan. 1, 1866, in *Report of the Joint Committee on Reconstruction*, 250; Swint, *Northern Teacher in the South*, app. 3, pp. 175–200 (names and locations of northern teachers in Virginia).

27. Reid, *After the War*, 330; Eric Foner, *Reconstruction*, 408; Osthaus, *Freedmen, Philanthropy, and Fraud*, 3, 15–18, 89, 103, 116.

28. Litwack, *Been in the Storm So Long*, 291, 392–99; Lucy Chase to "Dear folks at home," Mar. 4, 1863, in Swint, *Dear Ones at Home*, 49; Eric Foner, *Reconstruction*, 172–73.

29. Litwack, *Been in the Storm So Long*, 395; statement of the "Tobacco Factory Mechanicks of Richmond and Manchester," reprinted in Trowbridge, *South*, 230n–231n.

30. Reid, *After the War*, 301; Dennett, *South As It Is*, 73; Magdol, *Right to the Land*, 185; Litwack, *Been in the Storm So Long*, 406, 605.

31. Quoted in Eric Foner, "Rights and the Constitution in Black Life during the Civil War and Reconstruction," 871. A Freedmen's Bureau official estimated that by the late fall of 1865 at least 70,000 freedmen had been evicted from land they had been farming in eastern Virginia during the war (Reid, *After the War*, 326).

32. Cimprich, *Slavery's End in Tennessee*, found the same assertiveness and independence among Tennessee freedmen after the war.

33. *Equal Suffrage in Norfolk, Virginia*, in Philip Foner and Walker, *Proceedings of the Black National and State Conventions* 1:89.

34. Ibid., 102–3, 90–91, 94. Belz, *Emancipation and Equal Rights*, 148–50, notes the important point that American society rejected gradations of citizenship.

35. *Equal Suffrage in Norfolk, Virginia*, in Philip Foner and Walker, *Proceedings of the Black National and State Conventions* 1:92.

36. Ibid., 93.

37. *Equal Suffrage. Address from the Colored Citizens of Norfolk, Va., to the People of the United States*, in ibid., 83–89.

38. Ibid., xx; O'Brien, "Reconstruction in Richmond," 274–78; *New York Tribune*, June 17, 1865.

39. O'Brien, "Reconstruction in Richmond," 278–81.

40. *Proceedings of the Convention of the Colored People of Va., Held in the City of Alexandria, Aug. 2, 3, 4, 5, 1865*, in Philip Foner and Walker, *Proceedings of the Black State Conventions* 2:258–76.

41. Ibid., 262, 271.

42. Ibid., 271.

43. Ibid., 263, 267, 268. The modern authorities on the black conventions agree that "the main proceedings of the conventions were handled by the blacks" (ibid., 1:xxiii).

44. Ibid, 1:xxi, 44; Engs, *Freedom's First Generation*, 90–91, 131.

45. Philip Foner and Walker, *Proceedings of the Black National and State Conventions* 1:210, 213; *Report of the Joint Committee on Reconstruction*, 52–59.

46. Rachleff, *Black Labor in the South*, 31, 42–44; *Richmond Dispatch*, Apr. 12, May 1, 1867.

47. Philip Foner and Walker, *Proceedings of the Black National and State Conventions* 1:344–405. Cook's focus on black rights to the exclusion of women's rights was shared by another prominent black Virginian, Thomas Bayne of Norfolk, who gave his own definition of the role of women in the constitutional convention in 1868: "It is a woman's right to raise and bear children, and to train them for their future duties in life" (*Debates and Proceedings, 1867*, 524).

Chapter 6

1. *American Annual Cyclopaedia and Register of Important Events, 1867*, 761; Schofield's annual report for 1867, John M. Schofield Papers; *Registered Voters in Rebel States*, in *Senate Executive Documents*, 40th Cong., 2d sess., no. 53, p. 2; Maddex, *Virginia Conservatives*, 54.

2. *Petersburg Daily Index*, June 20, 1867, quoted in Henderson, *Unredeemed City*, 172–73; *Richmond Dispatch*, Oct. 10, 1867; *Charlottesville Chronicle*, June 18, 1867; Chesson, *Richmond*, 227; J. M. Schofield to Adjutant General of the Army, Dec. 13, 1867, in *Senate Executive Documents*, 40th Cong., 2d sess., no. 53, pp. 1–2. Blacks would retain their Richmond majority until July 1869 (ibid., 99). The *Richmond Whig* observed the same white disinterest in the capital; see issue of Sept. 17, 1867, quoted in Maddex, *Virginia Conservatives*, 47.

3. Born in upstate New York in 1832, Gilbert C. Walker was an alumnus of Williams College in Massachusetts and Hamilton College in New York. Admitted to the bar in 1855, he practiced law in New York State and soon involved himself with Democratic politics. A resident of Chicago by 1860, Walker supported Stephen A. Douglas for president and was a strong Unionist during the war. He moved to Norfolk in 1864, allegedly for his health but possibly for business reasons. There he helped to establish the Exchange National Bank and became its first president. He also owned stock in a metalworks plant and in the Norfolk and Petersburg Railroad, the subject of a political squabble after the war (Shifflett, "Gilbert Carlton Walker"; Cahill, "Gilbert Carleton [*sic*] Walker").

4. The son of a wealthy Nelson County merchant, Alexander Rives was closely related to the eminent Cabell family of central Virginia. Educated at Hampden-Sydney College and the University of Virginia, he was a prominent Whig state senator before the war and an outspoken Unionist in 1861. Governor Pierpont had appointed him to the state Supreme Court in 1866, and President Grant would move him to the United States district court for western Virginia in 1869 (*National Cyclopaedia of American Biography* 19:111).

5. Cahill, "Gilbert Carleton Walker," 23; *Charlottesville Chronicle*, Oct. 24, 1867; Ambler, *Francis H. Pierpont*, 305; *Richmond Whig*, Sept.–Oct. 1867.

6. Thomas Conway to O. O. Howard, Apr. 26, 1867, Oliver O. Howard Papers.

For the political activities of one bureau official, see Mugleston, "Freedmen's Bureau and Reconstruction in Virginia," 64–65, 76, 78–81.

7. O. Brown to O. O. Howard, June 13, 1867, Oliver O. Howard Papers; Charles H. Lewis to Henry Wilson, Nov. 19, 1867, Henry Wilson Papers; *Charlottesville Chronicle*, Oct. 24, 1867; Henry M. Bowden to Benjamin F. Butler, July 4, 1867, Benjamin F. Butler Papers.

8. This is also the conclusion of Alderson in "Influence of Military Rule and the Freedmen's Bureau on Reconstruction in Virginia," 193–96. See also Mugleston, "Freedmen's Bureau and Reconstruction in Virginia," 48, 56, 60, 88; Henderson, *Unredeemed City*, 56; Engs, *Freedom's First Generation*, 62, 64, 135; Abbott, *Republican Party and the South*, 133.

9. *Richmond New Nation*, Aug. 22, Oct. 3, 1867. Born in Greene County, New York, in 1833, Charles H. Porter was a graduate of the Albany Law School. He practiced law for a few years before the war, then served in a New York cavalry regiment until 1863. After settling in Norfolk that year (one year before fellow New Yorker Gilbert C. Walker arrived in the same city), he became attorney general in Pierpont's Restored government. In 1867 he moved to Richmond and became a leading radical (*Biographical Directory of the American Congress*, 1471).

10. *Richmond New Nation*, Oct. 1, 1867.

11. Ibid., Oct. 23, 1867, Dec. 18, 1868.

12. Trelease, *White Terror*, 65–68, 185, and Harahan, "Politics, Political Parties, and Voter Participation in Tidewater Virginia during Reconstruction," 97–98, agree that the Ku Klux Klan was not as active in Virginia as in some other areas.

13. Swint, *Northern Teacher in the South*, 129; Vance, "Negro in the Reconstruction of Albemarle County," 80–82.

14. *Richmond New Nation*, Oct. 23, 1867; *Norfolk Journal*, July 31, 1867; *Richmond Enquirer*, Oct. 29, 1867; *Lynchburg News*, Oct. 25, 1867; O'Brien, "From Bondage to Citizenship," 490; Lewis to Wilson, Nov. 19, 1867, Henry Wilson Papers.

15. Schofield to Grant, Oct. 26, 1867, Ulysses Grant Papers, LC; *New York Tribune*, Oct. 26, 1867; Chesson, *Richmond*, 227. For incidents at the Richmond and Lynchburg polls, see *New York Tribune*, Oct. 25, 1867; James Douglas Smith, "Virginia during Reconstruction," 24.

16. *Senate Executive Documents*, 40th Cong., 2d sess., no. 53, p. 2; Hume, "Membership of the Virginia Constitutional Convention of 1867–1868"; Lowe, "Virginia's Reconstruction Convention." These sources give a slightly different number for the Republican delegates. For a breakdown of delegates by race and party, see the appendix.

17. "Communication from General J. M. Schofield, Relative to the Registered Voters in the State, December 12, 1867," document no. 5, in *Documents of the Constitutional Convention*, 49–56; *Report of the Joint Committee on Reconstruction*, 86. Robinson, "Beyond the Realm of Social Consensus," maintains that social and economic class interests were important factors in southern Reconstruction politics.

18. Abbott, *Republican Party and the South*, 137; James Douglas Smith, "Virginia Constitutional Convention," 48; Gilbert C. Walker to William Mahone, [ca. Oct. 25, 1867], McGill Family Papers (hereafter cited as McGill Papers), UVA Lib.; Gilbert C.

Walker to General Schofield, Oct. 24, 1867, John M. Schofield Papers; *New York Tribune*, Oct. 26, 1867.

19. *Richmond Enquirer*, Nov. 1, 1867; *Charlottesville Chronicle*, reprinted in ibid., Oct. 29, 1867.

20. Maddex, *Virginia Conservatives*, 55–56. The proceedings and resolutions of the convention are in *Richmond Dispatch*, Dec. 12–13, 1867, and *Richmond Whig*, Dec. 12–13, 1867.

21. Avary, *Dixie after the War*, 253.

22. James Douglas Smith, "Virginia Constitutional Convention," 30–31; Hume, "Membership of the Virginia Constitutional Convention," 470–77. The exact numbers of the various political factions are difficult to determine. Smith identified thirty-three white Conservatives; General Schofield counted thirty-two (Lowe, "Virginia's Reconstruction Convention," 346–60); and Hume, an authority on southern "black and tan conventions," listed thirty-seven. As outlined in the appendix, I have identified twenty-four black Republicans, twenty-three carpetbaggers, twenty-one scalawags, and thirty-six Conservatives. One carpetbagger, J. Henry Williams of Amherst, Buckingham, and Nelson counties, consistently voted with the Conservatives, was regarded as a member of that group by the Republicans, and could therefore be classified with the Conservatives, giving the latter group a total of thirty-seven members.

23. In Texas, far removed from the northern states, the Republican party depended to a far greater extent on scalawags (80 percent of the constitutional convention's Republicans were scalawags) than did Virginia with its heavy influx of carpetbaggers (Moneyhon, *Republicanism in Reconstruction Texas*, 82). Eric Foner, *Reconstruction*, 296–97, 317, indicates that carpetbaggers made up about one-sixth of all the delegates in all the southern conventions, came primarily from black belt constituencies, and comprised less than 2 percent of any southern state's population. In Virginia they were nearly one-fourth of the total number of delegates and, as in other states, were elected from heavily black voting districts.

24. Lowe, "Virginia's Reconstruction Convention"; Hume, "Membership of the Virginia Constitutional Convention," 472–77; Hume, "Carpetbaggers in the Reconstruction South," 320–21, 323, 330; *Debates and Proceedings, 1867*, 743–44.

25. Lowe, "Virginia's Reconstruction Convention," 352, 355; Alderson, "Influence of Military Rule and the Freedmen's Bureau on Reconstruction in Virginia," 201; James Douglas Smith, "Virginia Constitutional Convention," 59. Underwood to A. A. Sparks, Dec. 16, 1867, with a Senate frank on the envelope, is in my own collection of Reconstruction materials.

26. Lowe, "Virginia's Reconstruction Convention," 352, 355; Baggett, "Origins of Upper South Scalawag Leadership"; McKinney, *Southern Mountain Republicans*, 56–60; Maddex, "Virginia: The Persistence of Centrist Hegemony," 130–32; Hume, "Membership of the Virginia Constitutional Convention," 472–77.

27. Jackson, *Negro Office-Holders in Virginia*; Lowe, "Virginia's Reconstruction Convention"; James Douglas Smith, "Virginia Constitutional Convention," 53–63 and passim; Hume, "Membership of the Virginia Constitutional Convention," 477; Hume, "Negro Delegates to the State Constitutional Conventions," 137, 149n; Meier, "Afterword," 393–406. See also Taylor, *Negro in the Reconstruction of Virginia*, for an early

treatment of the subject.

28. *Debates and Proceedings, 1867*, 485, 209–10, 151, 713, 486, 520–21, 155; *Journal of the Constitutional Convention,* 1867–68, 39–40; Eric Foner, *Reconstruction,* 210, 305, 375, 376. Teamoh, a literate former slave who had escaped to New York City with the connivance of his mistress in the 1850s, would later serve in the state Senate. See George Teamoh Journal (actually an autobiography), Carter Woodson Papers.

29. Taylor, *Negro in the Reconstruction of Virginia,* 227; *Journal of the Constitutional Convention,* 1867–68, 53; *Debates and Proceedings, 1867,* 63–64, 213; *New York Times,* Jan. 11, 1868. George Teamoh, a black delegate to the convention, was one of many Republican members who complained about the epithets directed at black members. Such tactics only hardened the resolve of the Republicans, according to Teamoh. See George Teamoh Journal, Carter Woodson Papers.

30. *Journal of the Constitutional Convention,* 1867–68, 221, 283–84; *Debates and Proceedings, 1867,* 331.

31. *Journal of the Constitutional Convention,* 1867–68, 364–65.

32. *Richmond Enquirer,* Apr. 20, 16, 1868.

33. *Journal of the Constitutional Convention,* 1867–68, 301.

34. *Debates and Proceedings, 1867,* 222–53, 300–350; Lowe, "Virginia's Reconstruction Convention," 349, 357.

35. *Debates and Proceedings, 1867,* 649ff., 665–66, 724, 732, and *Richmond Dispatch,* Jan. 31, Feb. 1, 19, 1868 (the *Debates and Proceedings* include only part of the proceedings; the debates for February through April can be found in Richmond newspapers); Eric Foner, *Reconstruction,* 328; Burton, "History of Taxation in Virginia," iv; Summers, *Railroads, Reconstruction, and the Gospel of Prosperity,* 24.

36. James Douglas Smith, "Virginia Constitutional Convention," 90–91. The Carolinas, Georgia, and Florida also limited state aid to private companies and corporations (Scroggs, "Carpetbagger Constitutional Reform in the South Atlantic States," 480–81). Summers, *Railroads, Reconstruction, and the Gospel of Prosperity,* 22, emphasizes the Republicans' "cautious" approach to economic matters in the 1867–68 southern constitutional conventions.

37. Abbott, *Republican Party and the South,* 146–47. The Reconstruction Acts disfranchised those persons disqualified for office in the Fourteenth Amendment, all men who, "having previously taken an oath, as a member of Congress, or as an officer of the United States, or as a member of any State legislature, or as an executive or judicial officer of any State, to support the Constitution of the United States, shall have engaged in insurrection or rebellion against the same, or given aid or comfort to the enemies thereof." In short, Congress had disfranchised the antebellum leaders of the South.

38. Although some of his fellow Republicans in Virginia favored heavy proscription of rebel rights, Bland said, he was "afraid to follow in the footsteps of the weakest *minds* and *nerves* the world have ever seen in party leaders" (Bland to Elihu Washburne, Mar. 15, 1868, Elihu Washburne Papers). See also Dennett, *South As It Is,* 27, and the essays in Rabinowitz, *Southern Black Leaders of the Reconstruction Era,* esp. the "Afterword" by Meier.

39. *Documents of the Constitutional Convention*, 155–56; *Richmond Dispatch*, Feb. 21, 22, Mar. 4, 7, 9, 25, 26, 1868; Eric Foner, *Reconstruction*, 42.

40. *Richmond Dispatch*, Mar. 14–25, 1868; *Journal of the Constitutional Convention, 1867–68*, 283–84; Abbott, *Republican Party and the South*, 148. The *Dispatch* of March 25 bitterly lamented that "the negroes and flibertigibbets made another stride in the work of cutting down the rights of white men and expanding those of negroes!"

41. Vaughn, *Schools for All*, 141–43; J. L. M. Curry, *Brief Sketch of George Peabody*, 37, 42. See also Pearson, "William Henry Ruffner," 31.

42. *Journal of the Constitutional Convention, 1867–68*, 340; James Douglas Smith, "Virginia Constitutional Convention," 109–14.

43. Henderson, *Unredeemed City*, 186; Vaughn, *Schools for All*, 141; Litwack, *Been in the Storm So Long*, 490; Perman, *Emancipation and Reconstruction*, 81. The same point is made in Hume, "Negro Delegates to the State Constitutional Conventions," 143–44.

44. James Douglas Smith, "Virginia Constitutional Convention," 121–23; Ed. R. S. Canby to W. T. Sherman, May 9, 1869, in *Senate Executive Documents*, 41st Cong., 2d sess., no. 13, pp. 9–10; Taylor, *Negro in the Reconstruction of Virginia*, 240.

45. For similar measures in other states, see Scroggs, "Carpetbagger Constitutional Reform," 479–80; Summers, *Railroads, Reconstruction, and the Gospel of Prosperity*, 24.

46. James Douglas Smith, "Virginia Constitutional Convention," 118–19, 125–26; *Richmond Dispatch*, Mar. 25, 1868.

47. *Debates and Proceedings, 1867*, 29, 250; *Richmond Dispatch*, Jan. 31, Mar. 25, 1868; *New York Times*, Feb. 6, 1868.

48. *Debates and Proceedings, 1867*, 431–35, 431; Abbott, *Republican Party and the South*, 147; *Richmond Dispatch*, Jan. 14, 1868; *Lynchburg Virginian*, Jan. 16, 1868.

49. John Hawxhurst to Editor, Mar. 24, 1868, in *Richmond Dispatch*, Mar. 25, 1868; Hawxhurst to Elihu Washburne, Mar. 24, 1868, Elihu Washburne Papers; various clippings in scrapbook of John C. Underwood Papers and Scrapbook, 164–65.

50. Alderson, "Influence of Military Rule and the Freedmen's Bureau on Reconstruction in Virginia," 229–30; *Richmond Enquirer*, Mar. 31, 1868; Henderson, *Unredeemed City*, 65–66.

51. Hickin, "Henry Horatio Wells"; *National Cyclopaedia of American Biography* 5:453.

52. Convention members had been considering Wells for the governorship as early as December 1867. By March 23, 1868, an observant officeholder in Richmond had learned that "Gen. Wells, of Alexandria, is certain to be *the* candidate for Governor. Sixty out of the seventy-odd [Republican] members of the Convention have signed a paper for him." A week later he added that "all the wires are fixed [for Wells]" (R. F. Walker to William Mahone, Dec. 10, 1867, Mar. 23, 30, 1868, McGill Papers).

53. Pierpont to Hunnicutt, Apr. 9, 1868, in *Richmond Independent Republican*, Mar. 20, 1869; autobiographical sketch, Pierpont Papers, Brock Collection, Henry E. Huntington Library.

54. *Richmond New Nation*, Apr. 11, 1867; *New York Times*, Oct. 9, 1868; R. F. Walker to Mahone, Apr. 9, 1868, McGill Papers. R. F. Walker, former editor of the moderate Republican *Richmond Republic*, was a native of Virginia and a protégé of General William Mahone, a Confederate hero and postwar railroad magnate.

55. Schofield to Grant, Dec. ?, 1867, John M. Schofield Papers; *New York Times*, Jan. 4, Mar. 3, 1868. U. S. Grant, general-in-chief of the army, and Schofield had wanted Alexander Rives, a Virginia native and Albemarle County moderate, to take the governorship. Rives refused, however, preferring his position as a state supreme court justice (Schofield to Grant, Apr. 8, 1868, John M. Schofield Papers).

56. Grant to Schofield, Apr. 3, 1868, John M. Schofield Papers; Schofield to Grant, Apr. 6, 1868, Ulysses Grant Papers. Some accounts state erroneously that Pierpont was removed in 1867; see, for example, Randall and Donald, *Civil War and Reconstruction*, 620.

57. Pierpont to Grant, Apr. 15, 23, 1868, Grant to Schofield, Apr. 5, 6, 1868, John M. Schofield Papers. See also Pierpont's autobiographical sketch, Pierpont Papers, Brock Collection, Henry E. Huntington Library. Disappointed, Pierpont left Richmond in the spring of 1868 and returned to his childhood home in Fairmont, now in West Virginia. He supported Grant for the presidency in 1868 and served one term as a Republican member of the West Virginia legislature before retiring from public life in 1869 (Lowe, "Francis Harrison Pierpont," 44).

58. *Richmond New Nation*, Apr. 1, Dec. 18, 1868; Abbott, *Republican Party and the South*, 135–36; *Richmond Whig*, Apr. 7, 1868; *New York Times*, Apr. 8, 1868.

59. *Richmond Enquirer*, Apr. 21, 10, 1868.

60. *Richmond Dispatch*, Apr. 18, 1868; Schofield to Grant, Apr. 18, 19, May 8, 1868, John M. Schofield Papers; Schofield, *Forty-Six Years in the Army*, 400–403.

61. Several Republicans, including scalawag Edward K. Snead and the carpetbagger Edgar Allen, refused to approve the constitution. They objected to several clauses, but especially the test oath (*New York Times*, Apr. 20, 1868). Gilbert C. Walker, another moderate carpetbagger and a future governor, called the convention a "farce" and believed the new constitution too radical for adoption (Walker to Schofield, Mar. 28, 1868, John M. Schofield Papers).

62. Scroggs, "Carpetbagger Constitutional Reform," 492–93. The constitution is in Thorpe, *Federal and State Constitutions* 7:3871–3904.

63. *Richmond Enquirer-Examiner*, Dec. 4, 1869; Maddex, *Virginia Conservatives*, 118, 120.

64. *Richmond Dispatch*, Apr. 20, 1868. See also Maddex, *Virginia Conservatives*, 58–59.

Chapter 7

1. *American Annual Cyclopaedia and Register of Important Events*, 1868, 760. The military governor of Texas, General Joseph G. Reynolds, used a similar maneuver in that state a few months later. After announcing that the Texas constitutional convention had exhausted all its funds, he refused to provide more money, thus bringing Reconstruction to a temporary halt (Moneyhon, *Republicanism in Reconstruction Texas*, 93).

2. Schofield to U. S. Grant, Mar. 21, 1868, John M. Schofield Papers. The convention, however, was not particularly extravagant. Its expenses ($145,068.55) were less than those of the 1850–51, 1861, and 1901–2 constitutional conventions (Brena-

man, *History of Virginia Conventions*, 105; James Douglas Smith, "Virginia Constitutional Convention," 136–37).

3. Schofield, *Forty-Six Years in the Army*, 400–403.

4. Thomas P. Jackson to Manly, Feb. 27, 1868, J. M. Stradling to Manly, Apr. 22, 1868, quoted in Alderson, "Influence of Military Rule and the Freedmen's Bureau on Reconstruction in Virginia," 233. Manly had been chaplain of the 16th New Hampshire Volunteers in the war (*Richmond Whig*, Sept. 26, 1867).

5. *Richmond New Nation*, Apr. 1, 27, May 1, 6, 1868.

6. Convention reports and documents are in ibid., May 8, 15, 1868.

7. The Orange and Alexandria Railroad, partly owned by the B&O, ran from Alexandria to Gordonsville and from Charlottesville to Lynchburg. It used the line of the Virginia Central Railroad to connect Gordonsville and Charlottesville. Thus, it cut southward from Alexandria on the northern border of the state down the middle of Virginia to Lynchburg.

8. Blake, *William Mahone*, 70–100.

9. Mahone had little or no influence in the removal of Pierpont or the appointment of Wells. The Republican convention delegates, General Schofield, and possibly Republicans in Washington had secured that appointment. Moreover, Mahone had no motive for removing Pierpont since the latter favored consolidation, too. For Mahone's 1868 search for a friendly Conservative, see Mahone to Gilbert C. Walker, Apr. 5, 1868, and Mahone to John Goode, Jr., Apr. 12, 1868, William Mahone Papers, Duke University Library.

10. *Richmond Enquirer*, May 8, 1868; Withers, *Autobiography*, 243, 247–49; Maddex, *Virginia Conservatives*, 61. Two historians of the period agree that railroad issues were of secondary importance to the Conservatives in May 1868. See Harahan, "Politics, Political Parties, and Voter Participation," 264; Maddex, *Virginia Conservatives*, 61.

11. *Proceedings of the National Union Republican Convention, 1868*, 5–58.

12. Ibid., 84–85; Mayer, *Republican Party*, 166–67; Porter and Johnson, *National Party Platforms*, 39–40.

13. *New York Times*, May 22, 1868.

14. *Proceedings of the National Union Republican Convention, 1868*, 91–134; Mayer, *Republican Party*, 166–67. Virginia was entitled to twenty votes, but for some unknown reason only twelve delegates attended the convention (*Proceedings of the National Union Republican Convention, 1868*, 58; John Hawxhurst to Benjamin F. Wade, May 8, 1868, Benjamin F. Wade Papers, LC).

15. *Richmond New Nation*, May 13, 15, June 17, Dec. 18, 1868; *New York Times*, May 28, 1868. W. H. Samuel had been a schoolteacher in Philadelphia, a reporter for the *Baltimore American*, and a lawyer in Baltimore before settling in Virginia (*Richmond Independent Republican*, Mar. 20, 1869).

16. *Bristol News*, June 5, 1868; *Abingdon Virginian*, June 19, 1868; Withers, *Autobiography*, 248–64; *Richmond Enquirer*, June 16, 1868.

17. *Congressional Globe*, 40th Cong., 2d sess., pt. 4, pp. 3887, 3990, and pt. 5, p. 4321.

18. Ibid., pt. 5, 4416–17.

19. Rachleff, *Black Labor in the South*, 50.

20. Perman, *Road to Redemption*, 23 and passim, explains the differences between the two strategies.

21. *Richmond New Nation*, July 11, Sept. 28, 1868; *Richmond Dispatch*, July 7, 9, 15, 1868; *Richmond Enquirer*, Oct. 30, 1868.

22. *Richmond New Nation*, July 11, Sept. 28, 1868; *New York Times*, Aug. 30, 1868. Born in Richmond in 1820, Williams C. Wickham was educated privately and at the University of Virginia. He was a Whig state senator before the war, voted twice against secession in the 1861 convention, then became a cavalry general in Robert E. Lee's army. He joined the Republican party a few weeks after Appomattox because he considered it the legitimate successor to the old Whig organization. Elected president of the Virginia Central Railroad in 1865, he remained with that road for several years and later served as vice-president of the Chesapeake and Ohio Railroad Company (Gaines, *Biographical Register of Members*, 79; *National Cyclopaedia of American Biography* 13:605–6).

23. L. E. Dudley to William E. Chandler, Aug. 1, 1868, William E. Chandler Papers, LC; *New Nation*, Dec. 18, 1868.

24. *Richmond Whig*, Sept. 22, 1868; *Richmond Enquirer*, Sept. 25, 1868; *Richmond New Nation*, Sept. 28–29, Oct. 1, 7, 1868. The leading excommunicators were Joseph M. Humphreys, a Virginia native, prewar Whig, and unconditional Unionist who had joined Hunnicutt in forming a Union League in Washington during the war; and Andrew Washburne, a Massachusetts man who had served in the Freedmen's Bureau in Virginia (*Richmond Independent Republican*, June 12, 1869; *Richmond New Nation*, Sept. 29, 1868).

25. A. B. Garland to Mahone, Aug. 18, 1868, A. Fulkerson to Mahone, Aug. 26, 1868, William Mahone Papers; H. H. Walker to Mahone, Sept. 10, 15, 1868, McGill Papers.

26. R. T. Wilson to Thomas H. Callaway, Oct. 29, 1868, William Mahone Papers; *Richmond Whig*, Mar. 17, 1869; Blake, *William Mahone*, 101.

27. *New York Herald*, June 2, 1869; *Richmond Whig*, July 7, 1869; Hickin, "Henry Horatio Wells," 51–52.

28. Stoneman's report, reprinted in Edward McPherson, *Political History of the United States*, 425; Alderson, "Influence of Military Rule and the Freedmen's Bureau on Reconstruction in Virginia," 225–29. General Schofield had appointed 532 men; Stoneman had appointed 1,972 in a much shorter period; 329 men could take the oath and did not have to be replaced; and 2,613 offices were vacant in March 1869.

29. Alderson, "Influence of Military Rule and the Freedmen's Bureau on Reconstruction in Virginia," 239; *Richmond Enquirer*, Oct. 23, 1868; Rives to Schofield, Feb. 25, 1869, John M. Schofield Papers.

30. *Richmond Enquirer*, July 10, 1868. Also see Hickin, "Henry Horatio Wells," 53.

31. *Washington Star*, Dec. 5, 1868; *Congressional Globe*, 40th Cong., 3d sess., pt. 1, pp. 31, 35, 37, 43.

32. This was essentially the suggestion of General Schofield in the spring of 1868. Other Virginians were thinking along the same lines in early December. See L. Q. Washington to R. M. T. Hunter, Dec. 2, 1868, Robert M. T. Hunter Papers, UVA Lib.

33. Stuart, *Narrative*, 15–25.

34. J. C. Walker to Kemper, Jan. 25, 1869, James Lawson Kemper Papers; Simp-

son, *A Good Southerner*, 299–300. A few prewar Democrats feared that the Stuart initiative, or New Movement, was an attempt by former Whigs to seize control of the Conservative party (L. Q. Washington to R. M. T. Hunter, Feb. 14, 1869, Robert M. T. Hunter Papers).

35. Stoneman encouraged the New Movement and believed it could "swallow up" the Wells-Underwood Republicans if it would ally with the national Republican party (Stoneman to John M. Schofield, Jan. 19, 1869, John M. Schofield Papers).

36. Stuart, *Narrative*, 26–29, 32–34, 47; *New York Tribune*, Jan. 4, 14, 27, Apr. 5, 1869. The *New York Times*, *Boston Advertiser*, and *Chicago Tribune* lined up with Greeley in supporting the movement (Stuart, *Narrative*, 47).

37. Stuart, *Narrative*, 34ff. President Grant's actions with regard to the Committee of Nine and the ratification of the Virginia constitution run counter to a recent argument that he was more sympathetic to blacks during Reconstruction than scholars have written. See Zilversmit, "Grant and the Freedmen," 136–40.

38. At about the same time (December 1868), moderate Republicans in Texas also began calling for universal amnesty and universal suffrage (Moneyhon, *Republicanism in Reconstruction Texas*, 100, 105–6). For southern Republican factionalism, see Eric Foner, *Reconstruction*, 348–49.

39. Colonel Frank Ruffin, a moderate Conservative, prominent gentleman farmer, and relative of the antebellum fire-eater Edmund Ruffin, believed that the Committee of Nine had accomplished little or nothing, that the effective lever in Washington had been the moderate Republicans led by Stearns, "slightly assisted by Gilbert C. Walker, who 'smelt roast meat' in the affair" (Frank G. Ruffin to Editors, Oct. 1, 1880, in *Richmond Dispatch*, Oct. 3, 1880). Maddex, *Virginia Conservatives*, 71, agrees that Virginia's centrist Republicans "probably changed more minds than did the nine." For Ruffin, see ibid., 70, 180, 291.

40. Stuart, *Narrative*, 34ff., 51; *New York Times*, Jan. 14, 1869; *New York Tribune*, Jan. 27, 28, 1869; Wells to John M. Schofield, Feb. 17, 1869, John M. Schofield Papers; Leslie Winston Smith, "Richmond during Presidential Reconstruction," 127–28.

41. Stuart, *Narrative*, 51–52. General Mahone had little or nothing to do with the New Movement or the Conservative-Republican agreement on the gubernatorial race. He was an interested bystander who stood to profit by Wells's defeat, but as yet he had done little to effect it. One "very distinguished Virginian" agreed that Mahone's role was insignificant: "Although I actively participated in the new movement from its beginning to the end, I never heard that General Mahone ever had anything to do with it, or even approved it. While we were being denounced and abused [by some Conservatives], he certainly remained very quiet" (*Richmond Dispatch*, Oct. 2, 1880).

42. The moderate Republicans' decision to divide the party if they could not control it came before the 1869 nominating convention, not after. For the older view, see Eckenrode, *Political History of Virginia during the Reconstruction*, 119.

Chapter 8

1. The general opinion in Richmond in late January was that the Committee of Nine had accomplished nothing (R. F. Walker to Mahone, Jan. 29, 1869, William

Mahone Papers; L. Q. Washington to R. M. T. Hunter, Jan. 31, 1869, Robert M. T. Hunter Papers).

2. Rye to Mahone, Feb. 27, 1869, McGill Papers; Eckenrode, *Political History of Virginia during the Reconstruction*, 116, claimed that Mahone was "directing" the moderates. This is highly doubtful in view of their differences in strategy.

3. Rye to Mahone, Mar. 3, 1869, Clements to Mahone, Feb. 22, 1869, McGill Papers. For Mahone's opposition to the moderates' strategy, see Blake, *William Mahone*, 102–3.

4. Born in New Hampshire, Tucker had been practicing law in Alexandria since 1862 when he left the Union army (*Report of the Joint Committee on Reconstruction*, 22ff; see also Henderson, *Unredeemed City*, 213–15).

5. Proceedings and comments on the convention are in *Richmond Whig*, Mar. 10–12, 1869; *New York Tribune*, Mar. 10, 1869; *New York Times*, Mar. 10–11, 1869. For Harris see Maddex, *Virginia Conservatives*, 128.

6. *New York Times*, Mar. 11, 1869.

7. Henderson, *Unredeemed City*, 215; Eckenrode, *Political History of Virginia during the Reconstruction*, 119; *Richmond Whig*, Sept. 30, 1880.

8. More than a decade later members of both groups, caught up in the politics of 1880, attempted to take full credit for initiating the True Republican movement of 1869. Based on their earlier agreement with the Committee of Nine, the Stearns men seem to have the better case. See the claims and counterclaims in *Richmond Whig*, Sept. 29–30, 1880; *Richmond Dispatch*, Sept. 30, Oct. 3, 7, 1880; G. K. Gilmer to Editors, Oct. 3, 1880, in ibid., Oct. 6, 1880. Stearns claimed that his group had initiated the 1869 movement and that Mahone had then become a valuable ally. This is probably the most accurate interpretation of the events (Stearns to Editors, n.d., in ibid., Oct. 5, 1880; *Richmond Whig*, Oct. 6, 1880).

9. *Richmond Whig*, Mar. 16, 1869; *New York Times*, Mar. 20, 1869.

10. *Richmond Whig*, Mar. 16, 1869. For Gilmer, see Ours, "Virginia's First Redeemer Legislature," 176. A similar split between radicals and moderates took place in the Texas Republican party a few months earlier, in August 1868 (Moneyhon, *Republicanism in Reconstruction Texas*, 98).

11. Ross, *Liberal Republican Movement*, 25, 26, 27; Eric Foner, *Reconstruction*, 500; Maddex, *Virginia Conservatives*, 133.

12. *Richmond Whig*, Mar. 16, 1869; *Richmond Enquirer*, Mar. 16–18, 1869; *Richmond State Journal*, Mar. 16, 1869.

13. *Richmond Independent Republican*, Mar. 20, 1869; *Richmond Whig*, Mar. 23, Apr. 2, 6, 1869.

14. *Richmond Whig*, Mar. 29, Apr. 9, 1869; *Lexington Gazette*, Mar. 31, 1869. Stoneman had asked Wells to resign in February. Wells had refused, however, and had evidently appealed to General Grant to protect him (Stoneman to John M. Schofield, Feb. 28, 1869, John M. Schofield Papers; R. F. Walker to Mahone, Feb. 19, 1869, William Mahone Papers; *Lynchburg Virginian*, Feb. 27, 1869).

15. Born and educated in Pennsylvania, Dr. Alexander Sharp had served on General Grant's staff during the war. President Johnson had appointed him deputy postmaster in Richmond in July 1865 (Siviter, *Recollections*, 383).

16. R. F. Walker to William Mahone, Apr. 2, 1869, William Mahone Papers; Alderson, "Influence of Military Rule and the Freedmen's Bureau on Reconstruction in Virginia," 246ff. Stoneman attributed his removal to his action against Wells and his refusal to make appointments to suit politicians (*Richmond Whig*, Apr. 9, 1869 [Stoneman interview]).

17. *Richmond Independent Republican*, May 8, 1869; *Richmond Whig*, Apr. 9, 1869.

18. Richardson, *Messages and Papers of the Presidents* 7:11–12; *Congressional Globe*, 41st Cong., 1st sess., 633–36, 653–62, 699–700.

19. A. Fulkerson to Mahone, Apr. 24, 1869, McGill Papers. See also McGill Papers and William Mahone Papers for March–April 1869.

20. Withers, *Autobiography*, 276; *Richmond Enquirer*, Apr. 29, 30, 1869; *New York Times*, May 3, 1869; John L. Marye, Jr., to Mahone, May 3, 1869, McGill Papers.

21. Basing his argument on a political pamphlet prepared by Mahone's friends for the general's 1887 senatorial campaign, Blake, *William Mahone*, 106, claims that Mahone "exerted considerable influence in calling the Conservative Convention and shaping the policy which it had adopted." The contemporary evidence suggests that Mahone was a powerful voice for withdrawal but not a director. On the other hand, the best study of the Conservative party does give Mahone a more central role in the politics of 1869 than I do. See Maddex, *Virginia Conservatives*, 67–82.

22. Richardson, *Messages and Papers of the Presidents* 7:13–15; Ed. R. S. Canby to W. T. Sherman, May 9, 1869, in *Senate Executive Documents*, 41st Cong., 2d sess., no. 13, pp. 9–10; Stuart, *Narrative*, 57.

23. Ed. R. S. Canby to W. T. Sherman, May 9, 1869, Canby endorsement on S. P. Lee to Louis V. Caziarc, June 28, 1869, Canby to Adjutant General, June 30, 1869, Canby's General Orders no. 83, June 30, 1869, in *Senate Executive Documents*, 41st Cong., 2d sess., no. 13, pp. 10, 14–15, 102.

24. *Richmond State Journal*, May 31, June 15, 1869, and passim.

25. Ibid., May 10, June 24, 1869, and passim.

26. Wells to Thomas Garland, May 1, 1869, in *New York Times*, May 6, 1869, and *Richmond State Journal*, May 4, 1869. The *State Journal* and other radical papers joined the governor in abandoning the disabling clauses (ibid., June 18, 1869).

27. J. C. Fowler to Mahone, July 4, 1869, C. W. Buttz to Mahone, Apr. 25, 1869, McGill Papers; Chesson, *Richmond*, 110; W. W. Wing to Mahone, May 21, 1869, William Mahone Papers; Maddex, *Virginia Conservatives*, 81; *Richmond Independent Republican*, May 29, June 5, 19, 26, 1869.

28. *New York Times*, May 29, 1869; *Richmond Independent Republican*, June 26, 1869.

29. W. L. Riddick to Mahone, May 12, 1869, A. Fulkerson to Mahone, May 26, 1869, McGill Papers; *New York Tribune*, July 7, 1869.

30. James R. Branch to Mahone, May 7, 1869, McGill Papers; *Congressional Globe*, 41st Cong., 2d sess., pt. 1, 400–407; *Richmond Whig*, May 29, 1869.

31. Mahone to G. C. Walker, May 3, 1869, James W. Walker to Mahone, July 7, 1869, William Mahone Papers; Edgar Allen to Mahone, June 15, 1869, McGill Papers.

32. Walker to Mahone, June 13, 1869, William Mahone Papers.

33. J. G. Randall and David Donald, *Civil War and Reconstruction*, 630–31, interpret this period in Virginia history as primarily a struggle between the railroad interests of Mahone and those of John W. Garrett of the Baltimore and Ohio.

34. For representative examples of radical speeches, resolutions, and editorials, see James D. Brady Scrapbook, 1:20, UVA Lib.; *Winchester Journal*, June 11, 1869; *Richmond State Journal*, May 18, 31, 1869. For True Republican and Conservative examples, see *Richmond Independent Republican*, May 29, June 26, 1869; *New York Times*, Mar. 31, 1869; *Petersburg Index*, Apr. 17, 1869; *Lexington Gazette*, June 24, 1869. In most cases the railroad question was ignored; in a few, it was one of several subordinate issues.

35. John R. Hathaway to Mahone, May 10, 1869, McGill Papers; Mahone to W. W. Wing, Mar. 31, 1869, William Mahone Papers.

36. The latest and most authoritative treatment of Republicans and railroad issues during Reconstruction agrees: "Conservatives [in the South] simply did not recognize economics as the main issue. To them, no issue outweighed sectional degradation brought about by racial equality." Moreover, "political questions—in particular equal rights—mattered more to the history of Reconstruction than the [railroad] questions I raise" (Summers, *Railroads, Reconstruction, and the Gospel of Prosperity*, 21, x; see also pp. 22, 27). This was also the conclusion of Alexander H. H. Stuart and Kemper's biographer (Stuart, *Narrative*, 62; Robert R. Jones, "Conservative Virginian," 124–25).

37. One of Mahone's closest advisers emphasized his commitment to the general's railroad plan. But, he warned, "I would not consent to a fusion with the Radical party to carry it into effect" (A. Fulkerson to Mahone, Dec. 2, 1869, William Mahone Papers).

38. *Norfolk Journal*, July 10, 1869, quoted in Harahan, "Politics, Political Parties, and Voter Participation," 164, 166; Ed. R. S. Canby to Adjutant General, July 22, 1869, in *House Miscellaneous Documents*, 41st Cong., 2d sess., no. 8, pp. 12–14, 23–24. Eric Foner, *Reconstruction*, 442, agrees that violence and the Ku Klux Klan "played little or no part" in the Virginia election.

39. Ed. R. S. Canby to Adjutant General, July 22, 1869, in *House Miscellaneous Documents*, 41st Cong., 2d sess., no. 8, pp. 12–14.

40. *Richmond Whig*, Jan. 4, 1870; Stuart, *Narrative*, 67. Like most observers, Alexander H. H. Stuart regarded the election as "a glorious victory" for the Conservatives.

41. *Biographical Directory of the American Congress*, 195, 498; *Richmond Whig*, Jan. 4, 1870.

42. See *Richmond Whig* and *Richmond Dispatch*, July 21, 1869, for a county-by-county table. Radical Republicans did enjoy some local successes. In predominantly black Petersburg, Mahone's hometown, Wells won a majority of the city's vote; carpetbagger James H. Platt won the congressional vote; white radical Franklin Wood was sent to the state senate; and two black candidates (Peter G. Morgan and George Fayerman) were elected to the House of Delegates. Petersburg would remain under Republican control until 1874, five years after most of Virginia had been "redeemed" by the Conservatives. Black Republicans would remain powerful in Hampton on the Peninsula even longer, until the late 1880s (Henderson, *Unredeemed City*, 223; Engs, *Freedom's First Generation*, 199 and passim).

43. Shifflett, "Gilbert Carlton Walker," 60.

44. *Lynchburg Virginian*, July 7, 1869; *Charlottesville Chronicle*, July 10, 1869; *New*

York Times, July 9, 1869; J. L. Marye, Jr., to Mahone, July 8, 1869, McGill Papers; *New York Tribune*, July 8, 1869.

45. *House Miscellaneous Documents*, 41st Cong., 2d sess., no. 8, pp. 9–11, 15–17, 24–25; J. W. Lewellen to Mahone, Sept. 10, 1869, McGill Papers.

46. *American Annual Cyclopaedia and Register of Important Events, 1869*, 714; *New York Times*, Oct. 8, 11, 1869; R. F. Walker to Mahone, Sept. 21, 1869, William Mahone Papers; Maddex, *Virginia Conservatives*, 83–84. As consolation, perhaps, President Grant appointed Wells United States attorney for the eastern district of Virginia a few months later. Wells served in that office until 1872 when he resigned and moved to Washington, D.C., to administer his Alexandria Canal, Bridge, and Railroad Company (Hickin, "Henry Horatio Wells," 54).

47. Lucy Chase to Miss Lowell, Feb. 28, 1870, in Swint, *Dear Ones at Home*, 246.

48. Rachleff, *Black Labor in the South*, 52; Taylor, *Negro in the Reconstruction of Virginia*, 260–61; *House Miscellaneous Documents*, 41st Cong., 2d sess., no. 8, pp. 1–3

49. *House Miscellaneous Documents*, 41st Cong., 2d sess., no. 8, pp. 4–7.

50. Grant accepted the inevitability of Virginia's readmission but was not happy about the rise of the Conservatives. In order to forestall similar developments in Texas and Mississippi, he delayed elections in those two states, to give radicals more time to organize, and focused Federal patronage on the radicals. Grant's ploy succeeded when Republican tickets won in both Deep South states (Moneyhon, *Republicanism in Reconstruction Texas*, 113–16, 122; Abbott, *Republican Party and the South*, 208).

51. Richardson, *Messages and Papers of the Presidents* 7:29; Kelly, "Congressional Controversy over School Segregation," 540–42; *New York Tribune*, Dec. 9, 1869; *Congressional Globe*, 41st Cong., 2d sess., pt. 1, pp. 325–36, 350–61, 380–94, 416–24, 458–78, 507–18, 539–49, 563–75, 597–614, 634–44, 715–21, esp. pp. 442, 716. The readmission act is in *United States Statutes at Large* 16:62–63.

52. Henderson, *Unredeemed City*, 197.

53. Even the carpetbagger Walker eventually joined the Conservatives after he was read out of his own party by Republicans unhappy with his patronage policies (Shifflett, "Gilbert Carlton Walker," 61).

Chapter 9

1. Maddex, "Virginia: The Persistence of Centrist Hegemony," 133; Maddex, *Virginia Conservatives*, chaps. 8–14; Younger, *Governors of Virginia*.

2. Maddex, "Virginia: The Persistence of Centrist Hegemony," 133, 143–45; Jackson, *Negro Office-Holders in Virginia*, vii.

3. Harahan, "Politics, Political Parties, and Voter Participation," 6, 155, 261, 265, 270, 294. This pattern held true in other states of the upper South also. See Eric Foner, *Reconstruction*, 590.

4. Maddex, "Virginia: The Persistence of Centrist Hegemony," 130–31, 148–50. On the Readjusters, see James Tice Moore, *Two Paths to the New South*.

5. Gay, "James Hoge Tyler," 155–56.

6. C. Vann Woodward, *Thinking Back*, chap. 4; Eric Foner, "Reconstruction Revisited," 82–100.

7. Roark, *Masters without Slaves*, 208. Some southerners considered it "humiliating" to be "compelled to bargain and haggle with our servants about wages." Another southerner, Confederate general Richard Taylor, a perceptive and intelligent observer, went further: "Society has been completely changed by the war. The [French] Revolution . . . did not produce a greater change in the 'Ancien Regime' than has this in our social life" (Eric Foner, *Politics and Ideology in the Age of the Civil War*, 98–99, 107).

8. While admitting that Reconstruction reforms were limited, a leading historian of the subject emphasizes that "all the same, civil rights laws were placed on the statute books of the southern states and hundreds of blacks held offices of public trust. Reconstruction may not have broken down racial barriers and ended discrimination, but it was certainly an era of improvement in southern race relations." It was clearly an "advance over the total exclusion from white institutions that blacks had experienced during slavery" and far better than the Jim Crow era thirty years later (Perman, *Emancipation and Reconstruction*, 82).

9. Olsen, "Introduction," in Olsen, *Reconstruction and Redemption in the South*, 10.

10. While there is no perfect way to estimate the proportion of each race that did register to vote, the census and the voting rolls do provide a rough approximation of the percentages. In the 1869 election 120,103 blacks were registered to vote. According to the United States census of 1860, the total black population in Virginia in 1860 (using post–1863 borders) was 527,763. Thus, about 23 percent of the total black population was on the voting rolls in 1869. The white figures—149,781 registered voters and 691,773 total white population—yield a percentage of roughly 22 percent. The 1870 census, although generally less dependable than that of 1860, shows a similar pattern (23 percent for blacks and 21 percent for whites). Of course, these numbers are imprecise, but they do imply that there was no significant difference between the races as far as voter registration in the late 1860s (U.S. Bureau of the Census, *Statistics of the Population, Ninth Census*, 68–70; *House Miscellaneous Documents*, 41st Cong., 2d sess., no. 8, p. 24).

11. Perman, *Emancipation and Reconstruction*, 96, explains southern Republican factionalism in much the same terms.

12. Siepel, *Rebel*, xvii.

13. See James Tice Moore, *Two Paths to the New South* and "Black Militancy in Readjuster Virginia."

14. Perman, *Emancipation and Reconstruction*, 92, demonstrates that Republicans throughout the South were denied legitimacy by their opponents.

15. *Debates and Proceedings, 1867*, 72. Eric Foner, *Reconstruction*, 346, emphasizes the denial of legitimacy to southern Republicans.

16. C. Vann Woodward, in "Reconstruction: A Counterfactual Playback," wonders whether Reconstruction ever had a chance for true long-term success, given the countervailing will of the dominant white majority (Woodward, *The Future of the Past*, esp. pp. 199–200).

17. Perman, *Emancipation and Reconstruction*, 63, makes the same point about Republican parties throughout the former Confederacy.

18. As Herman Belz makes clear, while Reconstruction did not measure up to the

hopes of more radical Republicans then or to the standards of equality deemed acceptable today, Republicans did succeed in steering the nation away from an even gloomier
alternative, the one offered by Democrats in both North and South: the black codes, legal sanctions against blacks, inequality before the law, and an exclusively manual-labor
status for black Americans (Belz, *Emancipation and Equal Rights*, xii–xiii). See also Eric
Foner, *Reconstruction*, 410.

19. Perman, speaking of the tendency of southern Republican parties to ally with
white moderates, observed that "this choice was probably unavoidable for a newly
formed political party whose right to exist was being challenged and whose survival in
a competitive electoral system required that it appeal successfully to a majority of the
voters" (Perman, *Emancipation and Reconstruction*, 73).

20. See, for example, Carter, *When the War Was Over*, 231, 275.

21. The most knowledgeable historian of the Readjuster movement concluded that
white reaction to black radicalism in the 1880s had a similar outcome—the end of
Readjuster-Republican power in the Old Dominion (James T. Moore, "Black Militancy
in Readjuster Virginia," 184, 186).

Bibliography

Abbreviations

AHR	*American Historical Review*
CWH	*Civil War History*
JAH	*Journal of American History*
JSH	*Journal of Southern History*
NCHR	*North Carolina Historical Review*
VMHB	*Virginia Magazine of History and Biography*
WVH	*West Virginia History*

Manuscripts

Bowdoin College Library, Brunswick, Maine
    Oliver O. Howard Papers
Brown University Library, Providence, R.I.
    Eli Thayer Papers
Duke University Library, Durham, N.C.
    William Mahone Papers
Friends' Historical Library, Swarthmore, Pa.
    Samuel Janney Papers
Henry E. Huntington Library, San Marino, Calif.
    Francis H. Pierpont Papers, Brock Collection
Indiana State Library, Indianapolis
    Daniel D. Pratt Papers
Library of Congress, Washington, D.C. (LC)
    Benjamin F. Butler Papers
    William E. Chandler Papers
    Ulysses S. Grant Papers
    Andrew Johnson Papers

Abraham Lincoln Papers (Robert Todd Lincoln Collection)
Edward McPherson Papers
John M. Schofield Papers
Thaddeus Stevens Papers
John C. Underwood Papers and Scrapbook
Benjamin F. Wade Papers
Elihu Washburne Papers
Henry Wilson Papers
George Teamoh Journal in Carter Woodson Papers
New York Public Library
Horace Greeley Papers
Syracuse University Library, Syracuse, N.Y.
Gerrit Smith Papers
University of Rochester Library, Rochester, N.Y.
William E. Seward Collection
Thurlow Weed Collection
University of Virginia Library, Charlottesville (UVA Lib.)
James Barbour Papers
James D. Brady Scrapbooks
Robert M. T. Hunter Papers
John D. Imboden Papers
James L. Kemper Papers
McGill Family Papers
Rives Family Papers
Alexander H. H. Stuart Papers
Virginia State Library and Archives, Richmond (VSL)
John Letcher Executive Papers
Francis H. Pierpont Executive Papers
Frank Gildart Ruffin Scrapbooks
Gilbert C. Walker Executive Papers
Henry H. Wells Executive Papers
West Virginia University Library, Morgantown
Archibald Campbell Papers
Granville D. Hall Papers
Francis H. Pierpont Papers
Waitman T. Willey Papers

Newspapers

Virginia
Abingdon Virginian
Alexandria Gazette
Alexandria Virginia State Journal
Ceredo Crescent
Charlottesville Chronicle

Fredericksburg Christian Banner
Fredericksburg Ledger
Fredericksburg News
Hampton True Southerner
Harrisonburg Rockingham Register
Leesburg Mirror
Lexington Gazette
Lynchburg News
Lynchburg Virginian
Norfolk Journal
Norfolk Post
Norfolk True Southerner
Norfolk Virginian
Petersburg Index
Richmond Dispatch
Richmond Enquirer
Richmond Examiner
Richmond Independent Republican
Richmond New Nation
Richmond Register
Richmond Republic
Richmond Southern Intelligencer
Richmond State Journal
Richmond Whig
Staunton Valley Virginian
Wellsburg Herald
Wheeling Intelligencer
Winchester Journal

Other Newspapers
New York Herald
New York Times
New York Tribune
Washington (D.C.) Chronicle
Washington (D.C.) Star

Public Documents

Acts of the General Assembly of the State of Virginia. Publisher and place of publication vary, 1861–69.

Biographical Directory of the American Congress, 1774–1961. Washington, D.C: GPO, 1961.

Calendar of Virginia State Papers and Other Manuscripts: From January 1, 1836, to April 15, 1869; Preserved in the Capitol at Richmond. Ed. H. W. Flournoy. 11 vols. Richmond: Secretary of the Commonwealth and State Librarian, 1875–93.

A Compilation of the Messages and Papers of the Presidents, 1789–1902. Ed. James D. Richardson. 10 vols. New York: Bureau of National Literature and Art, 1903.

Constitution of the State of Virginia and the Ordinances Adopted by the Convention Which As-
    sembled at Alexandria. . . . Alexandria, Va.: D. Turner, 1864.
The Debates and Proceedings of the Constitutional Convention of the State of Virginia, Assembled
    at the City of Richmond, Tuesday, December 3, 1867. Richmond: Office of the New
    Nation, 1868.
Debates and Proceedings of the First Constitutional Convention of West Virginia. Ed. Charles
    H. Ambler, William B. Mathews, and F. H. Atwood. 3 vols. Huntington,
    W.Va.: Gentry Bros., 1939.
Documents of the Constitutional Convention of the State of Virginia. Richmond: Office of the
    New Nation, 1867 [1868].
The Federal and State Constitutions, Colonial Charters, and Other Organic Laws. . . . Comp.
    Francis N. Thorpe. 7 vols. Washington, D.C.: GPO, 1909.
Journal of the Constitutional Convention of the State of Virginia [1867–68]. Richmond: New
    Nation, 1867 [1868].
Journal of the Constitutional Convention Which Convened at Alexandria. . . . Alexandria,
    Va.: D. Turner, 1864.
Journal of the House of Delegates of the State of Virginia. Publisher and place of publication
    vary, 1861–69.
Journal of the Senate of the State of Virginia. Publisher and place of publication vary,
    1861–69.
Proceedings of the Virginia State Convention of 1861: February 13 to May 1. Ed. George H.
    Reese. 4 vols. Richmond: Virginia State Library, 1966.
Report of the Joint Committee on Reconstruction. In *The Reports of the Committees of the House of*
    Representatives. 39th Congress, 1st session, vol. 2.
United States, Bureau of the Census. *Population of the United States in 1860; Compiled*
    from the Original Returns of the Eighth Census. Washington, D.C.: GPO, 1864.
——. *The Statistics of the Population of the United States; Compiled from the Original Returns*
    of the Ninth Census (June 1, 1870). Washington, D.C.: GPO, 1872.
United States, Congress. *Congressional Globe.* 37th through 41st Congresses.
——. *House Miscellaneous Documents.* 41st Congress, 2d session, no. 8.
——. *Senate Executive Documents.* 39th Congress, 2d session, no. 29; 40th Congress, 1st
    session, no. 14; 2d session, no. 53; 41st Congress, 2d session, no. 13.

Books

Abbott, Richard H. *The Republican Party and the South, 1855–1877: The First Southern*
    Strategy. Chapel Hill: University of North Carolina Press, 1986.
Abzug, Robert H., and Stephen E. Maizlish, eds. *New Perspectives on Race and Slavery in*
    America: Essays in Honor of Kenneth M. Stampp. Lexington: University Press of Ken-
    tucky, 1986.
Ambler, Charles H. *Francis H. Pierpont: Union War Governor of Virginia and Father*
    of West Virginia. Chapel Hill: University of North Carolina Press,
    1937.
——. *Sectionalism in Virginia from 1776 to 1861.* Chicago: University of Chicago Press,
    1910.

——, and Festus P. Summers. *West Virginia: The Mountain State.* 2d ed. Englewood Cliffs, N.J.: Prentice-Hall, 1958.

American Annual Cyclopaedia and Register of Important Events. 84 vols. New York: D. Appleton and Co., 1870–1903.

Andrews, J. Cutler. *The South Reports the Civil War.* Princeton, N.J.: Princeton University Press, 1970.

Ashby, Bernice M., comp. *Shenandoah County, Virginia, Marriage Bonds, 1772–1850.* Berryville, Va.: Virginia Book Club, 1967.

Avary, Myrta Lockett. *Dixie after the War: An Exposition of Social Conditions Existing in the South, during the Twelve Years Succeeding the Fall of Richmond.* New York: Doubleday, Page and Co., 1906.

Bates, Edward. *The Diary of Edward Bates, 1859–1866.* Ed. Howard K. Beale. In *Annual Report of the American Historical Association for the Year 1930.* Vol. 4. Washington, D.C.: GPO, 1933.

Belz, Herman. *Emancipation and Equal Rights: Politics and Constitutionalism in the Civil War Era.* New York: W. W. Norton & Co., 1978.

——. *A New Birth of Freedom: The Republican Party and Freedmen's Rights, 1861–1866.* Westport, Conn.: Greenwood Press, 1976.

——. *Reconstructing the Union: Theory and Practice during the Civil War.* Ithaca, N.Y.: Cornell University Press, 1969.

Benedict, Michael Les. *A Compromise of Principle: Congressional Republicans and Reconstruction, 1863–1869.* New York: W. W. Norton and Co., 1974.

Bentley, George. *A History of the Freedmen's Bureau.* Philadelphia: University of Pennsylvania Press, 1955.

Berlin, Ira, ed. *Freedom: A Documentary History of Emancipation, 1861–1867.* Ser. 2. *The Black Military Experience.* Cambridge: Cambridge University Press, 1982.

Berman, Myron. *Richmond's Jewry, 1769–1976: Shabbat in Shockoe.* Charlottesville: University Press of Virginia, 1979.

Blake, Nelson M. *William Mahone of Virginia: Soldier and Political Insurgent.* Richmond: Garrett and Massie, 1935.

Boney, F. N. *John Letcher of Virginia: The Story of Virginia's Civil War Governor.* University: University of Alabama Press, 1966.

Botts, John Minor. *The Great Rebellion: Its Secret History, Rise, Progress, and Disastrous Failure.* New York: Harper and Brothers, 1866.

Brenaman, Jacob N. *A History of Virginia Conventions.* Richmond: J. L. Hill Printing Co., 1902.

Browning, Orville H. *The Diary of Orville Hickman Browning.* Ed. Theodore C. Pease and James G. Randall. 2 vols. Springfield: Illinois State Historical Library, 1925, 1933.

Burnham, W. Dean. *Presidential Ballots, 1836–1892.* Baltimore: Johns Hopkins University Press, 1955.

Butler, Benjamin F. *Butler's Book: Autobiography and Personal Reminiscences of Major-General Benj. F. Butler.* Boston: A. M. Thayer & Co., 1892.

——. *Private and Official Correspondence of General Benjamin F. Butler during the Period of the Civil War.* Comp. Jessie Ames Marshall. 5 vols. Norwood, Mass.: privately issued, 1917.

Campbell, John A. *Reminiscences and Documents Relating to the Civil War during the Year 1865*. Baltimore: John Murphy & Co., 1887.

Cappon, Lester J. *Virginia Newspapers, 1821–1935: A Bibliography with Historical Introduction and Notes*. New York: D. Appleton-Century Co., 1936.

Carter, Dan T. *When the War Was Over: The Failure of Self-Reconstruction in the South, 1865–1867*. Baton Rouge: Louisiana State University Press, 1985.

Chambers, Lenoir, and Joseph E. Shank. *Salt Water and Printer's Ink: Norfolk and Its Newspapers, 1865–1965*. Chapel Hill: University of North Carolina Press, 1967.

Chase, Salmon P. *Inside Lincoln's Cabinet: The Civil War Diaries of Salmon P. Chase*. Ed. David Donald. New York: Longmans, Green and Co., 1954.

Chesson, Michael B. *Richmond: After the War, 1865–1890*. Richmond: Virginia State Library, 1981.

Cimprich, John. *Slavery's End in Tennessee, 1861–1865*. University: University of Alabama Press, 1985.

Crenshaw, Ollinger. *The Slave States in the Presidential Election of 1860*. Baltimore: Johns Hopkins University Press, 1945.

Curry, J. L. M. *A Brief Sketch of George Peabody, and a History of the Peabody Education Fund through Thirty Years*. Cambridge, Mass.: University Press: John Wilson and Son, 1898.

Curry, Richard O. *A House Divided: A Study of Statehood Politics and the Copperhead Movement in West Virginia*. Pittsburgh: University of Pittsburgh Press, 1964.

———, ed. *Radicalism, Racism, and Party Realignment: The Border States during Reconstruction*. Baltimore: Johns Hopkins University Press, 1969.

Dennett, John Richard. *The South As It Is, 1865–1866*. Ed. Henry M. Christman. New York: Viking Press, 1965.

Donald, David. *Charles Sumner and the Rights of Man*. New York: Alfred A. Knopf, 1970.

Dorris, Jonathan T. *Pardon and Amnesty under Lincoln and Johnson: The Restoration of the Confederates to Their Rights and Privileges, 1861–1898*. Chapel Hill: University of North Carolina Press, 1953.

Duke, Maurice, and Daniel P. Jordan, eds. *A Richmond Reader, 1773–1983*. Chapel Hill: University of North Carolina Press, 1983.

Eckenrode, Hamilton James. *The Political History of Virginia during the Reconstruction*. Baltimore: Johns Hopkins University Press, 1904.

Engs, Robert Francis. *Freedom's First Generation: Black Hampton, Virginia, 1861–1890*. Philadelphia: University of Pennsylvania Press, 1979.

Foner, Eric. *Politics and Ideology in the Age of the Civil War*. New York: Oxford University Press, 1980.

———. *Reconstruction: America's Unfinished Revolution, 1863–1877*. New York: Harper & Row, 1988.

Foner, Philip S., and George E. Walker, eds. *Proceedings of the Black National and State Conventions, 1865–1900*. Vol. 1. Philadelphia: Temple University Press, 1986.

———. *Proceedings of the Black State Conventions, 1840–1865*. 2 vols. Philadelphia: Temple University Press, 1979–80.

Gaines, William H. *Biographical Register of Members: Virginia State Convention of 1861, First Session*. Richmond: Virginia State Library, 1969.

Gerteis, Louis S. *From Contraband to Freedman: Federal Policy toward Southern Blacks, 1861–1865*. Westport, Conn.: Greenwood Press, 1973.

Gordon, George H. *A War Diary of Events in the War of the Great Rebellion, 1863–1865*. Boston: J. R. Osgood, 1882.

Gutman, Herbert G. *The Black Family in Slavery and Freedom, 1750–1925*. New York: Pantheon Books, 1976.

Hall, Granville D. *The Rending of Virginia*. Chicago: Mayer & Miller, 1901.

Halstead, Murat. *Three against Lincoln: Murat Halstead Reports the Caucuses of 1860*. Ed. William B. Hesseltine. Baton Rouge: Louisiana State University Press, 1960.

——. *Trimmers, Trucklers, and Temporizers: Notes of Murat Halstead from the Political Conventions of 1856*. Ed. William B. Hesseltine. Madison: State Historical Society of Wisconsin, 1961.

Hattaway, Herman, and Archer Jones. *How the North Won: A Military History of the Civil War*. Urbana: University of Illinois Press, 1983.

Henderson, William D. *The Unredeemed City: Reconstruction in Petersburg, Virginia, 1856–1874*. Washington, D.C.: University Press of America, 1977.

Heyman, Max L. *Prudent Soldier: A Biography of Major General E. R. S. Canby, 1817–1873*. Glendale, Calif.: Arthur H. Clark Co., 1959.

Historical U.S. County Outline Map Collection, 1840–1980. Ed. Thomas B. Rabenhorst. Baltimore: University of Maryland Baltimore County, 1984.

Hodges, Willis Augustus. *Free Man of Color: The Autobiography of Willis Augustus Hodges*. Ed. Willard B. Gatewood, Jr. Knoxville: University of Tennessee Press, 1982.

Holt, Thomas. *Black over White: Negro Political Leadership in South Carolina during Reconstruction*. Urbana: University of Illinois Press, 1977.

Howard, Oliver Otis. *Autobiography of Oliver Otis Howard, Major General, United States Army*. 2 vols. New York: Baker & Taylor Co., 1908.

Hunnicutt, James W. *The Conspiracy Unveiled. The South Sacrificed; or, The Horrors of Secession*. Philadelphia: J. B. Lippincott & Co., 1863.

Hunter, Robert M. T. *Correspondence of Robert M. T. Hunter, 1826–1876*. Ed. Charles H. Ambler. In *Annual Report of the American Historical Association, 1916*. Vol. 2. Washington, D.C.: American Historical Association, 1918.

Hyman, Harold M., ed. *New Frontiers of the American Reconstruction*. Urbana: University of Illinois Press, 1966.

——, ed. *The Radical Republicans and Reconstruction, 1861–1870*. Indianapolis: Bobbs-Merrill Co., 1967.

Jackson, Luther P. *Negro Office-Holders in Virginia, 1865–1895*. Norfolk, Va.: Guide Quality Press, 1945.

Jay, John. *Slavery and the War*. 21 vols. in 1. Pamphlet collection, Library of Congress, Washington, D.C.

Kendrick, Benjamin B., ed. *The Journal of the Joint Committee of Fifteen on Reconstruction*. New York: Columbia University Press, 1914.

Klingman, Peter D. *Neither Dies nor Surrenders: A History of the Republican Party in Florida, 1867–1970*. Gainesville: University Presses of Florida, 1984.

Kousser, J. Morgan, and James M. McPherson, eds. *Region, Race, and Reconstruction: Essays in Honor of C. Vann Woodward*. New York: Oxford University Press, 1982.

Leech, Margaret. *Reveille in Washington, 1860–1865*. New York: Harper & Brothers, 1941.

Lewis, Virgil A., ed. *How West Virginia Was Made*. Charleston, W.Va.: News-Mail Co., 1909.

Lincoln, Abraham. *The Collected Works of Abraham Lincoln*. Ed. Roy P. Basler. 9 vols. New Brunswick, N.J.: Rutgers University Press, 1953–55.

Linden, Glenn M. *Politics or Principle: Congressional Voting on the Civil War Amendments and Pro-Negro Measures, 1838–1869*. Seattle: University of Washington Press, 1976.

Litwack, Leon F. *Been in the Storm So Long: The Aftermath of Slavery*. New York: Alfred A. Knopf, 1979.

McConnell, John P. *Negroes and Their Treatment in Virginia from 1865 to 1867*. Pulaski, Va.: B. D. Smith & Bros., 1910.

McDonough, James L. *Schofield: Union General in the Civil War and Reconstruction*. Tallahassee: Florida State University Press, 1972.

McFeely, William S. *Yankee Stepfather: General O. O. Howard and the Freedmen*. New York: W. W. Norton and Co., 1970.

McGregor, James C. *The Disruption of Virginia*. New York: Macmillan Co., 1922.

McKinney, Gordon B. *Southern Mountain Republicans, 1865–1900: Politics and the Appalachian Community*. Chapel Hill: University of North Carolina Press, 1978.

McKitrick, Eric. *Andrew Johnson and Reconstruction*. Chicago: Univerity of Chicago Press, 1960.

McPherson, Edward. *The Political History of the United States of America during the Period of Reconstruction, April 15, 1865–July 15, 1870. 1871*. Rept. New York: Da Capo Press, 1972.

McPherson, James M. *Ordeal by Fire: The Civil War and Reconstruction*. New York: Alfred A. Knopf, 1982.

Maddex, Jack P., Jr. *The Virginia Conservatives, 1867–1879: A Study in Reconstruction Politics*. Chapel Hill: University of North Carolina Press, 1970.

Magdol, Edward. *A Right to the Land: Essays on the Freedmen's Community*. Westport, Conn.: Greenwood Press, 1977.

Maslowski, Peter. *Treason Must Be Made Odious: Military Occupation and Wartime Reconstruction in Nashville, Tennessee*. Millwood, N.Y.: KTO Press, 1978.

Mayer, George H. *The Republican Party, 1854–1966*. 2d ed. New York: Oxford University Press, 1967.

Miller, Thomas C., and Hu Maxwell. *West Virginia and Its People*. 3 vols. New York: Lewis Historical Publishing Co., 1913.

Mohr, James C., ed. *Radical Republicans in the North: State Politics during Reconstruction*. Baltimore: Johns Hopkins University Press, 1976.

Moneyhon, Carl H. *Republicanism in Reconstruction Texas*. Austin: University of Texas Press, 1980.

Moore, George E. *A Banner in the Hills: West Virginia's Statehood*. New York: Appleton-Century-Crofts, 1963.

Moore, James Tice. *Two Paths to the New South: The Virginia Debt Controversy, 1870–1883*. Lexington: University Press of Kentucky, 1974.

Morton, Richard L. *The Negro in Virginia Politics, 1865–1902*. Charlottesville: University of Virginia Press, 1919.

Nathans, Elizabeth Studley. *Losing the Peace: Georgia Republicans and Reconstruction, 1865–1871*. Baton Rouge: Louisiana State University Press, 1968.

National Cyclopaedia of American Biography. 63 vols. New York: James T. White & Co., 1898—.

Nevins, Allan. *The Emergence of Lincoln*. 2 vols. New York: Charles Scribner's Sons, 1950.

Nicolay, John G., and John Hay. *Abraham Lincoln: A History*. 10 vols. New York: Century Co., 1890.

Olsen, Otto H., ed. *Reconstruction and Redemption in the South*. Baton Rouge: Louisiana State University Press, 1980.

Osthaus, Carl R. *Freedmen, Philanthropy, and Fraud: A History of the Freedman's Savings Bank*. Urbana: University of Illinois Press, 1976.

Parker, Granville. *The Formation of the State of West Virginia, and Other Incidents of the Late War*. Wellsburg, W.Va.: Glass and Son, 1875.

Perman, Michael. *Emancipation and Reconstruction, 1862–1879*. Arlington Heights, Ill.: Harlan Davidson, 1987.

——. *Reunion without Compromise: The South and Reconstruction, 1865–1868*. New York: Cambridge University Press, 1973.

——. *The Road to Redemption: Southern Politics, 1869–1879*. Chapel Hill: University of North Carolina Press, 1984.

Pierpont, Francis H. *Letter of Governor Peirpoint, to His Excellency the President of the United States, on the Subject of Abuse of Military Power in the Command of General Butler in Virginia and North Carolina*. Washington, D.C.: McGill-Witherow, 1864.

Porter, Kirk H., and Donald B. Johnson, eds. *National Party Platforms, 1840–1956*. Urbana: University of Illinois Press, 1956.

Proceedings of the First Three Republican National Conventions of 1856, 1860, and 1864. Minneapolis: Charles W. Johnson, 1893.

Proceedings of the National Union Republican Convention, Held at Chicago, May 20 and 21, 1868. Chicago: Evening Journal Print, 1868.

Rabinowitz, Howard N., ed. *Southern Black Leaders of the Reconstruction Era*. Urbana: University of Illinois Press, 1982.

Rachleff, Peter J. *Black Labor in the South: Richmond, Virginia, 1865–1890*. Philadelphia: Temple University Press, 1984.

Randall, James G. *Constitutional Problems under Lincoln*. Rev. ed. Urbana: University of Illinois Press, 1964.

——. *Lincoln the President*. 4 vols. New York: Dodd, Mead & Co., 1945–55.

——, and David Donald. *The Civil War and Reconstruction*. 2d ed. Lexington, Mass.: D. C. Heath and Co., 1969.

Reid, Whitelaw. *After the War: A Tour of the Southern States, 1865–1866*. Ed. C. Vann Woodward. New York: Harper & Row, 1965.

Report of the Proceedings of the Conference at Richmond, June 11 and 12, 1867. New York: Union League Club, 1867. In John Jay, *Slavery and the War*. 21 vols. in 1. Pamphlet collection, Library of Congress, Washington, D.C.

Roark, James L. *Masters without Slaves: Southern Planters in the Civil War and Reconstruction*. New York: W. W. Norton and Co., 1977.

Robertson, James I., Jr. *Soldiers Blue and Gray*. Columbia: University of South Carolina Press, 1988.

Rose, Willie Lee. *Rehearsal for Reconstruction: The Port Royal Experiment*. Indianapolis: Bobbs-Merrill Co., 1964.

Ross, Earle Dudley. *The Liberal Republican Movement*. New York: Henry Holt & Co., 1919.

Schofield, John M. *Forty-Six Years in the Army*. New York: Century Co., 1897.

Sefton, James E. *The United States Army and Reconstruction, 1865–1877*. Baton Rouge: Louisiana State University Press, 1967.

Shanks, Henry T. *The Secession Movement in Virginia, 1847–1861*. Richmond: Garrett and Massie, 1934.

Siepel, Kevin H. *Rebel: The Life and Times of John Singleton Mosby*. New York: St. Martin's Press, 1983.

Sifakis, Stewart. *Who Was Who in the Civil War*. New York: Facts on File Publications, 1988.

Simpson, Craig M. *A Good Southerner: The Life of Henry A. Wise of Virginia*. Chapel Hill: University of North Carolina Press, 1985.

Siviter, Anna P. *Recollections of War and Peace, 1861–1868*. Ed. Charles H. Ambler. New York: G. P. Putnam's Sons, 1938.

The Southern Loyalists' Convention [Proceedings]. New York: Tribune, 1866.

Squires, W. H. T. *Unleashed at Long Last: Reconstruction in Virginia, 1865–1870*. Portsmouth, Va.: Printcraft Press, 1939.

State Maps on File: Southeast. New York: Facts on File Publications, 1984.

Stuart, Alex. H. H. *A Narrative of the Leading Incidents of the Organization of the First Popular Movement in Virginia . . . and of the Subsequent Efforts of the "Committee of Nine"* . . . . Richmond: W. E. Jones, 1888.

Summers, Mark W. *Railroads, Reconstruction, and the Gospel of Prosperity: Aid under the Radical Republicans, 1865–1877*. Princeton, N.J.: Princeton University Press, 1984.

Swint, Henry L., ed. *Dear Ones at Home: Letters from Contraband Camps*. Nashville: Vanderbilt University Press, 1966.

——. *The Northern Teacher in the South, 1862–1870*. Nashville: Vanderbilt University Press, 1941.

Taylor, Alrutheus Ambush. *The Negro in the Reconstruction of Virginia*. Washington, D.C.: Association for the Study of Negro Life and History, 1926.

Thomas, Emory M. *The Confederate State of Richmond: A Biography of the Capital*. Austin: University of Texas Press, 1971.

Trefousse, Hans. *Ben Butler: The South Called Him Beast!* New York: Twayne Publishers, 1957.

Trelease, Allen W. *White Terror: The Ku Klux Klan Conspiracy and Southern Reconstruction*. New York: Harper & Row, 1971.

Tribune Almanac and Political Register [published yearly, 1861–68]. New York: H. Greeley and Co., 1861–68.

Trowbridge, J. T. *The South: A Tour of Its Battle-fields and Ruined Cities, a Journey through the Desolated States, and Talks with the People.* Hartford: L. Stebbins, 1866.

Vaughn, William Preston. *Schools for All: The Blacks and Public Education in the South, 1865–1877.* Lexington: University Press of Kentucky, 1974.

Wayland, John W. *A History of Shenandoah County, Virginia.* Strasburg, Va.: Shenandoah Publishing House, 1927.

Welles, Gideon. *Diary of Gideon Welles.* Ed. Howard K. Beale. 3 vols. New York: W. W. Norton & Co., 1960.

———. *Selected Essays by Gideon Welles: Civil War and Reconstruction.* Comp. Albert Mordell. 2 vols. New York: Twayne Publishers, 1959–60.

Wertenbaker, Thomas J. *Norfolk: Historic Southern Port.* Durham, N.C.: Duke University Press, 1931.

Whitelaw, Ralph T. *Virginia's Eastern Shore: A History of Northampton and Accomac Counties.* 2 vols. Richmond: Virginia Historical Society, 1951.

Who Was Who in America: Historical Volume, 1607–1896. Rev. ed. Chicago: Marquis, 1967.

Wiggins, Sarah Woolfolk. *The Scalawag in Alabama Politics, 1865–1881.* University: University of Alabama Press, 1977.

Willey, William P. *An Inside View of the Formation of the State of West Virginia.* Wheeling, W. Va.: News Publishing Co., 1901.

Wilson, Theodore B. *The Black Codes of the South.* Tuscaloosa: University of Alabama Press, 1966.

Withers, Robert E. *Autobiography of an Octogenarian.* Roanoke, Va.: Stone Printing Co., 1907.

Woodward, C. Vann. *The Future of the Past.* New York: Oxford University Press, 1989.

———. *Thinking Back: The Perils of Writing History.* Baton Rouge: Louisiana State University Press, 1986.

Work Projects Administration Writers' Program. *The Negro in Virginia.* New York: Hastings House, 1940.

Younger, Edward, et al., eds. *The Governors of Virginia, 1860–1978.* Charlottesville: University Press of Virginia, 1982.

Articles and Essays

Abbott, Richard H. "Yankee Farmers in Northern Virginia, 1840–1860." *VMHB* 76 (Jan. 1968): 56–63.

Alderson, William T., Jr. "The Freedmen's Bureau and Negro Education in Virginia." *NCHR* 29 (Jan. 1952): 64–90.

Baggett, James Alex. "Origins of Upper South Scalawag Leadership." *CWH* 29 (Mar. 1983): 53–73.

Bean, William G. "John Letcher and the Slavery Issue in Virginia's Gubernatorial Contest of 1858–1859." *JSH* 20 (Feb. 1954): 22–49.

Benedict, Michael Les. "Equality and Expediency in the Reconstruction Era: A Review Essay." *CWH* 23 (Dec. 1977): 322–35.

——. "Preserving the Constitution: The Conservative Basis of Radical Reconstruction." *JAH* 61 (June 1974): 65–90.

Bogue, Allan G. "Bloc and Party in the United States Senate, 1861–1863." *CWH* 13 (Sept. 1967): 221–41.

Bond, Donovan H. "How the Wheeling *Intelligencer* Became a Republican Organ." *WVH* 11 (Apr. 1950): 160–84.

Bromberg, Alan B. "The Virginia Congressional Elections of 1865: A Test of Southern Loyalty." *VMHB* 84 (Jan. 1976): 75–98.

Campbell, John A. "Papers of John A. Campbell—1861–1865." *Southern Historical Society Papers*, n. s., 4 (Oct. 1917): 3–81.

Cappon, Lester J. "The Yankee Press in Virginia, 1861–1865." *William and Mary College Quarterly*, 2d ser., 15 (Jan. 1935): 81–88.

Cardoso, Jack J. "Southern Reaction to *The Impending Crisis*." *CWH* 16 (Mar. 1970): 5–17.

Carter, Dan T. "The Anatomy of Fear: The Christmas Day Insurrection Scare of 1865." *JSH* 42 (Aug. 1976): 345–64.

Chambers, Lenoir. "Notes on Life in Occupied Norfolk." *VMHB* 73 (Apr. 1965): 131–44.

Chesson, Michael B. "Richmond's Black Councilmen, 1871–1896." In Howard N. Rabinowitz, ed. *Southern Black Leader of the Reconstruction Era*. Urbana: University of Illinois Press, 1982. Pp. 191–222.

Coates, Alice M., ed. "The Civil War Experiences of a Northern Family Settled in Virginia." Fairfax County Historical Society *Yearbook* 8 (1962–63): 45–62.

Crenshaw, Ollinger. "The Psychological Background of the Election of 1860 in the South." *NCHR* 19 (July 1942): 260–79.

Current, Richard N. "Carpetbaggers Reconsidered." In David H. Pinkney and Theodore Ropp, eds. *A Festschrift for Frederick B. Artz*. Durham, N.C.: Duke University Press, 1964. Pp. 139–57.

Curry, Richard O. "A Reappraisal of Statehood Politics in West Virginia." *JSH* 28 (Nov. 1962): 403–21.

Ellem, Warren A. "Who Were the Mississippi Scalawags?" *JSH* 38 (May 1972): 217–40.

Errett, Russell. "Formation of the Republican Party in 1856." *Magazine of Western History* 7 (Dec. 1887): 180–89.

Foner, Eric. "Reconstruction Revisited." *Reviews in American History* 10 (Dec. 1982): 82–100.

——. "Rights and the Constitution in Black Life during the Civil War and Reconstruction." *JAH* 74 (Dec. 1987): 863–83.

Fraser, Walter J., Jr. "William Henry Ruffner and the Establishment of Virginia's Public School System, 1870–1874." *VMHB* 79 (July 1971): 259–79.

Gara, Larry. "Slavery and the Slave Power: A Crucial Distinction." *CWH* 15 (Mar. 1969): 5–18.

Gay, Thomas E., Jr. "James Hoge Tyler: Rebellious Regular." In Edward Younger et al., eds. *The Governors of Virginia, 1860–1978*. Charlottesville: University Press of Virginia, 1982. Pp. 147–58.

Gray, Myra G. "A. W. Campbell—Party Builder." *WVH* 7 (Apr. 1946): 221–37.

Greenough, Mark K. "Aftermath at Appomattox: Federal Military Occupation of Appomattox County, May–November 1865." *CWH* 31 (Mar. 1985): 5–23.

Harris, William C. "The Southern Unionist Critique of the Civil War." *CWH* 31 (Mar. 1985): 39–56.

Hickin, Patricia. "Henry Horatio Wells: The Rise and Fall of a Carpetbagger." In Edward Younger et al., eds. *The Governors of Virginia, 1860–1978*. Charlottesville: University Press of Virginia, 1982. Pp. 47–56.

———. "John C. Underwood and the Antislavery Movement in Virginia, 1847–1860." *VMHB* 73 (Apr. 1965): 156–68.

Hume, Richard L. "Carpetbaggers in the Reconstruction South: A Group Portrait of Outside Whites in the 'Black and Tan' Constitutional Conventions." *JAH* 64 (Sept. 1977): 313–30.

———. "The Membership of the Virginia Constitutional Convention of 1867–1868: A Study of the Beginnings of Congressional Reconstruction in the Upper South." *VMHB* 86 (Oct. 1978): 461–84.

———. "Negro Delegates to the State Constitutional Conventions of 1867–69." In Howard N. Rabinowitz, ed. *Southern Black Leaders of the Reconstruction Era*. Urbana: University of Illinois Press, 1982. Pp. 129–54.

James, Felix. "The Establishment of Freedman's Village in Arlington, Virginia." *Negro History Bulletin* 33 (Apr. 1970): 90–93.

Johnson, Ludwell H. "Contraband Trade during the Last Year of the Civil War." *Mississippi Valley Historical Review* 49 (Mar. 1963): 635–52.

Jones, William Deveraux, ed. "A British Report on Postwar Virginia." *VMHB* 69 (July 1961): 346–52.

Julian, George W. "The First Republican National Convention." *AHR* 4 (Jan. 1899): 313–22.

Kaczorowski, Robert J. "To Begin the Nation Anew: Congress, Citizenship, and Civil Rights after the Civil War." *AHR* 92 (Feb. 1987): 45–68.

Kelly, Alfred H. "The Congressional Controversy over School Segregation, 1867–1875." *AHR* 64 (Apr. 1959): 537–63.

Kiplinger, John L. "The Press in the Making of West Virginia." *WVH* 6 (Jan. 1945): 127–76.

Kolchin, Peter. "Scalawags, Carpetbaggers, and Reconstruction: A Quantitative Look at Southern Congressional Politics, 1868–1872." *JSH* 45 (Feb. 1979): 63–76.

Langford, Victor. "Constitutional Issues Raised by West Virginia's Admission into the Union." *WVH* 2 (Oct. 1940): 12–36.

Litwack, Leon F. " 'Blues Falling Down Like Hail': The Ordeal of Black Freedom." In Robert H. Abzug and Stephen E. Maizlish, eds. *New Perspectives on Race and Slavery in America: Essays in Honor of Kenneth M. Stampp*. Lexington: University Press of Kentucky, 1986. Pp. 109–27.

Lowe, Richard. "Another Look at Reconstruction in Virginia." *CWH* 32 (Mar. 1986): 56–76.

———. "Francis Harrison Pierpont: Wartime Unionist, Reconstruction Moderate." In

Edward Younger et al., eds. *The Governors of Virginia, 1860–1978*. Charlottesville: University Press of Virginia, 1982. Pp. 33–46.

——. "Republican Newspapers in Antebellum Virginia." *WVH* 28 (July 1967): 282–84.

——. "The Republican Party in Antebellum Virginia, 1856–1860." *VMHB* 81 (July 1973): 259–79.

——. "Virginia's Reconstruction Convention: General Schofield Rates the Delegates." *VMHB* 80 (July 1972): 341–60.

McDonough, James L. "John Schofield as Military Director of Reconstruction in Virginia." *CWH* 15 (Sept. 1969): 237–56.

Maddex, Jack P., Jr. "Virginia: The Persistence of Centrist Hegemony." In Otto H. Olsen, ed. *Reconstruction and Redemption in the South*. Baton Rouge: Louisiana State University Press, 1980. Pp. 113–55.

Maddox, Robert F. "The Presidential Election of 1860 in Western Virginia." *WVH* 25 (Apr. 1964): 211–27.

Majeske, Penelope K. "Virginia after Appomattox: The United States Army and the Formation of Presidential Reconstruction Policy." *WVH* 43 (Winter 1982): 95–117.

Mallam, William D. "The Grant-Butler Relationship." *Mississippi Valley Historical Review* 41 (Sept. 1954): 259–76.

Meier, August. "Afterword: New Perspectives on the Nature of Black Political Leadership during Reconstruction." In Howard N. Rabinowitz, ed. *Southern Black Leaders of the Reconstruction Era*. Urbana: University of Illinois Press, 1982. Pp. 393–406.

Moger, Allen W. "Railroad Practices and Policies in Virginia after the Civil War." *VMHB* 59 (Oct. 1951): 423–57.

Montague, Ludwell Lee. "Letters Home to Maine from Virginia, 1841–1859." *VMHB* 79 (Oct. 1971): 436–61.

Monteiro, Margaret K. "The Presidential Election of 1860 in Virginia." *Richmond College Historical Papers* 1 (June 1916): 222–58.

Moore, George E. "The West Virginia Incident: An Appraisal." *WVH* 26 (Jan. 1965): 80–85.

Moore, James T. "Black Militancy in Readjuster Virginia, 1879–1883." *JSH* 41 (May 1975): 167–86.

Moore, John Hammond. "The Norfolk Riot, 16 April 1866." *VMHB* 90 (Apr. 1982): 155–64.

Morton, Richard L. " 'Contrabands' and Quakers in the Virginia Peninsula, 1862–1869." *VMHB* 61 (Oct. 1953): 419–29.

——. "Life in Virginia by a 'Yankee Teacher,' Margaret Newbold Thorpe." *VMHB* 64 (Apr. 1956): 180–207.

Mugleston, William F., ed. "The Freedmen's Bureau and Reconstruction in Virginia: The Diary of Marcus Sterling Hopkins, a Union Officer." *VMHB* 86 (Jan. 1978): 45–102.

Nichols, Roy F. "United States vs. Jefferson Davis, 1865–1869." *AHR* 31 (Jan. 1926): 266–84.

O'Brien, John T. "Reconstruction in Richmond: White Restoration and Black Protest, April–June 1865." *VMHB* 89 (July 1981): 259–81.

O'Grady, Joseph P. "Immigrants and the Politics of Reconstruction in Richmond, Virginia." *Records of the American Catholic Historical Society of Philadelphia* 83 (1972): 87–101.

Olsen, Otto H. "Reconsidering the Scalawags." *CWH* 12 (Dec. 1966): 304–20.

Pearson, Charles C. "William Henry Ruffner: Reconstruction Statesman of Virginia." *South Atlantic Quarterly* 20 (Jan. 1921): 25–32 and (Apr. 1921): 137–51.

Pierpont, Francis H. "History of the Reorganization of the Restored Government of Virginia and the Formation and Organization of the State of West Virginia." In *Calendar of Virginia State Paper and Other Manuscripts.* Ed. H. W. Flournoy. 11 vols. Richmond: Secretary of the Commonwealth and State Librarian, 1875–93. 11:351–508.

Powell, Lawrence N. "The Politics of Livelihood: Carpetbaggers in the Deep South." In J. Morgan Kousser and James M. McPherson, eds. *Region, Race, and Reconstruction: Essays in Honor of C. Vann Woodward.* New York: Oxford University Press, 1982. Pp. 315–47.

Reidy, Joseph P. " 'Coming from the Shadow of the Past': The Transition from Slavery to Freedom at Freedmen's Village, 1863–1900." *VMHB* 95 (Oct. 1987): 403–28.

Rice, Otis K. "Eli Thayer and the Friendly Invasion of Virginia." *JSH* 37 (Nov. 1971): 575–96.

Robinson, Armstead L. "Beyond the Realm of Social Consensus: New Meanings of Reconstruction for American History." *JAH* 68 (Sept. 1981): 276–97.

Scroggs, Jack B. "Carpetbagger Constitutional Reform in the South Atlantic States, 1867–1868." *JSH* 27 (Nov. 1961): 475–93.

——. "Southern Reconstruction: A Radical View." *JSH* 24 (Nov. 1958): 407–29.

Sefton, James E., ed. "Aristotle in Blue and Braid: General John M. Schofield's Essays on Reconstruction." *CWH* 17 (Mar. 1971): 45–57.

Shanks, Henry T. "Disloyalty to the Confederacy in Southwestern Virginia, 1861–1865." *NCHR* 21 (Apr. 1944): 118–35.

Shifflett, Crandall A. "Gilbert Carlton Walker: Carpetbagger Conservative." In Edward Younger et al., eds. *The Governors of Virginia, 1860–1978.* Charlottesville: University Press of Virginia, 1982. Pp. 57–68.

Smith, George Winston. "Ante-Bellum Attempts of Northern Business Interests to 'Redeem' the Upper South." *JSH* 11 (May 1945): 177–213.

Squires, J. Duane. "Lincoln and West Virginia Statehood." *WVH* 24 (July 1963): 25–31.

Stiles, Robert. "Reconstruction in Virginia." In Hilary A. Herbert et al. *Why the Solid South?* Baltimore: R. H. Woodward, 1890.

Stuart, Meriwether. "Of Spies and Borrowed Names: The Identity of Union Operatives in Richmond Known as 'The Phillipses' Discovered." *VMHB* 89 (July 1981): 308–27.

Trelease, Allen W. "Who Were the Scalawags?" *JSH* 29 (Nov. 1963): 445–68.

Turner, Charles W. "The Chesapeake and Ohio Railroad in Reconstruction, 1865–1873." *NCHR* 31 (Apr. 1954): 150–72.

Van Deusen, Glyndon G. "Why the Republican Party Came to Power." In George H. Knoles, ed. *The Crisis of the Union*. Baton Rouge: Louisiana State University Press, 1965.

Vance, Joseph C. "Freedmen's Schools in Albemarle County during Reconstruction." *VMHB* 61 (Oct. 1953): 430–38.

Wicker, J. Tivis. "Virginia's Legitimization Act of 1866." *VMHB* 86 (July 1978): 339–44.

Williams, Robert A. "Haw's Shop: A 'Storm of Shot and Shell.'" *Civil War Times Illustrated* 9 (Jan. 1971): 12–19.

Woodward, C. Vann. "Seeds of Failure in Radical Race Policy." In Howard M. Hyman, ed. *New Frontiers of the American Reconstruction*. Urbana: University of Illinois Press, 1966.

Woodward, Isaiah, ed. "Opinions of President Lincoln and His Cabinet on Statehood for Western Virginia, 1862–1863." *WVH* 21 (Apr. 1960): 157–85.

Zilversmit, Arthur. "Grant and the Freedmen." In Robert H. Abzug and Stephen E. Maizlish, eds. *New Perspectives on Race and Slavery in America: Essays in Honor of Kenneth M. Stampp*. Lexington: University Press of Kentucky, 1986. Pp. 128–45.

Unpublished Works

Alderson, William T. "The Freedmen's Bureau in Virginia." M.A. thesis, Vanderbilt University, 1948.

——. "The Influence of Military Rule and the Freedmen's Bureau on Reconstruction in Virginia." Ph.D. diss., Vanderbilt University, 1952.

Burton, Robert C. "The History of Taxation in Virginia, 1870–1901." Ph.D. diss., University of Virginia, 1962.

Cahill, Audrey Marie. "Gilbert Carleton [*sic*] Walker: Virginia's Redeemer Governor." M.A. thesis, University of Virginia, 1956.

Eckenrode, Hamilton J. "History of Virginia since 1865: 1865–1945, a Political History." Typescript, n.d., in Hamilton James Eckenrode Papers, University of Virginia Library.

Fahrner, Alvin A. "The Public Career of William 'Extra Billy' Smith." Ph.D. diss., University of North Carolina, 1953.

Harahan, Joseph Patrick. "Politics, Political Parties, and Voter Participation in Tidewater Virginia during Reconstruction, 1865–1900." Ph.D. diss., Michigan State University, 1973.

Hickin, Patricia P. "Antislavery in Virginia, 1831–1861." Ph.D. diss., University of Virginia, 1968.

——. "John Curtis Underwood and the Antislavery Crusade." M.A. thesis, University of Virginia, 1961.

Jennings, George W. "The Fiscal History of Virginia from 1860 to 1870." Ph.D. diss., University of Virginia, 1961.

Jones, Robert R. "Conservative Virginian: The Post-War Career of Governor James Lawson Kemper." Ph.D. diss., University of Virginia, 1964.

Lowe, Richard Grady. "Republicans, Rebellion, and Reconstruction: The Republican Party in Virginia, 1856–1870." Ph.D. diss., University of Virginia, 1968.

McFarland, George M. "The Extension of Democracy in Virginia, 1850–1895." Ph.D. diss., Princeton University, 1934.

O'Brien, John Thomas, Jr. "From Bondage to Citizenship: The Richmond Black Community, 1865–1867." Ph.D. diss., University of Rochester, 1974.

Ours, Robert M. "Virginia's First Redeemer Legislature, 1869–1871." M.A. thesis, University of Virginia, 1966.

Rice, Franklin P. "The Life of Eli Thayer." Manuscript, n.d., Library of Congress, Washington, D.C.

Smith, James Douglas. "The Virginia Constitutional Convention of 1867–1868." M.A. thesis, University of Virginia, 1956.

——. "Virginia during Reconstruction, 1865–1870: A Political, Economic, and Social Study." Ph.D. diss., University of Virginia, 1960.

Smith, Leslie Winston. "Richmond during Presidential Reconstruction, 1865–1867." Ph.D. diss., University of Virginia, 1974.

Vance, Joseph C. "The Negro in the Reconstruction of Albemarle County, Virginia." M.A. thesis, University of Virginia, 1953.

Wayland, John W. "The German Element of the Shenandoah Valley of Virginia." Ph.D. diss., University of Virginia, 1907.

Index